UNDERSTANDinu uuuJ

In the series

Animals, Culture, and Society

edited by Clinton R. Sanders and Arnold Arluke

UNDERSTANDING
DOGS

LIVING AND
WORKING
WITH CANINE
COMPANIONS

Clinton R. Sanders

Temple University Press
PHILADELPHIA

Temple University Press, Philadelphia 19122
Copyright © 1999 by Temple University
All rights reserved
Published 1999
Printed in the United States of America

Library of Congress Cataloging-in-Publication Data

Sanders, Clinton.
    Understanding dogs: living and working with canine companions /
Clinton R. Sanders.
        p.   cm. — (Animals, culture, and society)
    Includes bibliographical references and index.
    ISBN 1-56639-689-1 (cloth : alk. paper). — ISBN 1-56639-690-5
(pbk. : alk. paper)
    1. Dogs.   2. Dogs—Social aspects.   3. Guide dogs.   4. Dog owners.
5. Human-animal relationships.   6. Dogs—Diseases—Treatment.
7. Veterinarians.   I. Title.   II. Series.
SF426.S25   1999
636.7—dc21   98-38816

On frontispiece: The author's maternal grandfather Fred Bowie Horne (1891–1936).
Photographer unknown

Contents

Preface

The world exists through the understanding of dogs.
Friedrich Nietzsche (Comfort 1994, 174)

will admit at the beginning that I really love dogs. Not *all* dogs, actually; I am most taken by members of the more substantial breeds and tend to regard canines[1] that are less than around sixty pounds as more on the par with hamsters— frequently cute and friendly but not the sort of creature I would want to have sleeping at the foot of my bed.

My attraction for the large "working" breeds developed late in my dog owning career. As a boy I lived with a long-eared beagle named Beepo. The beagle is not the most tractable or intelligent of canines, and Beepo was an exemplary member of his breed. Despite his failings, I loved that dog with all my heart, spent many happy hours in his company, and wept when my parents called me at college to tell me of his passing.

My mother soon prevailed upon my father to acquire another dog, and they purchased a Saint Bernard pup from a local breeder. Challie was wonderfully good-natured and drooled constantly. Spending time with her became the high point of my vacation time at home, and our relationship initiated my abiding affection for big dogs. My fondness for the larger breeds was furthered by the two bull mastiffs my mother acquired after Challie's death. Having moved from the East Coast to rural Colorado, my mother wanted dogs that would provide some measure of security. Other than their imposing bulk and thunderous barks, the mastiffs were a dismal failure in the protection department since they were both rather timid and tended to either run away, or be embarrassingly sycophantic, when confronted by intruders.

When I was finally in a suitable situation where I was able to adequately feed and house a dog of my own, I remembered Pushkin, the kindly old Great Pyrenees that belonged to a friend of my partner Eleanor. We did our homework and soon were moving to rural Connecticut with a bouncing white furball of Pyr puppy. In retrospect, our orientation to dog rearing was entirely too Spockian (the baby doctor, not the Vulcan). Not wanting to "break the dog's spirit," we postponed training the poor animal until he was nine months old and developed a rather permissive approach to daily discipline. Despite his refusal to agree to stay off the bed and his intense desire to explore the countryside on his own, Cloud was a good-natured and relatively healthy member of our family. He eventually departed this veil of tears at the ripe old age of twelve, and we buried his remains under a white rhododendron.

After an appropriate period of mourning, we initiated the search for another canine companion. The major criteria were that the new dog be large, tractable, and long-haired. I was sitting in the local public library looking at American Kennel Club publications when I came upon Lord Byron's epitaph for his Newfoundland Boatswain that reads, in part:

> Near this Spot
> are deposited the Remains of One
> who possessed Beauty without Vanity,
> Strength without Insolence,
> Courage without Ferocity,
> and all of the Virtues of Man without his Vices.
> This Praise, which would be unmeaning Flattery
> if inscribed over human Ashes,
> is but a just tribute to the Memory of
> BOATSWAIN, a DOG . . .

I was sold. Eleanor and I soon contacted a Newfoundland breeder who had a kennel close to our house and, after running the members of the latest litter through our crude version of the "puppy test" we had read about, picked out two female Newfs. Since one cannot live with too many Newfs, we later acquired another and as I write this, three Newfoundlands are lying in the hallway leading to my study just waiting for me to finally do something interesting—that is, some activity involving food or walking in the woods.

As my experience living with the dogs has proceeded, I have come to realize that we share some important basic orientations to life. Most importantly, we all are fond of a calm and fairly routine daily pattern. We also agree that being in one's home territory is preferable to being away and that walking together in the woods is good for the soul. The Newfs are somewhat more taken with chasing sticks and swimming in frigid streams than I am, but I have come to accept that.

Like many of the dog owners presented in this book, I find the interweaving of my daily life with those of my dogs to be a somewhat mixed experience. Serious dog caretaking requires one to adopt a "cyno-centered" existence and to accept some related adjustments to what might otherwise be one's preferences. What I have noticed most is how I have had to adjust my deeply rooted inclination for maintaining a neat and hygienic living space. When I was young I remember seeing parents blithely changing baby diapers and scraping milky vomit off their shoulders. I vowed to avoid these experiences if at all possible. Now, however, I find myself cleaning up the liquids, solids, and semi-solids produced by my dogs with nary a passing thought. I also have come to accept muddy footprints on the floors, balls of fur in the corners, claw marks on door frames, and the other visible evidence that dogs are part of my family. Of course, the dogs agree to adjust their preferences in return. They accept that they cannot eat whenever and whatever they want, should restrain their enthusiasm when guests come to the house, and must restrict their toilet activities to areas outside the "den" if at all possible.

Living with dogs also requires one to adjust his or her schedule, especially when the animals are young. Regular feeding and housebreaking place significant demands on time and attention. While my Newfs tend to sleep eighteen hours a day or so, they frequently bark to ward off imaginary intruders in the middle of the night and are committed to engaging in vigorous physical activity around five in the morning. I have come to be able to forcefully suggest that the dogs quiet down while remaining semi-asleep and have decided that 5:00 a.m. isn't such a bad time to start one's day—especially if we can all agree to take a nap in the middle of the afternoon.

Living with dogs also has considerable impact on one's emotional experience. For the most part, the balance is tipped to the positive end of the scale as the dogs provide amusement, a sympathetic ear when it is needed, and loving devotion that is honest and not contingent on the vagaries of the immediate situation. Being in the company of dogs has yet another reward if one is open to their experience. While, as I discuss later, dogs clearly demonstrate a memory of past events and anticipate the future, they tend to live primarily in the present and derive tremendous pleasure from the most basic elements of living. As I share in my dogs' joy when they are offered a nourishing meal or the sensual satisfaction they get from simply being close to the warm bodies of their fellows, I come to realize that the most simple and immediate gratifications are to be most treasured.

Living in the here-and-now is difficult for mere humans, however. Intimacy and commitment open one up to the pain of worry and loss. Some of my blackest times have revolved around concern about my dogs' passing illnesses, and the chronic physical disorders such as hip dysplasia, cruciate ligament problems, and arthritis to which the large breeds are prone. Worst by far is the sorrow surrounding the inevitable decision to euthanize a canine friend and the tearing feelings of loss that follow the animal's passing. These significant and painful emotional elements of living with dogs are explored in depth later on.

My specific interest in service dogs began when I was a high school student in Morristown, New Jersey. Morristown is the home of the Seeing Eye Foundation, and I frequently would encounter dogs and their trainers on the street. Even then I was struck by the special quality of the relationship between guide dogs and people and resolved to explore the issue at some time in the future.

The opportunity presented itself many years later when, as a junior faculty member, I prevailed upon a blind student in one of my classes who was planning to acquire his first dog at the Seeing Eye to record his thoughts and experiences at the end of each day of training. The material he provided proved to be of limited use since he had many things to worry about during his training and producing a running account of his experiences turned out to be rather far down the list of his priorities.

My first real opportunity to explore the world of guide dogs came when another of my students was accepted as a trainer at a local guide dog program and agreed to help me gain access. I initially participated in a fund-raising event sponsored by the program and, after talking informally with various other people taking part, I realized that I needed to build a more secure foundation of knowledge about the everyday interaction between people and dogs before I could do an adequate job exploring the special relationships between guide dogs and their trainers and owners. I began then to look for a research setting where I could observe and interact with ordinary dog owners and their pets.[2]

In the fall of 1988 I enrolled, along with Eleanor and our two Newfoundland puppies, in an eight-week "puppy kindergarten" class that met in a local veterinary clinic and was led by an academically trained animal behaviorist. The class included some ten dogs (ranging in age from twelve to fifteen weeks) and their owners. The purpose of the training was basic socialization—to accustom the animals to interacting more or less agreeably with other dogs and humans and to teach the owners elementary techniques for developing satisfactory relationships with their pets. As a direct participant in the setting I began to record observations of the interactions within the class following each two-hour session. The next spring, with permission of the trainer, I attended another class sequence and, from an unobtrusive location, systematically recorded field notes detailing the interactions and activities I observed. Since I was primarily interested at this point in exploring the early stages of people's relationships with canine companions, the puppy classes provided an excellent opportunity to see aspects of this developmental process in action.

At the same time I was doing fieldwork in the puppy kindergarten, I was also recording incidents that occurred in both our home territory and public settings while I was watching and interacting with my own newly acquired puppies. Since it merges autobiography and ethnography, this methodological approach is commonly referred to as "auto-ethnography."[3] My auto-ethnographic notes proved to be an especially rich source of insight into many of the issues discussed in this book, especially in Chapter 2 where I examine the everyday owner's understanding of his or her dog as an individual and the experiences that dogs and owners have when they are together in public.

What follows is also based on information collected during approximately fourteen months of participant observation in a major veterinary hospital in New England. Ten veterinarians, together with some two dozen veterinary technicians and administrative personnel, worked in the clinic. I was able to enter this setting fairly easily because I was sponsored by one of the five partners in the hospital corporation—a veterinarian who had cared for my dogs for some fifteen years and with whom I had developed a close friendship. My initial interest in doing research in the hospital was in finding additional situations where I could watch people interacting with their dogs. I soon found, however, that the day-to-day work of the veterinarians was as interesting as were the owner-animal exchanges with which I was initially concerned. My field notes soon reflected this dual focus as I began to observe and interact with the doctors and other hospital personnel as they socialized and worked outside of the six examination rooms within which clinical encounters normally occurred.

I visited the clinic an average of three times a week, typically spending between two and five hours each visit observing, interacting, reading available journals, and—eventually—assisting with the ongoing business of the clinic. In my role as participant, I commonly helped with the tasks usually assigned to veterinary technicians. I restrained animals during exams, "held veins" in animals' forelegs while blood was drawn, fetched equipment and supplies, carried and positioned anesthetized patients in surgery, comforted frightened and injured animals, assisted in limited ways during surgeries and necropsies, and accompanied veterinarians on "farm calls" as they ministered to dairy herds.

One of my major functions was to act as what one vet referred to as "official greeter." Especially when the clinic was busy, I routinely would enter examination rooms and chat with owners as they waited to be seen by a veterinarian. These field conversations proved to be especially fruitful since they provided an opportunity to briefly interview owners about their pets. At the same time I could directly observe interactions between caretakers and their animal companions. I usually did not specifically explain my role when I introduced myself upon entering the examination room. Typically, clients assumed I was a visiting doctor or a veterinary student. If they asked directly, I explained that I was a sociologist from "the university" interested in relationships between people and companion animals. Clients generally seemed satisfied with this explanation and on only one occasion was I asked to leave.[4]

The guide dog training program I have already mentioned was the third setting in which I did fieldwork. In this program guide dogs were bred, trained, and placed with visually disabled owners. During the nine months I did research in this setting, I spent my time observing and talking with the dog trainers and kennel personnel as they went about their daily routines. In addition to finding out what the job of raising and training service dogs was like, I was especially interested in how the trainers came to understand and interact with the dogs for whom they were responsible. As will be seen in Chapter 5, trainers' ambivalent views of their trainees—as "things" whose behaviors are shaped through conditioning or individuals who are taught about how to act in certain situations—emerged as an issue of special importance.

Formal interviewing is a conventional element of doing ethnography. Typically, semistructured interviews are conducted with key participants in the setting being studied not long before the researcher intends to leave the field. I usually find this part of my work to be the most pleasurable and instructive since it allows people to talk at length about their views and experiences while providing me with an opportunity to explore and refine hunches I have had about matters that seem significant. These interviews also yield the rich personal narratives that are at the heart of any good ethnography. In the course of the three related research projects briefly described above, I conducted formal interviews with twenty-four ordinary dog owners, ten veterinarians, six guide dog trainers, and seven guide dog owners. These interviews were tape-recorded and lasted from one to three hours. In the chapters that follow, I make considerable use of these interviews since they allow the people in whom I was interested to speak eloquently and at length about their personal experiences.

This book deals with the experiences of people who live and work with dogs. I am well aware of the ideological debate that surrounds the words used to describe the everyday relationship between humans and the nonhumans with whom they live. Nonetheless, I have chosen to use the terms "pet" and "companion animal" and "owner" and "caretaker" interchangeably. Though many members of the rather heterogeneous "animal rights community" recoil at the "oppression" symbolized by the words "pet" and "owner," they are commonplace designations and I use them largely for variety rather than to make a political statement.

That being said, I will admit to disagreeing with those animal rights advocates who see petkeeping as an intrinsically oppressive relationship.[5] Domestic dogs are not wolves and house cats are not miniature tigers. Centuries of purposive breeding and the symbiotic relationship that has developed between humans and dogs and other companion animals have transformed these animals into creatures that are radically different from their relatives in the wild.[6] The view that petkeeping is tantamount to slavery and that all animals are better off in their "natural state" severely romanticizes the "state of nature." The relationships upon which this book focuses are *familial*[7] rather than intrinsically oppressive. While members of the political and cultural right tend to romanticize the family as vigorously as some animal rights advocates idealize the state of nature, social scientific analyses of the family offer a very mixed picture. The family may be the source of love, mutual aid, pleasurable interaction, and other social rewards for its various members. But this basic social structure can also offer intense pain, neglectful relationships, and virtual slavery. Like all family members, dogs and other companion animals can be subjected to mental, physical, and social abuses.[8] At best, however, dogs and other pets are cherished, given responsibilities, and lovingly cared for. The nonhuman animals with whom we share our homes and everyday lives commonly are the recipients of what is best about being the member of a family.

Much of this book focuses on the issue of whether companion dogs are thoughtful and intentional individuals with whom we have ongoing interactions that parallel our social exchanges with fellow humans. For those who live with dogs, this is an issue about which there is little doubt. My own view, based on years of research and lifelong personal experience, is that dogs are purposive and minded. My own dogs definitely display the individual tastes, perspectives, habits, and interests that make up what is commonly seen as "personality." They consistently demonstrate that they have expectations and recognize that they can affect my actions by behaving in particular ways. My dogs, for example, are well aware that I am the source of their food and believe that I will provide it for them around 7:30 in the morning. When these expectations are not met at the appropriate time, they actively inform me that things are not as they should be and do all they can to get me to do what they want. I would have to be fairly obtuse not to understand their expectant looks, impatient barks, and runs to the cabinet where their food is kept as anything other than their expression of their expectations and their attempts to manipulate my behavior. It is hardly an anthropomorphic delusion to regard the empirical data drawn from this and many similar daily incidents as persuasive evidence of the existence of canine mindedness. Like the owners and others whose lives revolve around relationships with dogs presented in this book, I base my understanding of dogs on my routine interactions with them.[9] In turn, acting on these understandings has practical outcomes. My dogs and I communicate effectively and share in the mutual interactions that comprise our relationships.

I have done fieldwork in a variety of settings and with a diverse collection of people. Some of the groups I have studied have been made up of people with whom I had little in common and found it difficult to establish any degree of honest rapport, and whose activities and perspectives I experienced with some measure of distaste. My early research with narcotics police comes immediately to mind. Other of my field studies involved people with whom I got along fairly well but, except for a few with whom I developed close friendships, most were individuals that I could easily either take or leave. The people whose lives revolved around their association with and love for dogs—the people I focus on in this book—were different. The owners, trainers, kennel workers, veterinarians, and veterinary staff I worked with and whose lives and perspectives I attempt to present here were—almost to a person—kind, open, and helpful and earned my sincerest admiration. I will always remember them with fondness and am indebted to them for their friendship and their willingness to put up with me and the seemingly endless array of stupid questions with which I was inclined to burden them.

Acknowledgments

n addition to the human and nonhuman participants in the settings I studied, I am indebted to the following for their interest, assistance, and advice: Patricia Adler, Peter Adler, Steve Alger, Arnold Arluke, Myrna Armstrong, Russell Belk, Robert Broadhead, Spencer Cahill, Albert K. Cohen, Carolyn Ellis, Myra Ferree, Gary Alan Fine, Michael Flaherty, Lee Freese, Barry Glassner, Ann Goetting, David Goode, Michael Gordon, Amanda Han, Douglas Harper, Douglas Heckathorn, Rosanna Hertz, Harold Herzog, Elizabeth Hirschman, James Holstein, Jonathan Imber, Jack Katz, George Laties, Doni Loseke, Steve Markson, Robert Mitchell, Lisa Penaloza, Bob Prus, D. W. Rajecki, Julius Roth, Andrew Rowan, James Serpell, Kenneth Shapiro, Mary Stewart, Jo Swabe, John Swan, Marcello Truzzi, Gaye Tuchman, Melanie Wallendorf, Francoise Wemelsfelder, and Melissa Young. Special thanks are due to the various members of the "qualitative methods group" at the University of Connecticut (especially Naomi Reich, Silke Roth, and Angus Vail) and the people who helped me with the hateful task of transcribing interviews (Amy-Joy, Doris Basset, Debbie Crary, Jarrod, Dawn Stabley, and Lynn Paradiso). I am grateful to Janet Alger, Ron Baenninger, and (especially) Marc Bekoff for their careful reading of an earlier draft of the manuscript and their supportive and helpful comments. Yvonne Ramsey's skilled editing helped to smooth out my sometimes tortured prose, and her encouraging words lifted my spirits. Through it all, Janet Francendese of Temple University Press has been a good friend while providing encouragement, advice, and a sympathetic ear. As always, Eleanor Lyon put up with my moods, listened to my complaining, and helped immeasurably to refine the often nebulous ideas I had about the matters on which this book focuses. And finally, none of this could have been possible were it not for Cloud, Emma, Isis, Raven, and Shadow.

Portions of this book are adapted from previously published articles:

"The Animal 'Other': Self Definition, Social Identity, and Companion Animals," in Gerald Gorn, Richard Pollay, and Marvin Goldberg (eds.), *Advances in Consumer Research*, 17, Provo, UT: Association for Consumer Research, 1990, pp. 662–668, with the permission of the Association for Consumer Research.

"Excusing Tactics: Social Responses to Companion Animals," *Anthrozoös*, 1990, 4 (2): 82–90, with the permission of the Delta Society.

"Understanding Dogs: Caretakers' Attributions of Mindedness in Canine-Human Relationships," *Journal of Contemporary Ethnography*, 1993, 22 (2): 205–226, copyright © 1993 by Sage Publications. Reprinted by permission of Sage Publications.

"Annoying Owners: Routine Interactions with Problematic Clients in a General Veterinary Practice," *Qualitative Sociology*, 1994, 17 (1): 159–170, with the permission of Plenum Publishing Corporation.

"Biting the Hand That Heals You: Encounters with Problematic Patients in a General Veterinary Practice," *Society and Animals*, 1994, 1 (2): 47–66, with the permission of White Horse Press.

UNDERSTANDING DOGS

Introduction

The Relationship between People and Pets

few years ago in the journal *Anthrozoös,* the editor, Andrew Rowan, wrote an editorial defending the use of "anecdotal" evidence in building an understanding of the relationship between people and animals. In support of his contention that we can only fully grasp the emotional elements of this relationship by listening to the stories people tell, he described a luncheon at the meetings of the Delta Society at which awards were given to acknowledge the services of special therapy animals. Here is his description of one award:

> The final award went to a hearing ear dog. The owner of the dog was a stockman who worked with dairy cows. He stood on the stage and could not speak for about ninety seconds. He then began haltingly, but with increasing confidence, to describe what his dog meant to him. The dog had brought him out of his self-imposed isolation and even learned to identify (by the sound they made) milking machines that were not working properly. The stockman's description of the change his companion had wrought ended when he broke down in tears.[1]

In the preface to her outstanding book on women primate researchers, Sy Montgomery describes her own ethological work with emus (flightless birds related to the ostrich) in Australia. She writes:

> On my last day [in the field], of course, I went out again to the emus. They seemed to be looking for me. I followed them all

1

day, and toward evening they stopped to graze on some wild mustard. Then I thought: I wish I could tell you what you have given to me. How could I express to creatures whose experience of the world was so different from mine what they had allowed me to feel? I said aloud, in a low voice: "You have eased in me a fear more gripping than that you feel when you are separated from the others. You have given me a comfort more soothing than the feel of your feathers passing through your beaks under the warm sun. I can never repay you, but I want you to feel my thanks." . . . This speech was one of those expressions like laying flowers upon the graves of the unknowing dead. The recipient doesn't know or care. But the human species is like this: we have to utter our prayers, even if they go unheard. So while I sat with them that night, deep in the bush, I whispered over and over: "I love you, I love you." [2]

I recall how moved I was when I first read both of these passages. These simple examples (and, perhaps, your own response to them) reveal the intensity of the relationships we have with animals—both the companions with whom we share our homes and lives and those with whom work brings us in contact. This book is about this unique and emotional social connection and the people who, because they live and work with dogs, foster and are most familiar with it. Those readers drawn to this book because of their interest in dogs will find a rich collection of stories and descriptions that will doubtless speak to their own experiences. The core chapters focusing on everyday dog owners, guide dog users, veterinarians, and guide dog trainers are likely to be most engaging to the casual reader. While these stories told by dog owners and those who work with canines are at the literal heart of this work, it is, at the same time, a sociological discussion. This means that some sections may be of somewhat less interest to readers who are, at best, minimally concerned with the often arcane process of doing academic sociology. Nonetheless, I believe that it is important to focus a sociological eye on the common and emotionally significant interactions we have with dogs and other companion animals. The conventional inattention to and discounting of this key form of human association has left a considerable gap in the sociological exploration of everyday life. My goal is to fill in some of this gap since it is, to my mind, inexcusable that sociologists have typically ignored or trivialized a type of relationship that holds such meaning for and touches the hearts of so many.

Most of this introductory chapter will offer a general overview of pet keeping and the sociological significance of people's association with dogs and other companion animals—especially the ways in which pets enhance and extend the owner's self. Chapter 2 focuses on the everyday dog owner. Specifically, we will see how caretakers come to understand their dogs as individuals—as thoughtful, reciprocating, emotional beings with uniquely individual tastes and personalities. Thus defined, owners include their dogs in the rituals and routines that make up the social life of the household. Since the interactions people have in public are of considerable interest to sociologists, the discussion in this chapter moves the owner and his or her dog outside the confines of the home. While, as we will see, being with a dog in public may increase a person's positive social exchanges with those encountered, this is not always the case. At those times when the dog threatens, jumps on, barks at, or otherwise annoys strangers, the owner may feel it necessary to make excuses for the animal's "inappropriate" behavior. Caretakers typically are held to be accountable for their dog's misbehavior. They are, after all, the responsible party and expected to be "in charge." Since the dog's misbehavior disrupts the normal flow of public interaction and potentially diminishes the identity of the owner, people with dogs commonly take certain steps to get public interactions back "on track." In Chapter 2 we will examine some of the most common "excusing tactics" owners use to explain their canine companions' problematic actions and thereby restore their own degraded public identities.

Chapter 3 describes another, more specialized, form of dog ownership. The experiences of people who live with and regularly depend on guide dogs[3] have some interesting similarities to and differences from those of the commonplace owner. In this chapter I describe the "career" of the guide dog user—his or her decision to get the dog, the development of the relationship with the assistance animal, and the ways in which living with a guide dog changes the owner's everyday experience. Like those of the commonplace owner, the public encounters of guide dog users are significantly affected by being accompanied by a dog. There are, however, some striking differences. We will look at both the tribulations and the pleasures guide dog users encounter as they and their canine assistants move about in public.

Having examined the experiences of people who live their lives in the company of dogs, we turn to look at two occupations that revolve around dogs and their owners. Chapter 4 deals with the work lives of veterinarians and the triangular relationship of owner/client, animal/patient, and doctor inherent in veterinary medicine. The chapter focuses on the routine problems vets encounter in their interactions with dogs and other patients and with the owners who purchase their services. One factor that significantly distinguishes human medical practice from veterinary medicine is that vets routinely are required to end the lives of their patients. Since the practice of euthanasia is a central and emotionally traumatizing part of what goes on in veterinary clinics, I discuss the exchanges surrounding the purposive delivery of an "easy death" in some detail.

Chapter 5 focuses on another "cyno-centered" occupation—that of the guide dog trainer. Here I examine the often serendipitous career path of the trainer and key elements of his or her on-the-job experience. Since working with the dog-owner "team" is central to the trainer's job, I discuss how both owners and dogs are evaluated and matched. As I did with both blind and everyday owners, I will look at how trainers understand dogs generally, and their trainees specifically. Here definitions of "hard" versus "soft," emotionality, how dogs think, and the ways in which dogs manipulate people are of special interest. The chapter closes with some observations about a potential conflict that arises in all dog training situations. Dogs may routinely be seen as animated objects to be "shaped" through behaviorist manipulations or as individual beings who are "taught" in the context of a social relationship. As we will see, guide dog trainers hold onto elements of both these orientations. While this object-being dichotomy is seen in a number of settings in which people routinely interact with animals—for example, in scientific laboratories and animal shelters—in those settings people usually experience some measure of ambivalence about the conflicting definitions and make attempts to adjust their perspectives so as to ease or make sense of their feelings of ambivalence. In this light, the relative lack of ambivalence felt by the guide dog trainers with whom I worked is a matter of some interest and the focus of the thoughts that conclude this chapter.

In Chapter 6 I attempt to lay the groundwork for a sociology of human interactions with dogs and other nonhuman animals. The chapter opens with a presentation of conventional ways in which animals and their behaviors have been understood—from Descartes's view of animals as machines to contemporary cognitive ethologists' understandings of animals as communicative, thoughtful, emotional interactants who are possessors, to a certain degree, of culture. After a relatively brief outline of the typical discounting of the abilities of animals and humans to participate together in "authentic" social exchanges, I outline key elements of a sociological view of the relationships of people with dogs and other companion animals. Specifically, I propose that animals have at least a rudimentary ability to construct meaning—to purposefully define situations and devise coherent plans of action on the basis of these definitions. I further maintain that animals possess a self-definition and from this subjective perspective can engage in the elemental social activity of "taking the role of the other." Given these abilities, I argue that the conventional sociological view that the interactions between people and companion animals are qualitatively different from those between human social actors is, to put it mildly, open to serious debate.

Pet Keeping and Social Identity

Throughout history the types of companion animals that people have kept, the treatment they received, and the ways in which they were symbolically defined have varied greatly.[4] While the major reason human beings fostered relationships with pet animals was, and continues to be, the desire for companionship, there has been a consistent linkage between companion animals and social status in Western culture. In most complex societies pet keeping typically has been associated primarily with upper-class status. Those with power and economic resources symbolized their advantage by owning nonfunctional and expensive animal property.[5] In turn, pet possession by members of the lower classes commonly was condemned as inappropriate and wasteful:

> Throughout the nineteenth century, for example, even as pets were made increasingly welcome at respectable domestic hearths, the pets of the poor were castigated as symbols of their owners' depravity—an unwarranted

indulgence that led them to neglect important social duties. A typical complaint criticized colliers who "have more dogs than they know what to do with" and "starve their children and feed their dogs on legs of mutton." In addition, pet dogs were alleged to intensify the squalor of impoverished accommodations. . . . Thus reformist critics presented their efforts to deprive the poor of their pets as straightforward humanitarian efforts on behalf of suffering people with animals. But the juxtaposition of such efforts with explicit attempts to regulate the behavior of lower class humans suggest an additional dimension. . . . The underlying symbolism of domination may have defined pet ownership as the prerogative only of those whose social position justified some analogous exercise of power over their fellow human beings.[6]

To some degree, ownership of certain animals such as pedigreed dogs, cats, and horses continues to symbolize social privilege since they are relatively expensive to acquire and maintain.[7] However, the commonality of pet ownership and the problems most people have in distinguishing between a rare and expensive animal and a cheap one has tended to dilute the importance of companion animals as status symbols. Instead, pets have come to represent other aspects of social identity. Rather than demonstrate elite status, pets—especially dogs—symbolize the owner's caring nature; love for fun; and, especially for those in the upper class, one's populist connection to the "common person." It is, for example, now conventional for American presidents to own and routinely be photographed with a pet dog (Johnson hoisting his beagle by the ears, Nixon and Checkers, the Bushes' well-known "first dog" Millie, and Bill Clinton's Labrador Buddy).[8]

The type and temperament of the companion animal one chooses and the instrumental purpose for which it is bred also work to demonstrate features of owners' identities. Powerful and aggressive dogs such as rottweilers and German shepherds, for example, not only have a protective function but also reflect the owner's desire to present a social self that is correspondingly aggressive. Possession of an Afghan dog, a poodle, or cats, in contrast, generally is regarded as indicating the owner's soft and "feminine" character. The animal is, in a sense, a decorative addition to the self.[9] In turn, hunting dogs (or, more rarely, trained birds-of-prey) are effective in informing others about the owner's "outdoorsy" interests.

The distinction between dog fanciers and those who favor cats is a related feature of social identity frequently encountered in contemporary popular culture. One early study[10] found that those who strongly agreed with the statement "dogs are much more admirable animals than cats" rated high on measures of authoritarianism. Later research, however, indicated that childhood experience with either dogs or cats, rather than one's personality characteristics, was the major factor shaping pet preference.[11]

In general, it appears that possession of a companion animal does, in fact, have a positive impact on the owner's social identity. Randall Lockwood,[12] for example, found that people pictured with animals were judged by undergraduate students to be more sociable, content, and easygoing. It is most likely that this apparent effect on social definition is related to the fact that companion animals act as facilitators of interaction—an identity enhancing feature that I will discuss later in this chapter and will return to in Chapter 2.[13]

Although there is a connection between one's income and the likelihood of his or her owning a pet,[14] owners themselves rarely define their pet primarily as a publicly displayed symbol of their social and/or economic status. Mary Harris[15] found that only .4 percent of pet owners admitted to having chosen their companion animal primarily because they thought it helped to enhance their status. Another study of Australian pet owners found only 1 percent of owners saying that they saw prestige as the primary benefit they derived from their possession of a pet.[16] As I stress in the chapters on everyday and visually handicapped dog owners, by far the most common value that dogs and other household pets have for their caretakers is the companionship and affection they provide.

Pets and Extended Social Involvements

A variety of studies demonstrate that dogs and other companion animals act as effective "social facilitators." For example, 83 percent of those questioned in a Swedish study[17] agreed with the statement "my dog gives me the opportunity of talking with other people." Similarly, 37 percent of the respondents in Ann Cain's[18] study of pets in the family said that their companion animals helped them to make friends or increased their social contacts. In one of the best known studies of dog owners in public settings, Peter Messent[19] observed seven owners walking through Hyde Park in London both with and without their dogs. Owners accompanied by dogs spoke with strangers an average of three times but engaged in no social exchanges when walking the same route without their animals. In the second stage of the study Messent observed forty owners walking their dogs on their normal daily routes. On average, the owners spoke to other people on three occasions during each walk; 60 percent of these interactions simply involved exchanges of greeting. Conversations were significantly longer when the other person encountered was also accompanied by a dog.

Like a wide variety of the objects displayed in public—children, kites, unique articles of clothing, tattoos, and so on—dogs act as sources of "mutual openness."[20] Dogs and other items displayed by people in public settings provide a shared focus of nonthreatening interaction between strangers. Shared affinity for and experience with dogs offer a relatively neutral and accessible topic of conversation. Since, as Charles Horton Cooley[21] emphasized, interactions with others are the major sources of information we use to construct a definition of our selves, being in the public company of a dog or other companion animal increases the quantity and enhances the quality of self-defining encounters. In this way, pets help to reinforce the owner's positive feelings about his or her self.

Pet facilitated interactions with other people, together with the positive information about the self one gains from intimate and loving interactions with companion animals, appear to enhance owners' feelings of self worth. James Serpell,[22] for example, found that female dog owners perceived themselves to be significantly more attractive than did non-owners. Another study of chief executive officers in Fortune 500 firms[23] found that these high status individuals were more likely than the average American to own a cat or dog. The CEOs attributed the character traits they saw as being responsible for their success—discipline, empathy, and compassion—to the experience they had of owning and interacting with companion animals.[24]

Pets facilitate social interaction and extend the situations in which caretakers receive self-definitional information in yet another way. Shared possessions, activities, and interests act as the organizational focus of what Herbert Gans[25] refers to as "taste publics." Like antique cars, comic books, polkas, or other items of taste culture, companion animals can act as central elements in extensive social rituals and organizations. Dog and cat shows, breed-specific organizations, and animal activity competitions such as obedience work extend the social interactions of pet enthusiasts. Within these subcultural contexts, owners can acquire status and prestige. Animal focused activities increase participants' positive social contacts as well as provide a pleasurable way to spend leisure time. In addition, rewarding outcomes of competitive animal focused activities are sources of considerable pride and enhance the positive relationship between the animal and his or her human companion. In this way, enthusiastic involvement and cooperative work with dogs and other companion animals expand the owner's social encounters and enhances his or her self-esteem.[26]

Companion Animals and the Social Self

The construct sociologists refer to as the "self" is built on the foundation of information derived from a person's interactions with others. As discussed above, companion animals facilitate human-to-human interactions, thereby increasing (and enhancing) self-defining situations. However, the connection between companion animals and the caretaker's self concept is *direct* as well as *mediated*. As is made clear in later chapters, owners consistently define their pets as "persons" with whom they share lasting, intimate, and emotionally involving relationships.[27] Studies show that somewhere between half[28] and three-quarters[29] of pet owners define their companion animals as "persons" or as having "person status." In this role as person the animal is talked to and confided in.[30] Pet owners typically see these exchanges as "real" conversations since they believe that the animal understands what they say and responds appropriately.[31]

One of the most simple forms of personhood assigned to companion animals is seen when they act as surrogates for other people.[32] Here the animal may act as a "stand-in" for a human parent, child, friend, or other significant person. In the course of interacting with the animal-as-surrogate, the human caretaker commonly engages in the process of "playing at a role"—assuming the appropriate complimentary role (i.e., friend to friend, parent to child) and imaginatively trying it out. Clark Brickel,[33] for example, emphasizes the importance of the animal-as-surrogate in the socialization of the child when he observes:

> Role play with real or imaginary companions is important for the child. This play satisfies needs for companionship, self-aggrandizement, collaboration, and a release of forbidden impulses. . . . Pets satisfy such needs. . . . As children grow they take on a number of roles in play, feeling what it might be like to have a certain status. Pets invite such activities of fantasy. The child assumes roles of parent, teacher, or anything else with an animal and has no fear of rejection. . . . Success in this role play is virtually assured.[34]

In the defined role of "person," the companion animal is incorporated into the owner's network of relationships. The most common form this incorporation takes is for the owner to regard the animal as either a family member or close friend. Studies show that somewhere between 70 and 99 percent of pet caretakers define their animals as members of the family,[35] and from 30 to 83 percent consider the pet to be a "special" or "close" friend.[36] In the following chapter we will take a detailed look at the ways in which dogs owners incorporate their companion animals into their families and define them as "virtual" persons. But, in short, the human caretaker comes to construct the personhood of the animal by seeing him or her as a unique, communicative, emotional, reciprocating, and companionable being who is a true member of the family. From this socially defined position the companion animal acts as a "significant other" for the owner, and their face-to-face interactions provide important, commonly rewarding, social experience.

As is also emphasized in the following chapters, human interaction with the companion animal/person presents a rich variety of rewards. Like all primary relationships, those between people and their pets offer intrinsic, rather than instrumental, social benefits. People see companionship and affection as being the primary advantages of this unique relationship. The animal is seen as nonjudgmental, accepting, and genuine, requiring nothing from the relationship other than the affectionate reciprocation of attention. As James Serpell describes it:

> Most pet-owners believe that their animals are sensitive to their moods and feelings, and many confide in their pets verbally. In other words, the animal

is perceived as empathic. It listens and seems to understand, but it does not question or evaluate. . . . Lacking the power of speech, animals cannot participate in conversation or debate but, by the same token, they do not judge us, criticize us, lie to us or betray our trust. Because it is mute and non-judgmental, their affection is seen as sincere, innocent, and without pretence. It is essentially reliable and trustworthy.[37]

My own research with dog owners and other studies of pet caretakers clearly show that companionship and affection are key rewards people derive from their relationships with animals.[38] These stable, emotionally rewarding, nonjudgmental relationships with the animal are defined by caretakers as reflecting their self worth; their self definition as deserving affection is reinforced by their experiences with their dogs or other companion animals. As Clark Brickel puts it:

Activity provides role supports required to reaffirm self-concepts and enhance psychological self-maintenance. The more frequent and intimate the activity, the more potent its validating ability. . . . [In] the struggle for self-identity . . . animals are enlisted as sources of emotional support, since animal oriented activities help carve out definitions of self. . . . They provide emotional anchors during the tempest, giving comfort and solace through their stability.[39]

The two most common shared activities through which the intimate relationships people have with their animal companions are expressed and reinforced are mutual play and touch. Observational studies of dog owners have found that object-oriented games (forms of play that employ physical objects and entail rudimentary rules known to all players) such as fetch, tug-of-war, and keep-away are, together with play wrestling and chasing, the major types of play. These mutually pleasurable interactions often merge into each other, require the dog to inhibit his or her natural inclinations to bite or otherwise act in an overly aggressive manner, and help to enhance the human-animal bond.[40] Similarly, "hand contacts" ranging from "sound pats" to "idle play" are forms of physical interaction directed by the owner (though commonly initiated by the animal) that are mutually defined as pleasurable and reinforce the primary relationship between the person and his or her dog.[41]

In a society in which everyday interaction is typically secondary, fleeting, noninvolving, and instrumental, many of us experience a lack of social connectedness and intimacy. In the absence of emotionally rewarding human interactions, people often turn to companion animals as sources of these positive experiences. As Sharon Smith puts it in the conclusion to her discussion of dog-person interactions in the family:

> Despite belonging to different evolutionary orders, these dogs and people cooperated in coordinating their interactions so that interaction continued at least momentarily. They responded to each other behaviorally in a variety of ways. Yet it appeared that at any given moment their behavior was not random. They appeared to interact for the purpose of interacting; no material outcomes were apparent, such as access to a limited resource like food. In this way the interactions of these people and their dogs resembled those of members of the same species.[42]

The intimate association between humans and companion animals provides more than the direct social and affective rewards inherent in the relationship, however. It is probable that the relationship between dogs and humans, for example, has its basis in the functional mutual benefits wolves and early humans derived from their earliest association—primarily cooperative hunting and security. These key features of mutual assistance have been, and continue to be, key elements of the relationships between humans and animals (particularly dogs).[43] The functional importance of dog companions as instruments of protection continues to be a significant factor for many owners. Bruce Fogle, for example, notes the significant increase in the size of the average dog in Britain and the United States over the past decade as well as the growing popularity of more aggressive breeds such as the rottweiler and pit bull.[44] As such, companion animals have acted as, and continue to be, extensions of the owner's physical self—supplementing his or her limited senses and enlarging his or her control of the environment. Guide dogs for the visually impaired and other assistance animals for the physically challenged are contemporary examples of the way in which companion animals act as direct extensions of the human's physical self.[45] As the visually handicapped dog owners presented in Chapter 3 stress, it is through their functional relationship with animals that people enhance their physical abilities. Guide dogs and other assistance animals extend one's ability to control his or her physical surroundings. As Serpell stresses, increased physical control leads, understandably, to enhanced feelings of self-esteem:

An example of neoteny. Infantile physical features call forth emotional responses.
Photographer: Clinton Sanders

> We have here people with overt physical and mental disabilities who lack self-esteem and confidence because of this. The physical control of an animal lacking such disabilities and the use of it as an *extension of the self* increases coordination, mobility and skill and, hence, improves confidence and self-esteem.[46]

Given these clear connections among self-definition, feelings of self-esteem, and a person's relationship with a companion animal, it is eminently understandable that the death of a pet should generate the intense pain described by the bereaved owners presented in Chapter 4. In essence, the owner experiences a *loss of self* in addition to the loss of a loving companion.[47]

As I noted briefly above and will discuss in detail in the following chapter, people who live and work with dogs and other companion animals consistently talk to the animals with whom they interact. Owners, in particular, value these exchanges because their pets, unlike many humans, are typically attentive, responsive, and noncompetitive.[48] It is reasonable to see our "conversations" with our companion animal as an extension of the way in which we routinely "talk to ourselves." For some people—for example, children interacting with imaginary companions—or in certain situations—for example, when one is praying in a religious setting—a person's talking to him- or herself out loud is regarded as legitimate and understandable. However, for most social actors in most social situations, overtly verbalizing one's internal dialogue is regarded as a violation of what the sociologist Thomas Scheff[49] refers to as "residual rules." Those who regularly talk to themselves in public run the risk of being seen by others as mentally disordered.[50] But when the person engages in verbal self dialogue in the presence of his or her dog or other companion animal and speaks directly to the animal—a very common situation, indeed—this legitimates the potentially discrediting act both for the talker and, if it takes place in public, in the eyes of other people. Publicly talking to an animal companion—as opposed to one's self—typically is seen as being normal or, at worst, somewhat eccentric. It is not, within the confines of fairly flexible social expectations, seen as indicating that the speaker is suffering from "mental illness."

This then is yet another way in which companion animals relate to the owner's self. They act as socially legitimated self-surrogates allowing the caretaker to engage in externalized self-dialogue while avoiding the potential for having other people (or the person doing the talking) define the verbal activity as pathological. In my field notes, I noted my own tendency to direct self-speech to my dogs early in my systematic observation of our developing relationship:

> I notice that I have begun to do something rather interesting. Being home alone so much I know I have developed a habit of talking to myself out loud. I remember having jokingly expressed some concern about this one time when I was having lunch with [a veterinarian friend]. Today it struck me that I still do this but I often direct these verbalizations to Emma and Isis [two of my three Newfoundlands]. I was getting ready to go to the grocery store today and started nattering—"Well, we better not forget to get something for dinner tonight. How does chicken sound to you? Did you see where I put my

keys?" They are very attentive, and I am comfortable about doing it because it is in line with the comments of [the dog trainer in the puppy kindergarten] about the importance of ongoingly talking to the puppies as an aid in the bonding process. I am apparently talking with them, but I am really talking to myself.

A client at a veterinary clinic studied by Alan Beck and Aaron Katcher expressed this point much more succinctly when he stated: "I just talk. Just what's in my head, like I was talking to myself, only I don't feel I'm nuts, because the dog listens." [51]

In this chapter I have attempted to situate the relationships and interactions we have with companion animals in a sociological context. In the typically ambivalent way animals are regarded in our culture, pets can be seen as both social objects and as subjects. As objects they are possessions that display and help enhance their owners' status and function as assistants and physical extensions. But the social place of companion animals as subjects is far more significant and sociologically interesting. As co-actors in our everyday lives, the dogs and other non-human companions with whom we associate are cast in the role of persons. Like human persons they listen, offer affection, and—in a variety of other important ways—provide us with those social things we need in order to feel that we are valuable, individual, and have a place in a world that is often experienced as alienating and chaotic.

While I believe it is necessary and worthwhile to locate our associations with dogs, cats, and other animals in an abstracted context such as that provided by the sociological perspective, this analytical standpoint does not get at the *heart* of these matters. To actually *feel* the central role that dogs and other animal companions play in our lives, it is necessary to examine closely the real experiences and listen carefully to the words of those who love, educate, depend upon, and care for the nonhuman members of our society. We turn first to the familiar world of the everyday dog owner.

2

The Everyday Dog Owner
Knowing and Living with Dogs

f the encounters that people experience in their daily lives, those with companion animals are second only to those with other humans in frequency and importance. According to recent data from the American Veterinary Association, some 37 percent of American households contain an average of 1.7 dogs (over 52 million dogs) and 38 percent contain an average of 2.2 cats (around total of 63 million cats).[1] A study by the American Animal Hospital Association found that 69 percent of dog owners and 60 percent of cat owners say they give as much attention to their companion animals as they would to their children. The majority of dog and cat owners (54 percent) said they felt an emotional attachment to their pets.[2]

This chapter focuses on dog owners' understandings of the companion animals with whom they share their lives. Based on routine, intimate interactions with his or her dog, the caretaker comes to regard the animal-other as a thinking, playful, empathetic being who is well aware of basic rules and roles that govern and comprise the relationship. The owner also sees the dog as consciously acting so as to achieve the animal's goals in the course of routine social exchanges with people and other canines. In other words, the dog is seen as a purposive social "performer" possessing at least a rudimentary ability to "take the role of the other," as sociologists put it, and from that imaginative perspective act in ways that bring about desirable outcomes.

Because the animal is "mute," caretakers often find themselves in situations in which they must "speak for" their nonhuman companions. In so doing, they make use of a rich body of knowledge derived from an intimate understanding of the animal-other built up in the course of day-to-day experience. Dog owners commonly give voice to what they perceive to be their animals' mental, emotional, and physical experiences.[3] Caretakers also interpret and make excuses for their animals' misbehaviors when they see these violations as creating problems during encounters with other people.

This chapter examines the ongoing, intimate, day-to-day interaction between people and their dogs and how owners typically come to view their animals as socially defined "persons" possessing unique personalities, tastes, and responses to specific situations. Having established an understanding of owners' relationships with their dogs, we move from the home into more public spaces to look at how being with a dog shapes and constrains public interactions. As outlined in the last chapter, being accompanied by a dog affects one's social identity in important ways. At times the dog draws positive attention from other people. However, at other times the dog may act in ways that cause problems.

Conflict, especially that which occurs in public settings, is a particularly interesting aspect of human interaction. Consequently, we will look at those situations in which dogs misbehave in public and the methods owners use to deal with these impositions. Since the experiences of a person accompanied by a dog are remarkably similar to those of an adult who is with a child in public, I will draw out some key elements of this similarity at the end of the chapter. The central themes that run through this chapter are the intimacy of the canine-human bond, the ways in which owners understand their animals as individuals, and the common tendency of caretakers to assign a child-like status to their animals.

Knowing One's Dog

The Dog as Conscious and Thinking

Grounded on their ongoing, intimate contact with their dogs, the owners with whom I spoke had little doubt of their animals' cognitive abilities and all could recount examples of what they defined as thoughtful behavior. Dogs' thought processes were generally seen as fairly basic. As one owner observed when asked about his dog's intellect, "Well, he's not exactly a Rhodes scholar." To a certain extent, owners saw intelligence as varying from animal to animal and from breed to breed. Because they were dogs and not humans, the companion animals were typically described as engaging in thought processes that were "wordless."[4] Their thoughts were presumed to be nonlinear, composed of mental images, and driven largely by emotion. When asked if she thought that her malamute could think, one owner cited a parallel example in her own experience when she replied:

> Yes, I do. I don't think their heads are empty. I think their thinking process is different from ours. I think they think on emotions. If the environment is happy and stable, they are going to act more stable—pay more attention to what you are doing. They are going to be more alert. If everything is chaotic they would not be thinking externally, but be more concerned with themselves internally—protecting themselves and not paying attention to my cues. I would call that thinking, but it is not what you would call linear thinking. It is more of a stimulus thinking. The reason I relate to that is that I was real depressed for a long time. And when you are really really depressed and your mental abilities are not sharp, you are not really thinking. You are just responding to emotional stimuli. I think that is how they are—they respond with emotion. But I would call that a type of thinking. They are making decisions based on those emotional cues.

No matter what the mode of thought defined by caretakers, most agreed that the issues their dogs thought about were rather basic. Owners saw their dogs as focusing primarily on events and matters of central concern to their ongoing physical and emotional experience:

> I think that [my dogs] are here just to get approval. [They are here for] feeding or to get petted or get their ears rubbed. I think they think enough not to get yelled at, not to get into trouble. That's the way dogs are. I don't think they can reason like people.

Some owners did see their animals as going beyond these basic physiological and emotional concerns. One typical sort of description offered by caretakers focused on their dog's play activities and the adjustments he or she made while being trained. In the course of play and
training, the dog's purposive modification of behavior was seen as demonstrating a basic ends-means process of reasoning. For example, one
owner proudly described how his hunting dog acted intelligently while
learning to retrieve objects from the water:

> This is the smartest dog I have ever had. We are having him trained profes-
> sionally, and we were with the trainer with my dog and some of the other
> dogs he was training. He said, "Look here. I'll show you how smart your dog
> is." He threw the retrieving dummy out into the middle of this long pond
> there. My dog jumped in and swam to the thing, grabbed it in his mouth
> and took a right turn. He swam to the land and walked back to us with the
> dummy in his mouth all proud. He was the only one smart enough to walk
> back. The other dogs all swam out, retrieved the thing, and swam all the
> way back.

In the course of watching my own dogs play, I was struck by the
adjustments they made—adjustments that, were they made by humans, would clearly indicate thought. Following the introduction of a
new puppy into my household, I made the following entry in my auto-
ethnographic observations after returning from a walk in the woods:

> Today Isis [my three-year-old Newfoundland] appeared to come to a realiza-
> tion about how she had been attempting to play "chase" and this prompted
> her to alter the play process somewhat—essentially altering the assumption
> of roles. On each of the walks so far, Isis has attempted to initiate chase by
> acting as the chaser. She runs off at a rapid pace, turns back, runs toward
> Raven [the puppy], bowls her over, runs past, etc. This doesn't work because
> of the size and strength difference. Raven just cowers, runs to one of us for
> protection, cries out. So, this time when Raven made a run at her at one point
> in the walk, Isis ran off a little ways until Raven followed. Isis then ran fur-
> ther and soon Raven was in hot pursuit. Isis led her a merry chase over fallen
> trees, through thickets, into gullies. It was particularly interesting to watch
> because Isis was adjusting the game on the basis of her knowledge of Raven's,
> as yet, limited abilities. She would run just fast enough so that Raven wouldn't
> get more than a few feet behind and would occasionally slow down enough
> that Raven could grab hold of some hair on her side or legs. Isis would also toy
> with the other player by jumping over larger falls or into gullies with deep,
> vertical sides—obstacles she knew were beyond Raven's limited abilities.[5]

Because play is such an important element of dog activity and is typically highly interactive,[6] I will examine it later when discussing role-taking and manipulation of others in the course of interaction.

The Dog as Emotional and Empathetic

As mentioned above, owners typically understand their dogs as having subjective experiences in which some form of reasoning is linked with emotion. The most common theme that emerged from my encounters in the veterinary clinic and interviews with owners was that dogs are eminently emotional beings. Their rich emotional lives involved a wide range of basic feelings. Dogs were, for example, described as experiencing loneliness, joy, sadness, embarrassment, and anger.[7] The owners I interviewed often focused on this last emotional experience—anger—because it was linked to incidents in which dogs responded in ways owners saw as indicating vindictiveness. For example, one owner described her shar pei puppy's displeasure at being abandoned and his playfully vengeful response to her absence:

> It's funny, usually after I have been at work all Friday I don't go out unless I am sure that somebody is going to watch him. But one time I left him alone and when I got home HE WAS ANGRY. He just let me know.
>
> [How did he let you know?]
>
> He'd follow me around and he would look up at me and he would just bark. It was like he was yelling at me. And I would say, "What is it with you?" and when I would stop talking he would look at me and bark—like "You left me. How could you do that?" You could read it in his face. When he was younger and I would go to work and leave him during the day he would find some way to let me know that he wasn't pleased. . . . Like he would shred all his newspapers. Every day was something new. He would move his crate, or he would flip his water dish, or something like that.

I routinely asked owners whether they thought that their dogs had a "conscience." Though there was some considerable variation among respondents with regard to how effective their animal's conscience was in constraining unwanted behavior, all saw their dogs as having at least a sense of the rules imposed by the human members of the household. In turn, they all could offer accounts of incidents where their animals violated the rules and subsequently responded in ways indicating the subjective experience of guilt. Typical guilt responses entailed clearly readable body language—bowed head, tucked tail, ears down, sidelong glances. For example:

> Some major problems existed with him when he has younger and learning the house rules—what's proper and what's not proper. In some ways he has modified us because there are things we do with him that we would find obnoxious with someone else's dog. Because it is him and because it is in this house, its ok. . . . After a period of time, if you don't pay attention to him he will try and push the point a bit. But after a while if he realizes he is not going to get the attention, he will just go sit down. He more likely will mope, but at least he gets out of the way.
>
> [Do you think Diz has a conscience?]
>
> He knows what he should and shouldn't do. If he gets into something. . . . He came up the stairs with a big old flower in his mouth, this silk flower, and his ears go forward. That's his look, "Am I doing something I'm not supposed to be doing?" He'll get something in his mouth and he'll put his head down and his ears go down and his little tail is kind of wagging. It is a body language that says to me, "Am I supposed to be doing this?"

Since caretakers saw their dogs as experiencing a subjective world in which emotion played a central role, they frequently understood their relationships with the animals as revolving around emotional issues. The chief pleasure they derived from the animal-human relationship was the joy of relating to another being who consistently demonstrated love—an affection that was honestly felt and displayed and not contingent upon the personal attributes or even the actions of the human-other. One measure of the intensely positive quality of their relationships with their animals was the owners' perception that their dogs were attuned to their own emotions and responded in ways that were appropriate and empathetic. I quote from an interview in which a father and his teenage daughter speak of their golden retriever's ability to read their emotions and his attempts to comfort them when they feel sad:

> DAUGHTER: He's just fun. He keeps us lighthearted. And he certainly senses our moods. If you're sad and crying he will come snuggle next to you.
> FATHER: He just seems to sense it somehow. You can be in a different room and be down. Recently when Mary was in her room he just seemed to know where to go. . . . He sensed that somewhere in this house—his doghouse— there was something that was not quite right. He sought Mary out and was just there. One day I was sitting on the front porch kind of blue about some

things and he just snuggled in there—totally noninvasive. Just "If you want to pet me, pet me. I'm here if you need me."

This was the most essential theme that emerged from my interactions with owners. Like other intimate relationships, those with their dogs were intrinsically rewarding and premised on intersubjectivity and shared emotion. Unlike human-to-human associations, however, caretakers defined their relationships with their dogs as free from criticism and contingent feelings; they were honest and openly loving. These characteristics—unique attributes of relationships in which humans are involved—prompted owners to feel strong emotional ties to their dogs. The centrality of emotional connectedness is seen in this story offered by a client in the veterinary clinic when I asked her to tell me about how she had acquired her dog some years before:

> I just told my parents I wanted a dog. I was living with my parents then. A lady down the street had a litter. I went in and immediately he came right over to me. It was love at first sight—he chose me. I remember it was really snowing that night and we couldn't get to the grocery store. My mother made him chicken soup. To this day he goes wild when he smells chicken soup. Every time I make it he gets half. Sometimes this annoys my roommate— "Hey, I wanted some of that." But he is more important. He's not a dog to me. He's my best friend. He loves me and I love him. When I come home from work he's happy to see me and I am happy to see him. I try to spend quality time with him every day. . . . He gives me love. He can't live without me and I can't live without him. It's so hard to see him getting old. I just don't know what I would do without him.

The Dog as a Playful Performer

In order to effectively string together the individual actions that make up interaction, social actors must be able to—or at least believe they are able to—gain some sense of the subjective experience of the other. It is through this process of constructing one's own answer to the basic question "What's going on here?" and trying, in turn, to imagine how others are defining the immediate situation—its physical and social features, interactants' goals, strategies devised for self and anticipated from others, and so forth—that "collective action"[8] proceeds. This ability to imaginatively "take the role of the other" is central to all social exchanges. As we have seen, caretakers typically see their dogs as having the ability to understand their emotions and, in turn, they can read the emotional states of their dogs. The dominant vehicle for this intersubjective exchange of emotional information is the mutual "conversation of gestures" based on interactants' physical movements and posturings.[9]

Verbal cues are also mutually employed in the interactions of people with their dogs. Owners come to understand what their animals mean when they whine, bark, or engage in other forms of "proto-speech."[10] For example, one owner encountered in the veterinary clinic spoke of her family's developing ability to interpret what their dog was "saying":

> Our lives have really changed since we got him. He even talks to us.
>
> [How?]
>
> He makes these low grunting sounds deep in his throat. He tells us when he wants something and we have learned to understand him. He leans against us and looks up at us. You're sitting there and he will come over and put his head on your lap and look at you—he wants you to pet him. He communicates through different sounds and the way he acts. He even makes a special sound when he wants a popsicle.[11]

The interaction between people and their dogs is, then, premised on communicative acts. Typically, this communication proceeds, as seen in the above quote, in the context of mutually defined household routines and owner-defined rules.[12] One interviewee, a graduate student involved in writing her dissertation, spoke of the domestic routine and situated communication she shared with her great dane:

> [How does Jerry speak with you?]
>
> Well, if she really wants my attention she will bark and she won't stop until she gets me to do what she wants—which is mostly either to play with her or let her out. That's like at night when we are upstairs. Other than that we have such a routine that she doesn't need to overtly tell me much. We just sort of have this pattern of things that she and I do together. She gets up with me at 5:30 and she comes down and goes outside while I do my yoga. Then we go for a walk; then I feed her. I start work at 9 o'clock. She knows. I say, "Let's go," and we go up the stairs to the office. She climbs up into her chair and she goes to sleep while I work. At noon she goes out again. She is with me so much that we each know what the other wants.

One way in which sociologists commonly think of human interaction is by using a theatrical analogy. The "drama" of social interaction proceeds as people—individually or in cooperation with others—"perform" for an individual or group "audience." This performance involves the actor behaving in ways intended to present a particular definition of the immediate situation and using "expressive materials" such as costumes, sets, and props. The goal of the performance is to shape the audience's definition of the situation, thereby manipulating her/his/its behavior.[13]

This dramaturgical perspective has considerable utility in directing attention to certain elements of domestic canine social behavior both with people and with other dogs. Owners frequently offered stories in which their dogs acted in ways that were obviously intended to shape the owners' definitions of the situation and to manipulate their subsequent behavior to desirable ends. A number of the owners with whom I spoke described incidents such as the following:

> We have a beanpot that we keep filled with dog cookies. Every time the dogs go out and "do their business" they get a cookie. They have interpreted this as, "all we have to do is cross the threshold and come back and we get a cookie." So it will be raining and they won't want to go out and they will just put one foot outside the door and then go over to where the cookies are kept. "Well, technically we went out."

Though rarely successful, this represents an attempt by the dog to deceptively manipulate the owner's definition of the situation (dog went out) so as to shape his or her behavior (give cookie). Caretakers also provided descriptions of times when they observed their dogs engaging in deceptive actions while playing with other dogs. For example, a veterinarian offered the following story when we were discussing the issue of whether or not dogs think:

> I believe that dogs think. My dogs play a game called "bone." One of them will get the rawhide bone and take it over to the other one and try to get him to try and get it. Or one will try to get the bone if the other one has it. One day I was watching and the youngest one was trying to get the bone without much luck. So he goes over to the window and begins to bark like someone is coming up the driveway. The other dog drops the bone and runs over to the window and the puppy goes and gets the bone. There wasn't anyone in the driveway, it was just a trick. Maybe it was just coincidence but. . . .[14]

From the perspective of dog owners, then, the animals with whom they have ongoing, intimate relationships behave in ways that indicate they are actively involved in trying to view situations from the perspective of others and behaving in ways purposefully designed to shape the subsequent actions of others to their own ends. Caretakers are, in turn, able to imaginatively assume the perspective of their dogs. This mutual intersubjective exchange of definitions and their indications provides the foundation for successful and rewarding interactions.

Seeing the Dog as a Person

The designation of "person" is socially constructed and assigned. The exclusion of certain human beings from the category of person has been a fairly common sociohistorical phenomenon. "Primitives," African Americans, women, and members of various other human groups routinely have been, and continue to be, denied the full status of person,[15] and studies of interactions in total institutions[16] are filled with accounts of the "dehumanization" of inmates by staff members.

In their study of the interactions of nondisabled people with severely disabled family members, Robert Bogdan and Steven Taylor[17] discuss the ways in which the social meaning of humanness is created and the criteria "normals" use to assign a human identity to severely disabled intimates. This definitional activity entails attending to four basic factors. First, the nondisabled attribute thinking to the disabled other. The latter is seen as being able to reason, to understand, and to remember. The disabled individual is, then, regarded as a partner in the intersubjective play of social interaction and his or her gestures, sounds, postures, and expressions are interpreted as indicating intelligence. Nondisabled family members are adept at using information derived from intimate association to effectively take the role of the disabled other.

The nondisabled, according to Bogdan and Taylor, also see the disabled person as an individual, as having a distinct personality, identifiable likes and dislikes, authentic feelings, and a unique personal history. In turn, the disabled person is seen as reciprocating, as giving as much to the relationship as he or she receives from it. For nondisabled caretakers, disabled family members are true companions who help expand their lives by providing companionship, acting as objects of caring, and opening up situations in which they can encounter new people.

Finally, Bogdan and Taylor describe how the disabled person is humanized by being incorporated into a social place. Through defining the disabled person as an integral member of the family and involving him or her in ongoing domestic rituals and routines, the nondisabled actively include the other into the intimate network of the family.

The owners I interviewed and encountered in the veterinary hospital engaged in a process of identity construction very similar to that described by Bogdan and Taylor. They routinely used their day-to-day experience with their dogs as a source of information directed at understanding their animals as socially defined "persons."[18] As described earlier, caretakers defined their dogs as demonstrating an ability to think and as reciprocating partners in an honest, nondemanding, and rewarding social relationship.[19]

Although many caretakers did see certain personality characteristics as breed related—malamutes were tough and intelligent, golden retrievers were "goofy" and fun-loving, and so on[20]—they regularly spoke of their own dogs as unique individuals. Few of the people with whom I spoke had any trouble responding at some length to my routine request that they describe what their dog "was like." Owners currently living with multiple dogs or those who had had serial experience with dogs often made comparisons in presenting their animals' unique personal attributes. For the most part, these comparisons emphasized contrasts—one was aggressive, the other was shy; one was smart, the other was dumb; one was dependent, the other was independent. For example, an interviewee with two springer spaniels responded to my question about the personality of one of his dog's as follows:

> It's interesting. A good way to look at this is to compare her with my other dog. I look at my older springer and she is always begging for attention. Sometimes I misinterpret that as wanting something to eat. I'll just be studying and she is happy just to sit there and have her head in my lap while I scratch her behind the ears. On the other hand, Ricky really likes attention and she seeks it. But if you're not willing to give it to her, she'll go find something else to entertain herself. She's bold, she's aggressive. At the same time she is affectionate—willing to take what you will give her.

Owners also were readily able to describe their dogs' unique personal tastes. Respondents typically took considerable pleasure in talking about individual likes and dislikes in food, activities, playthings, and people. For example, when asked by the veterinarian whether her dog liked to chew rocks (he had noticed that the dog's teeth were quite worn), a woman described her female doberman's special passion:

She just loves rocks.

[VET: If you see her straining to go or walking hunched up, she may have a rock stuck in her craw.]

No. She just loves big rocks; the bigger the better. When she finds a new one she is so happy she howls. She'll lie and chew them all day. She puts them in her water bucket and sometimes it takes two hands to get them out.

As we have seen, caretakers routinely attribute feelings to their canine companions. Their dogs are individuals who feel pride, embarrassment, joy, and sorrow and have other emotional experiences that indicate their sentience and individuality. For example, one owner described the somewhat puzzling emotions he attributed to his female English bull terrier:

It's strange. She gets it into her head that I'm angry at her and she'll just stay away from me. Like I'll be eating and bend down to give her something and she'll shy away from me and then stay away from me for a month when I'm eating. I have just learned to accept it. It first started when she was young and she was playing with another dog and they were chasing a ball and the other dog kept getting it. She seemed to be embarrassed that the other dog was getting the ball and then she seemed to think I was mad at her for that. She'll come into the room and I'll say something to her and she'll just go into her cage like she is sulking. Then she'll come back in and I won't say anything—I just figure she wants to be left alone—and then she'll be upset because I'm not talking to her. She thinks I'm mad at her, that she's done something wrong. I just try to accept it. She has a mind of her own.

Finally, owners attribute individuality to their dogs by including them in a readily recountable narrative history. All interviewees seemed to take great pleasure in telling stories about how they came to acquire their dogs and about the dogs' exploits. The following historical narratives offered by owners are typical of the acquisition stories I heard:

I have had Fred since I was a sophomore in college. I found him when I was eloping. . . . I didn't get married as it turned out but I got a dog. We were driving down to the Cape and I had had a few beers so we stopped by the side of the road so I could take a leak. I was standing there and this puppy runs up. I thought that there must be someone around so I called and called but no one answered. We decided to just go ahead and take him with us. Every time we stopped at the shore I let him out and he ran off. But when we got back to the car there he was waiting for us. I figured it was fate—I was destined to have a dog.

FIELD NOTE EXCERPT: An old (16 years) mixed breed dog ("Randy") is brought in by retired owner for a routine check of his irregular heartbeat and to evaluate the effectiveness of the current medication. Marty (the veterinarian) takes Randy into the medical prep area for his EKG. The dog still seems to be having some problems so Marty talks about increasing the dosage. I am touched by the elderly owner's obvious love for his dog. He says, "Each time I come in here for this I think it is the end. But he always comes home. He's a good puppy. I still call him that. He likes it. . . . I got him for free at the animal hospital. He was a street dog—had a tire chain welded around his neck. He lived on the street and ate pizza and Mexican food out of the trash at "Sloppy Joes." He'd follow the gulls around on the shore and chase them until they dropped their clams and then he'd eat them. He had a bad case of colitis when I got him. (sighs) But he's getting old. It won't be long now. We're going to have to make a decision sometime soon."

As individuals with distinct personalities, unique tastes, identifiable feelings, and personal histories, the dogs were regarded as "persons" by their owners. This social assignment of personhood was furthered as owners actively involved their animals in both the routines and the special rituals of the family. The dogs typically were considered to be authentic family members.[21] Shared family routines commonly centered around feeding and food preparation, playing with or exercising the dog, and some more idiosyncratic routines that had emerged in the course of the shared relationship. One owner described her daily breakfast routine with her newly acquired puppies at some length and with obvious relish (notice the reference to the dogs as "kids" and the respondent's connection of their shared routine to one remembered from her own childhood):

I love these dogs; they are people dogs. We do have a set course of activities during the course of the day. We seem to meld very nicely with one another. Anywhere from 5:30 on the dogs will start to bark which means to me that it is time to get up—the activities of the day have begun. I come downstairs and they are on the back porch waiting to come in for breakfast. I bring them in the house and I talk to them. We talk about what we are going to do today and what do you want for breakfast. Of course they have no choice; they get the same thing every meal. But it is very important for me to talk to them, and I'm sure they know what I am saying because they will go into the pantry and get a biscuit. So I go in and get the bag of [dog food] and I show it to them and say, "This is what we're having for breakfast." They'll sit down and look and I will go to the refrigerator and get the yogurt out and I will put a spoonful in each dish and I will always be sure that I leave a little on the spoon so the kids can lick it. I do that because it reminds me of when I was a kid and whenever my mother made frosting she would leave a little on the spoon. That was always the highlight of frosting a cake—licking the spoon. Then I take the dishes out and they eat. I go get my coffee and read the paper and talk to them. They will walk around and poop. They will play for a while. The day has begun.

Another owner described a somewhat unusual routine that her dog had devised and fostered during the time he had been a member of her family. Notice how she constructs an understanding of the dog's purpose as played out in this routine:

If we are in the shower, Robin always comes in. He'll push the door open and he will sit right there or lie down by the shower. You get out of the shower— it's really funny—and then he stays there until you begin walking out. Then whatever it is we're carrying—a towel or sweatshirt—he's got to have it in his mouth and he will help us carry it upstairs. He's not really tugging. He doesn't try to take it away from you. He just wants to be part of it. He just wants to help. And you get upstairs and you pet him on the head, "Thanks, Robin," and he lets go.

Emphasizing the importance of shared rituals as a source of social cohesion is common in sociological analyses.[22] All of the owners with whom I raised the issue were able to describe key ritual activities they shared with their animals. Most, for example, knew the date of and celebrated their dogs' birthdays. They baked cakes, bought presents, organized parties, prepared their dog's favorite foods, and took other special steps to ritually commemorate their animals' births. The other family ritual in which the dog typically was included was that surrounding Christmas or other religious holidays. A young woman, for example, described her puppy's first Christmas:

He just loved Christmas. Somehow he figured out which were his presents under the tree, and he happily opened them all himself. He had his own ornaments on the tree—I got some that were unbreakable and put them on the bottom branches. He would take one carefully in his mouth and come running into the other room with it all proud to show it off. He loved the tree. He thought we had brought it in from the outside though it is just a fake tree. He started to sleep under it. Sometimes he would go and stand under it and scratch his back on the bottom branches.[23]

This then was one of the major themes that emerged from my conversations with and observations of dog owners. Like the nondisabled interacting with severely disabled people studied by Bogdan and Taylor, owners used their daily experiences with their animals as the source of the information they needed to assign the social status of "person." Their dogs had individual personalities, tastes, histories, and emotions and were incorporated as members of the family. Even when respondents found it difficult to verbalize the criteria they used to define their dogs as unique persons, they had no doubt about their personhood:

The only way I can describe the relationship [with my dog] is to use human terms. He certainly has as much personality as any of the people I know. I just use many of the same indicators to know what he is thinking and feeling that I use to understand my wife or other people.[24]

Again, the picture that emerges here is of the dog as an authentic, reciprocating, thoughtful, and feeling social actor. As such, canine companions are effectively involved with their caretakers in the play of social action in which interactants try to imagine each other's points of view, effectively define the physical and social situation, and adjust their behaviors in line with these essential determinations. Mutual intersubjectivity—the ability of the dog and person to interact in what the latter at least defines as an "open awareness context"[25] where interactants share knowledge of each other's identities—is the foundation of the rewarding collective action of people's relationships with their dogs. Unlike many of the painfully manipulative and inauthentic relationships people routinely have with their fellow humans, owners' relationships with their dogs typically are seen as significantly more satisfying and authentic.

This elemental reward of living in intimate association with a dog, of sharing activities and imaginatively experiencing the animal's subjective world, was vividly captured in the statements of a husband and wife just before they demonstrated their daily ritual "family hug" for me at the end of an interview session:

WIFE: He pulls us together as a family. He just melts you down. If there is ever any stress or conflict or something, Bones will come up—right when we are having an argument. I mean, how can you be mad when this sweet little dog is here? It is almost like a lesson. He reminds me just how simple things really are and not to get all overworked about things in life.

HUSBAND: He's very constant. He's very sensitive to everyone's moods, but he never really basically changes. He's always the same, you can always depend on him. I will seek him out if I am a little down about something. Or, if I realize I am uptight and I want to calm down, Bones is the source of that. I will want to sit with him and just have him nuzzle up. It just brings things into perspective. I think it is because he is constant.

Dogs and People in Public

The intimate connection between people and their dogs means that people are responsible for the behavior of their canine companions. One situation in which this expectation is most apparent is when the owner and his or her dog are together in public.[26] In this type of situation, the animal and the owner constitute what Erving Goffman[27] refers to as a "with," a group whose members are perceived to be "together." They typically maintain a physical closeness that ordinarily permits the members to engage in conversation and that excludes non-members who otherwise might overhear what is said. The mutual "togetherness" of the with is typically symbolized by "with markers"[28] or "tie signs"[29] that demonstrate the connection between the various members. Leashes, mutual gaze, physical contact (e.g., petting, nuzzling), the owner's calling the animal by name, and a variety of other tie signs are used to publicly demonstrate that the dog and caretaker constitute a with.[30]

When they are together in public, the dog and his or her human companion are bound by expectations of propriety and mutual responsibility. The weight of these expectations rests most heavily on the owner who is seen as being most capable of exercising "intelligent self-control."[31] Consequently, when the dog misbehaves or fails to perform in line with public expectations, the owner usually is held responsible.

Socially problematic behavior by the animal has the potential of degrading the social identity of the human partner—he or she is, for example, regarded as an "irresponsible" dog owner.[32] In turn, the negative responses of other people can have negative consequences for the owner's self-definition. Judgmental social response by others typically generates uncomfortable experiences such as guilt, shame, or embarrassment for the caretaker.[33]

The dog's failure to abide by widely shared expectations about proper behavior disrupts the smooth, more-or-less cooperative flow of public interaction and presents an uncomfortable situation for the owner. As in other situations where problematic events disrupt social interaction, the owner with a misbehaving dog often is obliged to take steps to reestablish the flow of "normal" public interaction. In so doing, the owner also attempts to restore his or her positive social identity and regain those aspects of positive self definition that have been degraded by the negative responses of human others.[34]

When encountering problematic situations generated by their dogs' misbehavior, owners typically take steps to make amends. They call up and present definitions of the immediate situation and/or offer accounts of their animals' (or their own) motives in order to smooth out the disrupted interaction and repair their own damaged images.

It is possible to identify at least seven kinds of such "excusing tactics"[35] that owners use in the face of their dogs' misbehaviors in public. These various approaches may be used separately or in combination and typically are chosen on the basis of the form of the dog's violation and the degree of apparent "harm" caused by his or her misbehavior.[36]

"Situating" is one of the most common excusing tactics used by owners in public. When using this approach the owner typically emphasizes the unfamiliarity or chaotic character of the immediate situation in which the animal is expected to perform appropriately. Below are two examples of situating drawn from the field notes I collected while observing the puppy kindergarten class. In the first, the owner offers an excuse focused on the structure of the situation in which the puppy is not meeting expectations. In the second example, the caretaker provides a rather unique situating explanation emphasizing observed changes in the dog's behavior based on the time of day:

> During free play (an activity that opened each class where all of the puppies were allowed to run around the classroom and interact without restraint) Hooter (a gawky, good-natured German shepherd) cowers under the bench at his owner's feet. The owner justifies this failure to socialize by saying, "He's always so rambunctious and wild at home. I don't know why he acts this way here. (pause) He does come from a small litter and he has never had much chance to play with other puppies. He likes people more than he likes other dogs."

> Ann (the trainer) is providing information about neutering. As she talks, Trots (a shy black lab) is biting his owner's hands. Ann notices this and asks about it, emphasizing once again that it is a behavior that should not be allowed. The owner ducks her head in embarrassment and responds, "He doesn't do this all the time. This is what he does at night. He only does it after 10. He's not like this at all during the day." Ann says, "He's just going to keep doing it until you get mad and say 'GOD DAMN IT! DON'T DO THAT!' He's having a great time controlling your behavior."

"Justifying" is another common excusing tactic. Owners use it to deflect responsibility for their animals' misbehavior by redirecting the blame on another person, usually the aggrieved party. Statements like, "You can't just walk up behind her like that" or "he gets really nervous when you touch him there" focus the blame for the infraction on the other person for having behaved stupidly or precipitously.

Owners also use "redefining" as an excusing tactic. Here owners attempt to defuse the negative feelings generated by their animal by presenting the behavior as a positive rather than negative action. Often the human companion labels the behavior as "cute" or "smart" in order to move it back into the realm of permissibility. In my experience, this tactic offers, at best, only limited success as a means of smoothing disrupted interaction. I quote again from my observations in the puppy kindergarten:

> After the rules have been explained, the dogs are all released to interact in "free-play" for the first time. In general, everything is going well and the owners sit and watch their dogs play with pleased smiles on their faces. Ann takes the three smallest dogs and their owners out into the hallway so the dogs can play together away from the general melee. One of the three, a rather hyper collie pup, is acting aggressively towards the other small dogs— growling, chasing them, nipping at their rumps as they frantically try to run or seek shelter and protection at their owners' feet. I notice the owners of the bullied pups are no longer smiling. The collie's owner laughs and says, "He sure is energetic. I guess he is going to be the class clown. He just thinks he's

Owners and their young dogs at puppy kindergarten.
Photographer: Mary Beth Kaeser

tough." The affronted owners manage weak, inauthentic smiles in response. One scoops up her pup and returns to the main room while the other pushes the aggressive collie pup away from her dog.

Embarrassed owners also use what I call "behavioral quasi-theorizing." John Hewitt and Peter Hall[37] speak of quasi-theories as commonplace cultural explanations that people employ during everyday interactions in order to "explain problematic situations and give them order and hope." "What we have here is a failure to communicate," or "those people are poor because they are just too lazy to work" are typical quasi-theoretical statements in contemporary society. When used as an excusing tactic, the quasi-theory tends to emphasize that the dog's misbehavior actually is "natural" (that is, justifiable) given that the animal is "just a dog" and "that's the way dogs are" or to focus on the dog's stage of development (for example, "I'm sorry she chewed up your purse. She's just a puppy and she's teething"). I quote from the auto-ethnographic notes I collected while spending time with my own dogs:

Something happened on the walk today that I realize is typical. As we were going along the trail we encountered a group of four people (an older couple and a young couple about our age) coming toward us. As usual, Emma and Isis were overjoyed to see someone and tore off to greet them tails wagging furiously and bounding in pleasure. Understandably taken aback by the sight of two sizeable dogs running towards them (we still define them as "small" since they only weigh around 75 pounds each), the four of them gather in an uneasy clump with Isis and, especially, Emma leaping happily around them. Not wanting to have trouble and fearing that the dogs could injure the older people, El and I began to shout commands and run toward the group. As we ran up I said, "It's okay. They're just puppies. They won't hurt you." I realize that "they're just puppies" is, along with, "we're still working on this" (i.e., trying to break them of doing whatever it is I am excusing), a kind of ritual incantation I trot out when we meet other people on walks.

Related to quasi-theorizing is "processual emphasis," an excusing tactic where the owner emphasizes that the dog will eventually acquire behavioral self-control as he or she matures or undergoes training (see the quote above). Owners often acknowledge that the violation is an example of troublesome behavior and present themselves as "working on" the animal's training in order to extinguish it from the dog's behavioral repertoire. The lesson is in process but has not as yet taken hold to the owner's—or, presumably, to the affronted other's—satisfaction.

Owners also commonly use "demonstrative disciplining" as an excusing tactic. When they confront problematic social situations precipitated by their pet, owners may combine the excusing move of "processual emphasis" with overt, often rather harsh, corrective actions directed at the animal. Through loudly shouting "NO!," jerking on the leash, striking the animal, and using other disciplining gestures, the embarrassed owner symbolically acknowledges that the dog's behavior was "wrong" while overtly demonstrating his or her desire to assert effective control. I quote again from field observations of the puppy kindergarten:

Franki (a barky, blond mixed breed) growls and snaps at his owner's hand when she reaches down to quiet him. Ann notices this serious infraction and goes over to them speaking emphatically. "Don't pull your hand away. That is the worst thing you can do. He thinks it's a game and he can win . . . that he can get you to do what he wants. Do this instead (she demonstrates the lip-pinching technique)." Owner: "I don't have the heart to do that to him." Ann observes, "Well then, you're going to lose a lot of blood." [later] Once again

Franki growls and nips at his owner. She lets loose with a loud "NO!" and gives the dog's lip a hearty twist causing it to yelp. She glances around at the other owners (most are looking at her) and says with a somewhat sheepish smile, "I guess he'll learn."

"Unlinking" is the excusing tactic of last resort. It is a public confession that the animal-human relationship itself is in serious trouble. Frustrated and confused, the guilt-ridden owner publicly acknowledges that the animal other is "out of control" ("I just don't know what to do. I can't get him to stop barking. I've tried and tried but nothing seems to work") and, in essence, symbolically dissolves the animal-human with. The fault for the disruptive action is presented as being the animal's and, in turn, the owner is absolved of responsibility. Understandably, the owner who comes to employ this type of excusing tactic with any frequency is well on the way to ending his or her relationship with the animal.[38]

Clearly, when appearing together in public, the caretaker and his or her dog are involved in a mutual social performance. When this performance fails to go smoothly or entails violations of the rules, interactions are disrupted, the collective social identity of the dog and owner is degraded, and the human actor's feelings of self-worth (and perhaps those of the animal member, as well) are subjected to attack. Interactional disruptions produced by the misbehavior of the companion animal typically prompt the owner to make restorative moves. By presenting the motives, developmental stage, and/or natural propensities of the animal, the owner attempts to couch the problematic behavior in an understandable, and therefore justifiable, context. Alternatively, the owner can engage in maneuvers intended to demonstrate that he or she is not emotionally or relationally attached to the animal and the latter's violation should not degrade the owner's social repute or be the source of human-to-human interactions that could potentially threaten the owner's positive definition of self.

This understanding of the public performance of the animal-human team and the steps taken to repair interactional damage caused by the animal's infractions is closely related to sociological discussions of a similar situation: the behavior of an adult-child pair in public settings.[39]

Spencer Cahill, for example, emphasizes that children acquire civil competence in the course of the instruction and disciplining meted out by adults when children overtly violate the expectations of public order. Failure of children to apply appropriate rules, in turn, reflects negatively on the social repute of the adult caretaker. As Cahill puts it:

> [People] are taught to have feelings attached to a self which is expressed through "face" or effective claims to positive self value. They are also taught that such claims are both made and validated through performances of the constituent interpersonal rituals of our religion of civility . . . and [they] come to experience some combination of anger . . . , embarrassment . . . , revulsion or shame . . . whenever they *or their coassociates* fail to fulfill the associated ceremonial expectations.[40]

Like companion animals, young children are rarely allowed to participate as individuals in public life and their relationship to the adult caretaker is publicly displayed through such tie signs as hand-holding or confinement in strollers. In turn, the problematic behaviors of children typically meet with remedial responses by the adult(s) in their with:

> To the extent that young children's caretakers are ritually competent actors who possess a defensive orientation toward saving their own face . . . , they can be counted upon to not only contain but to also ritually repair their charges' disruptions of the ceremonial order of public life.[41]

Remedial responses to children's tactless or otherwise violative public behaviors commonly entail the adult's interpreting the *motives* of the offender. Typical accounts emphasize that the violation was an "accident" or due to "forgetting."[42] As with the misbehavior of companion animals, these infractions are often redefined as "cute" or used by the adults as the focus of a lesson in the socialization process.

In addition to this processual emphasis, the excusing tactic of "demonstrative disciplining" is commonly employed by adult associates to realign public interactions disrupted by the child's actions. As Cahill puts it in his description of adults and children in public:

> Such admonitions as "you know you're not supposed to do that" and the exercise of physical control over a disruptive child seem designed not merely for the offender but for the offended as well. . . . Such admonitions and displays of physical control are designed to show that the "with" is ceremonially responsible even though one of its elements is not.[43]

Love, mutuality, and responsibility bind the everyday dog owner to his or her dog. While being with a dog in certain situations may have some problematic consequences and require explanations and disciplining, on the whole, caretakers value the time spent with their dogs and come to regard them as virtual persons. As such, they are seen as individual family members who offer day-to-day rewards that far outweigh the responsibilities of ownership and the problems their behaviors might occasionally cause. While the intimate relationship between the everyday owner and his or her dog is complex, touching, and sociologically interesting, it pales in comparison to the connection that arises when the owner must depend on the care and skill of a dog to negotiate the routines of daily life. We turn now to examine the unique and emotionally rich relationship between visually handicapped owners and the assistance dogs with whom they live.

The Guide Dog Owner

Dependence and Love

eople with guide dogs are, first and foremost, dog owners. Like the caretakers of common house dogs presented in the previous chapter, they know their dogs as individuals and feel intense affection for them. However, because their dogs are, in a real sense, extensions of their physical selves,[1] their relationships with their dogs take on some significant additional elements. Most essentially, the dog is a "tool" that functions to assist the visually impaired owner in moving though his or her daily life. Dependence on the animal's abilities, together with the almost constant interaction between the guide and the user, imbues this relationship with an intensity and emotional strength that significantly sets it apart from "ordinary" human associations with dogs.[2]

The guide dog owners with whom I talked typically were prompted to start the process of acquiring dogs by agents of the organizational structure Robert Scott refers to as the "blindness system."[3] Blindness workers would evaluate the psychological and physical condition of the potential owner and recommend that he or she might do well with an assistance animal. For example, one owner who lost his sight in an auto accident as a teenager described his initial movement into ownership:

About six months after [I lost my sight], I went to a place called the _____ Center for the Blind, a research and development center in _____, and I learned cane travel and I learned different adult living skills—cooking and braille and things like that. I was never very confident with a cane. I knew right away that [traveling with a cane was] not going to work. I was very frightened, very unsure of myself, and had zero confidence. So, I was back in my home and I really did not know were to go in my life or what to do. My counselor—my vocational rehabilitation counselor from the state service for the blind—came down to talk to me. They had a psychological evaluation done of me and said, "Well, you know, you have some spatial orientation problems, so you should probably get a guide dog." [The counselor] was on the board of directors of [the guide dog program] and said, "Why don't you apply to [the program]?" I did, was accepted, and about three or four months later they called me and said they had a dog for me.

Distaste for or problems with using the cane as mentioned by this interviewee were common for all those with whom I talked. One young woman derogatorily referred to her cane as "the icicle" while another young man observed that he mostly used his to have sword fights with his sighted friends. While recognizing that using a cane was considerably more convenient than living with a guide dog—it did not require extensive care and could be folded up and put away should one wish to "pass" as sighted—all those with whom I talked said that traveling with a cane required considerable concentration and the cane acted as a symbol of their difference to members of the sighted public.[4] In addition to helping the blind person navigate, the dog was seen as having the virtue of offering companionship as well as changing his or her social identity. One interviewee spoke of the dependency engendered by blindness and how acquiring a dog had changed his identity in others' eyes:

When you have been blinded there is an incredible amount of anger and frustration that you go through. . . . It's almost like a part of you dies and you are mourning a loss of who you are. Your identity is gone as a person. . . . I mean, [after I was blinded] I could not go into the kitchen and make a peanut butter and jelly sandwich. My grandmother would not let me. You basically lose adulthood; you are treated like a child. Forging my independence was a very difficult transition. . . . [Then I went away to college] and all of these new things are coming down on me and all of a sudden I get this dog who was a way out for me.

First Meetings

As one may well imagine, the anticipation novice guide dog owners feel just before they are introduced to their canine companions is incredibly intense. Guide programs construct dog-person teams based on a variety of criteria. They take into account the potential owner's age and mobility as well as his or her standard walking pace, physical strength, personality, and living situation. Dogs are chosen to enhance and compliment these attributes. One interviewee told about how program staff described the dog with whom she was to be paired and how they stressed the animal's appearance and personality:

> [The trainer] told me his name, and that he was a very beautiful dog. He said I would get a lot of compliments. He said he was a big dog, and that he was really good with children. I have nine nieces and nephews and it was really important for me to have a dog that was laid-back with kids. [The trainer] told me that he could be strong-willed and stubborn and that he was a very solid dog. I think they did a good job in matching. I needed a low-energy dog at the time I got him because [of my physical problems] and he is considered a low-energy dog. Niko doesn't have a lot of needs. If I need to walk ten miles in a day, he'll walk. If I lay in bed all day, he'll sleep right beside me. I didn't need his size, as much as his matching personality.

Another owner described the matching process as similar to computer dating:

> When they chose Millie they told me they took into account what I do for activities and everything from my body size, weight, height, what [activities] I was anticipating and, since Millie should be with me for approximately seven to ten years, what I expected to be doing in the future. Then they take all of the dog characteristics and wrap you together. It's sort of like a computer dating service. They told me they had two dogs in mind. [They said] one was a long-haired gray, and that she had a pretty face and markings. I don't know what the second dog was like because I said that whatever the first choice of dog was, I would go with that. I've been told by many people that we're a perfect match and I agree.

Since no amount of preliminary information can entirely prepare the new guide dog owner, most of those I talked to looked forward to their first encounter with a combination of anticipation and fear. One owner talked of her initial anxiety and the unanticipated consequences, both positive and negative, that followed upon her becoming a guide dog user. Again the theme of how being with a dog has impact on one's social identity comes to the fore:

> I was terrified. I started having nightmares the week before she came. The night before she came I didn't sleep. I was really afraid because, up until that point, I had been using my cane and I knew how to travel. I knew how to count and get from one place to another. I had no concept in my head for how this dog was going to do this. . . . I thought it would be like having a baby—making sure she was fed, taking her to the vet. . . . I knew she was going to be trained, but I didn't know exactly how. I wasn't sure how I was going to work with her. In some ways, I wondered if I was going to be giving up some of my independence to the dog. There are several ways to look at it. When you have a cane, it doesn't need to go out to go to the bathroom, it doesn't need to be fed, it doesn't need to go to the vet or stay home if you go to the beach. I knew Fanny would be a big help. She would be fully trained and I was going to be trained. I just didn't know if I was losing part of my independence, even a part of my identity.

Initial excitement soon gives way to an exhausting mixture of confusion and frustration. In their relative ignorance, some potential owners expect the dog to be, as one put it, "like a robot or a machine." They presume that the dog has been well trained and will, more or less automatically, perform his or her tasks. Instead, they soon realize that, as in any effective social relationship, the parties must learn about each other and experiment with various interactional strategies in a variety of situations. As seen in the following description, these initial experiments do not always go smoothly. But when the relationship begins to click it results in effective and intimate collective action:

> You know the blank slate theory of child development? That's what you are when you get your first dog—a blank slate. Here you are with this new animal and [the trainer] is telling you how you need to act and how to do this and that and everything is very structured. You stand a certain way and you say "left" and you say "right." It just really is all new. . . . It is overwhelming that there is so much to learn. But that first day just felt so good. I was like real hungry to learn more, to do more, and that sort of thing. It was also very frustrating. You know in your mind what you want but to communicate that to the dog in the beginning is really tough. The dog knows straight lines and curves, it knows left and right but they know nothing about were you want to go or what you want to do. That takes time. . . . The dog eventually learns, but in the beginning the dog is just like straight line material. . . . After working with Prophet for nine years I forget that it was really frustrating a lot of

times. He was a young dog and he was testing me. I was trying to let him know what I wanted and after a period of time working we got into our communication patterns. . . . It got to a very comfortable pattern where it was like I almost didn't even need to speak. I could just flick the handle [of the harness] and he would know what to do and [eventually] it got so that in any given situation he could second guess me and I could second guess him. And 99 percent of the time we would be right. It was amazing. It is an incredible thing.

Apart from the increased ease of moving about in public,[5] novice guide dog owners find their lives most changed by the impact of the assistance animal on their feelings about themselves. The dog increases the owner's confidence and self-esteem. When I asked one interviewee whether her initial experience with the dog was what she had expected it to be, she replied:

What I expected was only a fraction of what I got. I expected to have increased mobility, which I did. I expected to prove everyone wrong who said I shouldn't get a dog, which I did. What I didn't expect was the dignity, the self-esteem, the increase in my overall outlook on life. What I didn't understand was the dog wasn't a cane that you bring out walking with you and you hang up when you get home. Walking with a guide dog, at least for me, is a neat experience. It's great. I have an increased dignity that I never had before. Walking with a human guide or a cane, which I always hated, is horrible. You have no independence. You can't mobilize as well. With another person you're holding their arm, elbow. With a dog, you're a whole. You're not two people trying to function together; you're one unit. Even though you're two bodies, it doesn't feel that way. So there was a great deal of dignity and self-esteem that I didn't expect to happen.

Another owner told a story about the first day he was out with his dog and how that experience taught him that trust in the animal would be the basis of an enduring relationship and the foundation of the confidence he needed to get on with his life:

Anthem changed my life drastically. He really gave me the confidence to do a lot of things. I remembered the first day. I felt confident with him immediately. It's like we bonded immediately. We played together in the house and then we went for a walk out on [a busy street in town]. Like, immediately I knew that this is the way to go. This dog is like happening, you know. I mean, we were walking along just cruising. I felt really confident again and it just gave me a sense that I am going to be okay. That first day I was walking with him on the main street and this car comes speeding out between two buildings and [Anthem] stopped on a dime. If he hadn't that car would have hit me. So, that experience really helped me to say, "I need to trust this animal with everything that I have." I truly believe that the dog can sense whether you trust him or not and, if that trust is not there, then the team is probably not going to work. You really need to build a relationship, and it starts with that first step. I trust this animal with my life. [Anthem] gave me the confidence to try to go back to school; he made me think it was possible to do that. At the time he came into my life I could have gone either way. I could have just stayed home and said, "The heck with it," and not done anything. I think he was a real key part of me deciding to take the bull by the horns and do something with my life. . . . He gave me the confidence to try to do something else.[6]

Understanding the Dog

As I did with the caretakers of house dogs, I asked all the guide dog owners to tell me about how they saw their animals as individuals. How did their dogs' thought processes work? What where their dogs' emotional experiences? In what ways did their dogs try to manipulate them? Each interviewee was readily able to describe his or her dog as a unique individual with an active mental life, likes and dislikes, and personal styles of self presentation that, when displayed by fellow humans, we define as personality. Gauging the dog's distinctive temperament and demeanor was of special importance since the success of the person-dog team was seen as dependent on the correspondence between the owner's and animal's personalities:

> Asa is still just a puppy. He is very active and loves to play. I think of him as if he was a person, as someone that likes to have a good time and is very inquisitive. [If he was a person he] would be someone who likes to look things up when they don't understand it as opposed to saying, "Just forget about it." He is someone who likes to get things done, who does not like screwing around just doing nothing. . . . He's just kind of the way I am so we get along really good.

Because they had good basis for comparison, owners who had worked with more than one guide or who also lived with house dogs were most able to describe their dogs' unique personalities. Some were "needy" of attention while others were "aloof" and businesslike, some were playfully "goofy" while others were "regal," some were "timid" while others were "adventurous." Comparisons of individual dogs were frequently oriented around the "hard" versus "soft" dichotomy conventionally used within the training community.[7] Hard dogs are active, mentally tough, somewhat reserved, and require a "strong hand." Soft dogs are more timid, empathetic, and in need of supportive attention:

[You just made a distinction between hard and soft dogs. Explain the difference to me.]

The first thing is that in order to get a hard dog's attention, you've got to practically break its neck. I've seen hard dogs take people 6'3", 300 pounds and wrap them around door frames. Hard dogs don't slow down . . . and for a while it takes people who have hard dogs more time to correct [them] with the leash. They're really head strong. I never have to use the leash [correction] with Egan who is a soft dog. I've only had to use the leash when he is distracted by other dogs and when he wrapped me around something, which is fairly infrequent. When Egan sees me trip or hit something, he'll let out a little whine. The soft dog can anticipate the correction. The hard dog doesn't care or pay attention. [I heard this tape from a guide dog program] where they said the dog now is a lot more softer and a lot less strong than they used to be. Having had [experience with a previous hard dog], I tend to agree with them. The [current dogs are] good and they do the job, but they've bred out some of that single-mindedness they used to have.

Another owner used a similar distinction when she compared the demeanor and perspectives of the two guides with whom she had worked:

[My first dog] was regal; she was so responsible. I had to teach her how to play. . . . She was very hard-headed. A correction didn't affect her the way it affects [my current dog]. She was like, "Okay, fine, my mistake." Their guiding abilities were the same but she was very aloof. She would often be apart from the family group. If we were sitting in the living room she would be lying in the dining room doorway. She didn't need to be right there with me. She was completely confident with herself. She had a lot of autonomy and we worked well together. It wasn't that she wasn't affectionate because she was. It was in a more subtle way. [My current dog] is a lot more young acting. I don't think [the first dog] was ever young acting. [This dog] is very young acting; she's much more overtly affectionate.

Leading a visually handicapped person through the variety of circumstances that arise in everyday public life places considerable demands on the guide dog. While working, the animal must evaluate situations, decide among a variety of alternative actions, adjust his or her behavior, maintain an awareness of the owner's experience and, in many other ways, behave as a minded actor and interactant.[8] The daily demands of guiding have given rise within the guide dog community to a concept—intelligent disobedience—that encapsulates the necessity of the dog's making independent judgments in certain critical circumstances. The competent guide dog can recognize dangerous situations and, even when commanded to engage in a particular action, can decide to disobey in order to protect the owner's welfare. All the interviewees spoke of their dogs as regularly involved in behaviors that were not understandable if one were only to see dogs merely as automatons responding to instinct or behavioral conditioning. All, when prompted, were able to describe situations in which their dogs engaged in thoughtful decision making. Here are two examples that are similar in that they involve the dog working with two blind people. The first emphasizes the individuality of the dog's definition of the situation and choice of action while the second illustrates the dog's ability to thoughtfully evaluate and adjust to an unfamiliar predicament:

> I see [my dog] as thinking. I don't believe that she's got the same thinking ability as I do. I don't know a lot about the brain of a dog, but I don't think she has the same ability that I do. I do believe that she has the inherent intelligence and the training to make decisions in certain situations. She can help me solve problems related to me. I remember walking with another person and their guide dog, and the dogs made different decisions related to the obstacle in front of them. I thought this was really interesting, because normally the dog behind would slack off and let the dog in front make the decision and follow. But they didn't. They made totally different decisions. We went by this obstacle four times, and they made the same, consistent decision, each differently. One went under and one went around. I don't know why they did that. They just made their own decisions and so it is sure that there is an intelligence there.

> [Here's] an incident with my first dog that lends credibility [to the view] that they do think or that there's some communication going on between the dog and the master. I was walking with Bryan and I was actually guiding another blind person, which is taboo. We weren't really expecting him to guide for her, and I was going along and the person I was guiding realized she might bump some things, but we got to a particular street crossing, and Bryan stopped. I didn't understand why because he stopped before he got to the curb. There was room for me to go but there wasn't room for the person I was guiding. So, he had actually cleared for her. Further along on that same walk we were going to an apartment to check on its availability. I had been there on a previous night [but had come to it] from the opposite direction. I had

never been on that particular road and, when we got to the street we needed to turn on, I wasn't paying attention. I gave my dog a command to go forward and he wanted to go left. I corrected him for a minute, took a couple of steps in the street, and then realized that that was where I wanted to go. I hadn't really said anything to Bryan so I really believe that he thought it out.

While owners saw their dogs as actively involved in evaluating situations and deciding on certain actions, they did not overly anthropomorphize their animals. Like everyday owners, they saw their dogs as having rather basic thought patterns. Some interviewees described their dogs as involved in the elemental thinking process one would see in a human child. Others spoke of the dog's mind as specifically dog-like, filled with sensual concerns, thoughts about his or her owner, and the desire to work:

I think Millie mostly thinks about food and water and work. When she couldn't work, she kept going over to her harness because she wanted to work. I really think she thinks a lot about what we do together. I think she thinks about the people we're with. She really evaluates people and she tells me when she doesn't like people I'm with. I think she really thinks about how I am. She thinks about what's going on around her and what the kids outside are doing. If she hears things outside she likes to know what's going on. . . . She thinks about what the day's going to be like, what her schedule is, and if there are any changes. I know she doesn't like walking through puddles.

[Does she think about how you are feeling?]

She can tell my moods, especially when I'm upset. If I raise my voice because I'm upset, she'll go and hide because she thinks I'm mad at her. If she thinks I'm mad at my youngest daughter, whom she's very attached to, she'll go and sit next to her. She's very protective. . . . I talk to her all the time, so she's very familiar with different fluctuations in my voice. . . .

[Does Millie ever try to manipulate you?]

Yes, especially when she wants to go out and play. She loves to play and sometimes at night time she'll want to go out on her leash. She doesn't have to relieve herself at all; she just wants to see what the kids are doing. As soon as we get outside, she wants to see what's going on, not doing what she said she needed to do to get me outside. . . . But she's still a dog. She likes the affection and attention. She likes to eat and likes consistency, sort of like a small child.

Because of the intimacy and mutual dependence of their relationships, all the owners emphasized their dogs' empathetic abilities when describing their individual characteristics. The dogs were regarded as readily able to read their owners' emotions and respond appropriately. In addition to their abilities to understand and return emotion, the dogs were seen as having active, though simple, emotional lives. They experienced guilt, happiness, satisfaction with work, and shame when they failed to perform adequately. One interviewee stressed the close relationship between her dog's commitment to guiding and her emotional life. She saw the dog's occasional feelings of failure and guilt as indicating that the animal possessed a rudimentary conscience:

> I think dogs do have feelings although their feelings are very tied in with those of the people that they're with. They're going to feel bad if you do something that makes them feel bad. [When my dog feels that way] either I've done something to make her feel bad or I've done something to make her think I feel bad. I know that with Ellie, if I'm upset with her, she's upset. Dogs are in tune to feelings and if I'm upset then she knows it. She knows if I'm mad or if I'm scared. I know she feels pride. When she's working I know that she feels pride. She definitely takes pride in what she does and feels she deserves any praise anyone might have to give her. Therefore, I guess she feels shame, or has a lack of pride, when she does something wrong because she knows she's displeased me. She hasn't done her job quite right and that makes her not feel good. . . . I know they know when they've done something wrong. When she has made some kind of guiding mistake or any kind of mistake, she just physically droops. The tail and ears go down and she just hangs her head. It's awful. . . . A guide dog who's made a mistake will not make the same mistake for quite a while. . . . I don't think they have a conscience like humans do, but I think they know right from wrong. I think dogs clearly know, at least in their own little world through the things they've done, what's right and wrong.

Interactions in Public

Like everyday dog owners, people with guide dogs experience both problems and advantages when accompanied by their animals in public. These types of interactions are, however, rather different from the "excusing" situations discussed in the previous chapter. While blind owners are the focus of both positive and negative attention due to their being accompanied by a dog, the fact of their handicap and the public's misunderstanding of both blindness and the work of guide dogs tend to generate special difficulties. Most basically, the owner typically is not regarded as the more competent member of the person-dog "with." Needing to be led by a dog is an obvious sign to members of the public that one is less than entirely competent.

In this sense, the initial concern interviewees expressed about the dog acting as a stigma symbol was borne out. Their dogs—like the white cane—overtly identified them as disabled, and they commonly had public encounters in which they were forced to deal with the ignorance of the sighted. As one interviewee put it:

> [You lose] your anonymity. [When you are using a cane] people don't walk up to you and ask you the name of your cane. They don't want to pet your cane. . . . Having a dog makes me very visible. . . . People in my college classes to this day will say, "Hi, Fanny. Hi, Fanny's mommy." They remember the dog but they don't remember me. I'm an appendage of the dog. . . . Many times I feel like a person with a dog, and I'm not perceived as a person with my own abilities and self.[9]

These everyday slights and misunderstandings were frustrating for the owners I interviewed because they could not easily be dealt with directly and strongly. Interviewees spoke of themselves as "representatives of the blind" when in public and commonly took upon themselves the task of "educating" those with normal vision about blindness and guide dogs. One owner described his experience in public and his attempt to use humor to deal with an uncomfortable encounter:

> [Being in public] can be frustrating at times. The general ignorance of people is frustrating. Before I lost my sight I never knew a person who couldn't see or a person with a guide dog—not that I would have gone up and interrogated them about their life history if I did happen to see someone like that somewhere. Once in a while I get the person who thinks I am training the dog. Because I have been sighted I guess my mannerisms are like a sighted person's. So [some people will] ask, "How long have you been training the dog?" [I'll say], "Well, he's my guide dog." You don't want to become flip with people, because I think that is a bad representation of blind people and [the training program]. My attitude is that when you are out there you are representing blind people as a group. I don't want people to think all blind people are miserable, crummy people and all this other stuff, but it does get very frustrating. One time right after [my wife and I] had been told that we could not bring the dog into a restaurant something else happened at a grocery store. We were at the deli counter and this little girl is going, "Look Daddy, a doggy, a doggy," and the father is going, "Be quiet, be quiet." So I just turn and say, "That's okay. He knows he is a dog." Oh boy, it really can get overwhelming.

Like the dogs of everyday owners, guide dogs act as a source of "mutual accessibility." While, as we saw in Chapter 1, this commonly leads to positive public encounters for the typical owner accompanied by his or her domestic dog, the attention focused on the blind person working with his or her guide dog can be a problem. Guide dog owners often feel that members of the public violate their privacy:

> The major thing that annoys me the most about having a dog has nothing to do with the dog itself. It's going into public places like shopping malls and having people kind of invading your personal space. [They want to] pet the dog, talk about the dog, ask about the dog; their kids are going crazy over the dog. It is an invasion of personal space. It's like when you go to the mall you are a movie star or something. You can't get anywhere and you can't get done what you want to do. It's something you become used to, but it does get to you. I can generally stay in the mall no longer than two hours. It just starts to really bother me and I start to feel claustrophobic. I remember I started dating this woman one time and, the first time we went to the mall, after about two and a half hours she goes, "We have to leave. I can't take this." She was really freaked out by it. . . . That's difficult. You really can't go anywhere and just be left alone.

While being an "open person" [10] whom strangers feel free to engage in public conversation is occasionally troublesome, the fact that a guide dog draws attention and decreases the owner's public anonymity is not always seen as a bad thing. Owners also spoke of their positive encounters with members of the public. One guide dog user explicitly emphasized the way in which being with his dog enhanced his social identity:

> [Having a guide] dog changes your identity, changes the way society looks at you. People who see a person walking with a cane often pity that person. The posture of the person using the cane is often different than the posture of a person using a guide dog. I think that the air or presence of confidence is there when using a guide dog [that isn't there] when using a cane. . . . Your identity is influenced by the fact that you are a dog user, and [sighted] people see people who use dogs as kind people.

This mix of desirable and unwelcome attention precipitated by being in public with a guide dog is remarkably similar to that experienced by wheelchair users recently studied by Spencer Cahill and Robin Eggleston.[11] For both dog and wheelchair users their mobility aids identify them as "out of the ordinary" and lead "normals" to treat them as "open persons." Typically, members of the public approach users of the mobility aids and make "kinship claims." [12] Strangers commonly tell wheelchair users stories about people they know who also use chairs, and guide dog owners are offered more general stories about the dogs with whom the strangers are, or have been, associated. "Walkers" and members of the sighted public also offer chair and dog users unwanted assistance. While this assistance is, at times, appreciated, more commonly it is taken as a form of public insult in that it casts the handicapped person in the uncomfortable role of "virtual child." [13] The discomfort of both chair and dog users is amplified in these situations in that the unwanted and ignorant attentions they receive from the public require them to engage in a considerable amount of "emotion work" [14] as they hide their anger and other negative feelings. Wheelchair users regard this emotion work as necessary because they view themselves as representatives of the handicapped to members of the walking public.[15] Similarly, the guide dog owners with whom I spoke talked about having to display a friendly demeanor when confronted in public because they saw themselves as representing dog users as a group and upholding the reputation of the local guide dog program from which they had obtained their assistance animals.

All of the owners were disturbed with the general ignorance of people concerning the capabilities and experiences of guide dogs and the formal regulations allowing them access to public settings. One problem, fostered to a considerable degree by the public relations interests of guide dog programs, is that members of the sighted public tend to regard the animal as a "superdog," the "noble leader of the blind who can do no wrong" as one guide dog trainer put it. Having considerable personal stake in their dogs' abilities, the owners felt some conflict about the super-dog image. On the one hand, this conception led to unrealistic expectations. On the other hand, blind owners regularly were impressed by their dogs' capabilities. One interviewee clearly expressed this ambivalence in talking about her own experience of her dog and what she saw to be the public's ignorance:

> Wayne truly knows how to be a dog. He's like a five year-old who's into everything. . . . The most frustrating thing about dealing with the public is that they don't expect them to be dogs. If [the dog] makes a small mistake or does something that is "dog," people [don't understand]. . . . It's amazing

how people expect complete perfection from these dogs. Wayne can be looking at squirrels, enjoying himself, and then he remembers he's a guide dog
and should be working. They're humans, I guess, and make mistakes. The
majority of time when people see what appears to be a guide mistake, it's my
fault. . . . Most of the time I was goofing off and not listening to him, so I
walked through a puddle or into the bumper of a car. It appears that he made
the mistake, but I did. . . . But then again, they *are* superdogs. They *are* incredible. There are times when I'll be walking with him and he'll be doing
something really mundane, like stopping at curbs. It moves me to tears to
think that some dog could actually do this; that this animal who chews up
every ball he sees, who goes after pumpkins because they look like balls, also
has the intelligence and training to be able to do things for me that everyone
else who has sight takes for granted.

Another media-generated public misunderstanding causes problems
for guide dog users. Some people, often well-meaningly concerned with
the rights and welfare of companion animals, will approach owners and
express the opinion that the dog is being abused. One interviewee described this sort of encounter and how she attempted to use it as an
educational opportunity:

A lot of times I've even had [people come up to me with] questions concerning whether or not Millie is a working dog in a harness and whether or not
this is a form of abuse for Millie, a kind of enslavement, not natural to a dog
considered as a pet.

[How do you respond to that?]

I explain that Millie does sleep, runs around, goes to the park, and plays with
the kids. Most dogs who are domesticated were working dogs at one time. I
can remember sheep herding dogs when I was a child and they could herd a
thousand sheep. They were working dogs, not for pleasure or companionship. Millie has it much better than that. That explains it basically and it
seems to satisfy people.

The most irritating public experience guide dog users routinely encounter is being excluded from stores, restaurants, and other commercial establishments because they are with a dog. This slight typically is
seen as due to ordinary peoples' ignorance of the laws that allow them
access and misunderstanding of the dog's capabilities and routines. All
states have exceptions to the public health regulations that ban dogs
from certain public settings in order to accommodate guide dog users.
Further, a major aspect of training—typically begun when the poten-

tial guide dog is being raised in a foster family—is that the dog is taught to lie quietly out of the way under or next to the chair in which the owner is sitting. With considerable show of irritation, one interviewee told of a conflictual encounter in a restaurant and a subsequent experience in a national park:

> You would be surprised by some of the comments you get from people when you have a dog in a restaurant. I have partial vision, and some people want to know why I have the dog if I can see. You try and explain certain things to them, but if they are trying to get you and the dog out of there, then they're not really going to want to listen. I had one guy pull a gun on me to get me out of a restaurant. I was with a friend at the time who saw the gun and then later told me about it after we had decided to not press charges. I was surprised to find out that even the policemen who were called don't know the laws. I had to show them my guide dog identification card which had the state laws on the back before they'd help me. I had an interesting situation when I walked down to the bottom of the Grand Canyon with some friends. Guide dogs are allowed in state and public parks, so I didn't do anything about checking in. Part way down we ran into one of the mule trains that take people to the bottom and back, so we got over to the drop-off side of the trail to let the mules go by. A ranger told me I wasn't allowed to have the dog on the trail. When I told him it was a guide dog and that I was blind, he made some rhetorical comment about how cops are allowed to carry guns but that doesn't mean they go around shooting at everybody. When we got to the halfway point, there was a ranger station and we were waved inside because they had called down from the top. I talked to the ranger and told him about the federal law and he said, "Well, I don't know if that applies to trails." He had a problem with the mules and the dog, and I told him he ought to train his mules better if they have problems with a dog.[16]

The Owner-Guide Dog Relationship

The relationship that develops between a guide dog user and his or her dog is a unique and emotion-laden example of the human-canine bond. All the owners with whom I talked spoke of feeling "complete" or "made whole" because of their association with their animals. One interviewee, a student at a local university, talked about how the relationship became a central feature of her life, though she acknowledged, as did others, that some guide dog users see their animals as tools to be used rather than as individuals with whom one shares an intimate relationship:

It is a funny, subtle little thing how you start not wanting to do anything without the dog. It's not just wanting to go to the store, it's not really wanting to write your paper unless the dog's there, it's wanting the dog to be a part of your whole life. Anything that becomes an important thing in your life, you want the dog to be a part of it, even though sometimes it's not the most reasonable thing. Not all dog owners are going to have this same kind of interdependency. Maybe once a year I'll go on vacation without her. The bathroom and feeding routines are occasionally nice to get away from. One week is about all I can take, but it is kind of nice. Dogs aren't like coats where you put one on to go walking and take it off to put in the closet when you come home. . . . I could never view a dog simply as a mechanism to further mobility, but there are people who do. If it works for them and it works for their dog, I guess there's nothing wrong with it. I think it's kind of sad for the dog, and also [for] the person.

Like all effective and satisfying intimate relationships, that between the guide dog and the owner is based on mutual trust, commitment, and communication. Most essentially, the user must have confidence in the dog. Trainers consistently emphasize that the user must "let the dog find the way" or "give the dog control" when negotiating through traffic or traveling in public. Like the owner quoted above, another interviewee realized that some guide dog users relate to their animals as pieces of machinery; he stressed, however, that this sort of orientation stands in the way of developing the emotional communication that is the foundation of a satisfying relationship and effective team work:

[Guide dogs] think, have emotions, and catch your emotions. . . . All those things are really essential to develop the type of communication needed to work with a dog. I think that it is many things that come together to develop the team working together, especially learning communication style. . . . As you develop that bond with the dog, it becomes more and more refined and you are able to do it more and more. I think that there are some people who develop these characteristics less in their dog, you know. The person who sees their dog as like a vacuum [cleaner] is not likely to develop the kind of communication where they're dealing with an emotional dog on an emotional level. It is up to the person to handle it and to move toward that type of communication.

Later in our conversation this interviewee compared the guide dog-owner relationship to a human marriage, emphasizing that mutual trust, commitment, and affection are essential elements:

At first I think [my focus on myself] got in the way of Prophet and I developing a relationship because I kind of expected him to perform and didn't give

The cooperative work of the guide dog–owner team is based on mutual understanding.
Photographer: Bernice MacDonald

back as much as I could have. . . . I soon became aware that putting time and effort into this relationship was going to benefit me because it was going to make our working life easier. I guess I make the analogy to any relationship or marriage. If you just spent five minutes in the morning saying "hi" to your wife and five minutes giving her affection or attention before going to bed, your marriage is likely to be pretty unfulfilling—not a real partnership. If you do that to the dog it is the same thing. It really takes time and effort to build up a relationship. If you are going to receive the benefits of the relationship, I think that working on it and trusting in that bond [are] essential.

Like any relationship, that between the owner and dog has its ups and downs. The owner's occasional anger and frustration get in the way of the communication that facilitates team interaction. All of the guide dog owners acknowledged that their dogs sometimes had "off days" during which they tended to make mistakes. Avoiding anger and re-establishing communication were essential at these times:

Unfortunately, as with super human beings and wonderful people, the dogs have bad days. I've sat down on the sidewalk and talked to Shannon and said, "Listen, we haven't done so well today. I'm overreacting to you, which is causing you to make mistakes. Let's get back on track. We can do it." And it works. It calms me down, it calms her down, and we get back on track and there aren't as many mistakes. She isn't feeding off my frustration and anger. We're with each other 24 hours a day and, as with any partnership, at times I bug her and she bugs me.

The relationship between the guide dog user and his or her assistance animal is, then, uniquely interdependent, communicative, and emotionally binding. As one interviewee tearfully described it, "This dog is my life. I don't feel normal without him. He fills a void that nobody else can." Consequently, retiring the dog when he or she becomes too old or infirm to adequately perform routine tasks or having to euthanize the animal are painful and traumatizing experiences. One owner characterized the anticipation of retiring his first dog as having been "like having a terminal illness." Those who had had the experience of losing a dog to death or retirement typically spoke of how the parting precipitated a terrible feeling of loss. A blind therapist working in a social service agency who had lived with multiple guides told of his favorite dog and the grief he continues to feel because of the dog's passing:

Then there was Trucker, a black lab. He was just a sweet dog, my favorite. Trucker grew my kids up. He was there throughout their early growth. The family as a whole will tell you he was the best. When I do therapy, I often touch this model I have of him just to center myself. There was something special between us. He died a year ago June with liver problems, and then I went back [to the training program] and got this guy. (He pats the German shepherd lying by his chair.) There was one thing that I learned then that I had never quite internalized before. At times it looked like I was leading Trucker and he wasn't leading me. I think I should have retired him earlier. . . . Trucker was unbelievable. [My friends] mourned his loss with me. I still grieve. I've finally gotten to a point where I can accept it. I'm glad I didn't get a lab again, in some ways, because I needed a break.

Interviewees who had not yet retired or lost a dog anticipated that time with considerable fear. They realized that the parting was inevitable and that the decisions about when to retire their guides and whether to allow them to stay in the home or go to live with another caretaker would be extremely difficult.[17] One woman hugged her dog and began to cry as she spoke of that future time and her concern for the animal's feelings:

I know that some day I'm going to have to replace Freda, but I don't want to think about it. I wish she could live with me forever. But, for whatever reason she has to retire, I could never have her at home watching me go out the door with another dog. I just couldn't do that to her. I wouldn't want to have to say good-bye to her [when I left home] but, at the same time, I couldn't have her walk behind the other dog and have to share my attention. Even before I ever got her I had to come to terms with this. I knew, hopefully, it wouldn't happen for a long time, but even after the first week [we were together], I knew I could never do that to her.

Characterized by companionship, love, interdependence, trust, and communication, the bond between a guide dog and his or her owner has special qualities that set it apart from even the most intensely valued relationship between the everyday dog owner and his or her canine companion. The guide dog is literally experienced as an extension of the blind owner's self. One interviewee movingly summed up her relationship with her dog and what she had learned from their life together:

I think the most important lesson a person can learn working a guide dog is humility, because this highly trained and intelligent creature's entire existence is me. She doesn't really care about anything else. She likes the family and [our] other dogs, but when it comes down to brass tacks, her whole existence is to work for me, to make my life more manageable. That's the kind of relationship that we will never have with a human being, and it's not possible with human beings. . . . To have a creature whose greatest joy is found in making decisions for you should be very humbling in my opinion. . . . [There is a] really important lesson we can learn from working a dog. You can't take that dog for granted. The only way to thank [the dog] is through your actions. . . . People have often tried to find the human equivalent to the relationship I have with Winnie, but there isn't one. People ask me if she's my best friend, or if she's more like my child. *Winnie is my eyes.* What is your relationship with your eyes?

The guide dog user's relationship with his or her animal, like that of the everyday dog owner, is characterized by love and understanding. However, the intimacy of the bond between the blind owner and the dog is intensified by the dependency of the association. Those whose occupations are focused around dogs are also, though in a different way, dependent on canines. If they are to be successful in their jobs, they need to have an understanding of and, ideally, feel an emotional attachment to dogs. We turn now to look at key features of the occupational experience of one such worker—the veterinarian. Interactions with dogs and regular encounters with both the most joyful and most painful aspects of people's relationships with canines are, as we will see, central to the veterinarian's daily routines.

4

The Veterinarian
Caring for Canine Patients

Veterinarians, like all service workers, routinely categorize those with/for/upon whom they work in order to anticipate potential problems and devise ways of effectively dealing with those problems. Service workers make a basic distinction between those clients, patients, or customers who are "good" and those who are "bad." Problematic recipients of service, in general, act in ways that impede the normal flow of the commercial encounter, limit the worker's opportunity to gain financial or sociopsychological rewards, and/or display attributes that indicate some manner of character flaw or moral inadequacy.[1]

Like all workers involved in service occupations—from cab drivers[2] to surgeons[3]—veterinarians engage in this kind of categorizing activity. However, special features of the veterinary profession create unique problems and require unique responses on the part of the veterinarian.

While all medical encounters are negotiated exchanges balanced between cooperation and conflict,[4] the triangular nature of the veterinarian's occupational interactions with both a human client and an animal patient make for encounters that are uniquely challenging. Robert Shurtleff[5] captures a central aspect of this interesting challenge when he observes:

> Veterinary medicine is a human activity which treats animals as dictated by the needs and demands of other human beings; in many instances the needs or interests of the animal are secondary, if considered at all. . . . Unlike human medicine, wherein humans treat other humans and serve the interests of the common species of patient and doctor, veterinary medicine is often faced with an unwelcome choice: whether to act in the best interests of the patient, an animal, or whether to ignore the patient's interests and respond to the demands of the client, a fellow human being, who is actually seeking and paying for our services.

In addition to this troublesome ethical issue of determining responsibility and allegiance, the complexity of the triangular exchange among the doctor, client, and animal is compounded by the fact that the client and veterinarian cooperate to cast the animal in the role of what Stanford Gregory and Stephen Keto[6] refer to as the "virtual patient." Because the animal patient is a nonverbal and relatively powerless actor in the situation, the client and doctor exchange information and observations directed at determining the problem experienced by the animal and devising the appropriate treatment. In this exchange the client calls on his or her everyday, intimate experience of the companion animal while the veterinarian primarily employs technical expertise. Ideally, the sharing of these different types of information leads to a cooperative interaction and a mutually satisfactory clinical outcome. However, when everyday and technical evaluations and concerns do not coincide, significant conflict may result. The potential for conflict is increased by the emotional intensity with which the client commonly defines his or her relationship with the animal. The divided responsibilities for the interests of client and patient and this exchange of evaluative information based on differing sources and shaped by differing interests, combined with the emotionality of the human-companion animal relationship, make the technical "comfort work" and emotional "sentimental work"[7] that comprise the clinical activity of all medical specialists especially difficult for the veterinarian to balance and accomplish.

Evaluating and controlling both the client and the patient are central to what the veterinary literature commonly refers to as "practice management."[8] One of the veterinarians with whom I worked spoke of this endeavor as the "art of veterinary practice" and overtly connected it to the practitioner's learning to display caring for the animal-patient:

[The art of practice] refers to how you handle the client—something they don't usually teach you in vet school. The new kids come in here and they just don't know how to do it. I have to teach them how to "coochie-coochie" the client. . . . People tell me I'm lucky because I don't have to work with people. That's ALL it is! I was telling _____ (a younger vet) about how important it is to be good to the animal and he says, "Well, what if you don't like the animal?" ACT LIKE YOU DO! If people think you love their animal they will think you are the greatest vet in the world.[9]

This chapter focuses on veterinarians' definitions of and interactions with problematic patients. I will present the major criteria veterinarians use to place dogs and their other animal patients in the problematic category. In brief, veterinarians focus on the animal's controllability and aggressiveness, hygienic features of his or her physical condition, and evaluations of the patient's medical situation (especially, whether or not the illness can be effectively diagnosed and treated). Since animal patients and human clients are both, of necessity, dealt with by veterinarians, I will also discuss how veterinarians' evaluations of problematic patients are related to the apparent ignorance or neglectfulness of their owners. The chapter concludes by looking at the most troubling types of situations encountered by veterinarians, those in which the doctor is called upon to euthanize a dog or other companion animal. It is here that the key issue discussed in earlier chapters—the social assignment of the social designation of "person" to a nonhuman animal—arises most dramatically.

Veterinarians and Problematic Patients

Veterinarians define and interact with their animal patients in ways that largely depend on how long they have known the patient, the symptoms the animal presents or the reason he or she has been brought to the clinic, the species of the patient, and the animal's behavior in the course of the clinical exchange. On an impersonal level, animals are defined as either interestingly unusual or routine cases.[10] On a more personal level, patients with whom the vets and their support personnel are most familiar typically are regarded as distinct individuals. These familiar patients, as we will see, are often central characters in the continuing stories that are integral to the local lore of the hospital.

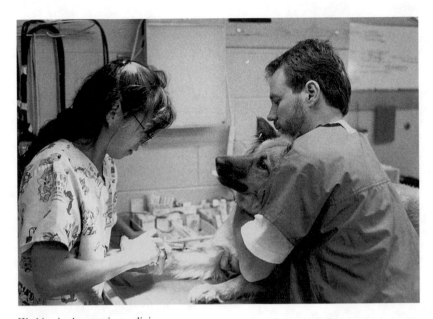

Working in the veterinary clinic.
Photographer: Clinton Sanders

Staff conversations frequently revolve around regular patients' exploits, physical problems, personality characteristics, and interactions with their owners and clinic personnel. Responding to key episodes in these ongoing stories, staff rejoice when a regular patient recovers, express concern when the animal's physical condition deteriorates, and mourn when he or she dies. In contrast to these positively regarded individual patients, other animals are notorious because of the problems they routinely present while interacting with doctors and support staff.

Uncontrolled Patients

One important attribute that determined whether an animal was regarded as a good or bad patient was how compliant and controllable he or she was.[11] Uncontrollable—or "hyper"—patients required the veterinarian to expend more time and energy in the clinical encounter than was typically justified by the limited rewards acquired. Here, for example, is a description drawn from my field notes of a typical veterinary encounter with an uncontrolled dog:

The case involves a young working class male who has brought in a year-old male chocolate Lab ("Bear") for shots. Bear is reasonably well-behaved while receiving the inoculation. Then the owner asks Nancy (the vet) to trim his nails. A major battle ensues. After some jockeying for position Nancy finally gets a major choke hold on the dog's neck (Bear appears to be tiring) and wrestles him over into the corner. All this time Nancy is shouting, "Be Good! Hold still!" in a deep command voice. After finally subduing the dog and trimming his nails we leave the exam room together. She is panting after it is over and makes a small joke to kind of defuse the situation: "Who needs aerobics when you have dogs like this?" During the battle the owner was not much help and was totally unapologetic when it was over. His only overt acknowledgment of the trouble Bear caused was to direct a mild "You've been a bad dog" to the animal as they were leaving. As we stand at the pharmacy counter I comment to Nancy about what a trial that case seemed to be. "Would you call Bear a 'bad patient'?" Nancy replies, "Well, I would say he was *difficult.*"

In this case, the veterinarian handled the problematic situation with what I saw to be considerable physical skill—the dog weighed around 80 pounds and the doctor was not an especially large woman. She was also fairly even-tempered about the encounter, interpreting the dog's behavior as due largely to fear rather than maliciousness. This tendency not to blame the patient for his or her misbehavior—to see it as a consequence of the stressful situation, physical discomfort, inadequate training by the owner or other factors outside the animal's voluntary control—was typical of the way veterinarians defined intractable patients.

Understandably, vets did not always interpret the patient's behavior so charitably and respond with such patience. Here is another episode recorded in my field notes in which an uncontrollable dog prompts the doctor to lose his temper:

I go into the exam room with Don and see Amber—a female golden retriever brought in by an older working-class couple. Amber has some skin problems on her hip and at the base of her tail. It is the result of a standard flea allergy, and the area has to be shaved and cleaned. I help hold the dog and hand Don gauze squares soaked with saline solution. He shaves the dog, who struggles and cries because of the pain involved. During this the owner stands over the poor animal, jerking her lead and screaming at her to "hold still." Despite the trouble caused, the dog appears to be a sweet animal. The procedure obviously hurts, but the dog still wags her tail submissively as Don shaves and cleans the sore area. After this is over the dog runs frantically around the exam room rubbing the itchy spot on the walls and leaving large splotches of blood. Don attempts to bandage the sore but the dressing falls off. He then puts sulfa powder on it, but this has no significant effect on the bleeding. The owner asks about "one of those things you put around their neck" and says he wants one put on so the dog will not worry at the spot. Don goes out and gets a white plastic Elizabethan collar out of a cabinet, assembles it with some difficulty, and takes it into the exam room. The dog does not want it around her head and begins to struggle wildly. Don eventually does get the collar on, but in the course of the renewed struggle it comes off again. He grabs the animal by the scruff of the neck, lifts her forefeet off the ground, and shakes her vigorously. He screams, "Bad dog! Hold it now! Be good!" He then takes the collar and storms out of the exam room with me following closely behind. In the pharmacy area he tries to put the collar back together and calm down. "I'm losing it," he says. "I'm usually better than this in these situations."

While patients who were, as one doctor put it, "so hyper that they won't relax enough for you to even examine them" often tried the veterinarians' patience, they were regarded with far less distaste than were "fractious" animals. Aggressive patients threatened more than the doctor's ability to effectively exercise control, complete an examination, and devise an appropriate treatment. Aggressive animals overtly threatened the practitioner's physical well-being.

Dangerous Patients

Far and away the most important characteristic that prompted the veterinarian to define an animal as a "bad patient" was if he or she acted threateningly or aggressively while being examined or treated.[12] Although all of the doctors maintained that they rarely were bitten by dogs or otherwise injured by patients, I observed them being snapped at, nipped, scratched, or pecked by animals with some frequency. Early in the research I mentioned the discontinuity between the doctors' statements that they were "rarely bitten" and the fact that I had already seen a number of such incidents. Here is a field note excerpt in which a vet accounts for the difference between what I had been told and what I had observed:[13]

I ask Dick if there is any dog he recommends that people avoid. Like Debra, he also mentions dalmatians. "Of course I am prejudiced since the worst bite I ever received was from a dalmatian." I ask how often he has been bitten, and he says that it has happened only once in his seventeen-year career. I observe, "This is really interesting to me. You all say you rarely get bitten, and yet I have been here only a few weeks and I've seen half a dozen incidents of biting." Dick replies, "Oh, you get nipped fairly often. Getting *bitten* is when you look down and the fat is hanging out of the holes in your arm and you have to be taken to the emergency room. You soon learn that cat scratches are the worst and they happen all the time. I always get them on my palm. They are always worse the next day. We have a hard time getting emergency room people to give us antibiotics, but we insist since [cat scratches] always get infected." [14]

When encountering an unfamiliar patient, veterinarians were generally watchful for signs of aggression. The breed of canine patients was of some relevance since certain breeds were not considered to be typically dangerous—golden retrievers, Labradors, Newfoundlands, for example—while others such as chows, dobermans, German shepherds, and malamutes were more commonly menacing, particularly when in the stressful situation of the veterinary clinic. [15] Familiar dogs who had proven to be aggressive in the past had this noted on their clinical records and a red tag was placed on the door of the cages holding dogs admitted to the hospital in order to warn vets and technicians that the animal was, as one doctor put it, "Q.O.F.—quick of fang."

During one clinical session with a large male doberman, I observed that the vet was working with noticeable caution. My mentioning this later prompted the doctor to launch into a series of "dangerous dog" stories:

"Yeah, I know that dog. See here." (He shows me the chart which has GO SLOW written on top with yellow highlighter.) Again I observe, "You must get bitten fairly frequently. Must be an occupational hazard." Martin shakes his head, "No, actually it's pretty rare. The worst was about eight years ago. I was examining a malamute and had had my face down by his and everything. I was just about done when I turned and he went for my hand. His owner jumps up on the little stool [in the corner of the exam room] and starts screaming, 'I knew he would bite someone. I knew it!!!' They ran in and got him off me and I was kind of in shock. I noticed that I didn't have any feeling in that hand. I went in the back there and just sat in the dark. I thought it was all over—my hands are my bread and butter. It took three years for the feeling to return completely." "It must have really made quite a mess," I said. "No, actually not," Martin replied. "A dog bite is usually just punctures and doesn't bleed all that much. Usually it isn't the dogs like Brutus in there you need to worry about. They are like Molly (a nice shepherd seen earlier). You aren't expecting it and they just turn on you. Dick got the end of his nose taken off one time. He had his head down examining the dog and it bit it right off. He was lucky. It didn't take the end off all the way and we rushed him to the hospital and they sewed it back on and there is hardly a scar."

Since regular patients' exploits are central to clinic lore, narratives often revolve around the aggressiveness of certain animals. Doctors and technicians typically took a regular patient's problematic reputation into account when interacting with the animal. Here is an incident in which a tech suffers the consequences for her initial failure to recognize a cat with a dangerous reputation. Notice the "excusing tactic" employed by the attending veterinarian:

Back in the surgical prep area (techs) Laura and Mary Sue and (vet) Don are gathered around a table with a large black Persian cat. An IV fluid bag is hanging up next to the table and Don is trying to insert a catheter into the cat's leg. The cat lets out a low growl and lunges at Mary Sue. She pulls back her hand and yells with pain—"He got me! He got me good! Hey! This is Midnight, Midnight Monroe. (I have noticed that patients are routinely referred to by their "call" names combined with the last name of their owners.) This is an evil cat! We never come near this cat unless it is anesthetized. And here I have been waving my hand in front of its face. This is the cat from hell!" Don says, "Well, he's not feeling very well right now." Mary Sue is still upset. "Yeah, that's why I still have a hand. You can't even walk by this cat's cage without him trying to get you. You open up the door and it lunges at you (places hand so it covers her face as a demonstration). He's like that creature in *Alien*. We never handle this cat without anesthesia. I thought it looked like Midnight Monroe, but I assumed that if it was it would be muzzled and in a bag. This cat would just as soon rip your face off as look at you."

If a doctor had reason to suspect that a patient presented a danger—the owner gave warning, the animal behaved aggressively, the animal's potential for trouble was noted on its records or was a feature of clinic lore—routine mechanical solutions were employed. Dangerous dogs were muzzled and "prickly" cats were put in a special sack or wrapped in a towel. A more extreme approach used to deal with dangerous patients was to tranquilize them. This was not a preferred method since the tranquilizer's effects could make some diagnoses more difficult and sedated animals commonly had to be admitted to the hospital to stay at least until the medication had worn off.[16]

Defiling Patients

In their comparison of large animal and small animal veterinarians, Clifton Bryant and William Snizek [17] observe that one of the reasons vets prefer clinical work with companion animals is that this type of office-based practice entails less physical defilement than does work with farm animals. While this may be the case,[18] I was struck by how routinely the doctors I observed were involved in "dirty work." In his discussion of this occupational issue, Everett Hughes [19] observes that those in prestigious positions commonly delegate the dirty work to lower status support personnel. Although veterinary technicians largely were responsible for the sometimes unsavory tasks of cleaning and deodorizing examination rooms and cages,[20] the veterinarians with whom I worked routinely were exposed to defiling substances and strikingly unappealing sights and odors. For example, the doctors were frequently called upon to express the rather pungent secretions that would build up in a dog's anal glands. This fluid is related to canine territorial marking and mutual identification. Impacted anal sacs—a common problem with the smaller breeds—cause the animal some discomfort and often must be lanced and drained. Even when a dog's anal glands are working properly, they can be the source of decidedly unsavory experiences for veterinarians. When frightened or upset—common emotions for canine veterinary patients—dogs' anal sphincters may contract causing anal secretions to be expelled, sometimes rather dramatically. Dogs who "blow their anals" were viewed with understandable distaste. Don tells a good defilement story:

> You weren't here Saturday, were you? You should have been. The grossest thing that has ever happened to me in my vet career happened. This client brought in an old English sheepdog. He was real nervous. I had the owner pick up the front of the dog [to put him on the examination table] and I picked up the rear. HE BLEW HIS ANALS ALL OVER ME! [It went] all down my pants leg, up my shirt, over my arm. His anals must have been the size of an egg. I almost puked. I just said, "I'll be back" and I went in the back and stripped off all my clothes and took a shower and eventually came back in [surgical] scrubs.

Odoriferous contamination with patients' body fluids and the unpleasant sights and smells related to maggot infestations of open wounds were most frequently cited by the veterinarians as the most unsavory aspects of their jobs. Different animals have differing secretions, and smells and the rising popularity of pot-belly pigs as companion animals and the continuing moderate favor enjoyed by ferrets (a rather musky member of the weasel family) presented veterinarians with a rising number of problematically dirty patients.

Defiling bodily excretions also hold some potential for danger to the veterinarians and technicians. A few of the parasites and diseases that afflict companion animals are communicable to humans. On one occasion I noticed one of the doctors coming in on his day off to give medication to a cat that was caged in the isolation area. When I asked what was going on, he replied:

> [The cat] was in the other day to be spayed and she blew diarrhea all over everything while she was being prepped. We checked it out and she has "X" [some serious sounding disease]. It's caused by a zoonotic organism, so Cassie (a tech) and I are both exposed. I didn't want anyone else exposed to it. I was trying to remember what I did afterwards. I think I ate two cookies without washing my hands. This is a parasite where you're supposed to wash your hands and scrub carefully under your nails and everything . . . but it is all coming out okay so far.[21]

Medically Problematic Patients

When asked to describe what she saw to be a "problematic patient," one veterinarian succinctly replied, "One that is going to die." Animals who arrive at the hospital so ill or damaged that they cannot be saved and those whose physical problems resist diagnosis are defined as especially troublesome in that they present cases in which the veterinarians feel powerless.

Similar feelings of powerlessness arise when patients are ill or injured and, despite being cared for competently, fail to respond appropriately to treatment. The vets I worked with regarded these animals with a mixture of puzzlement and disappointment. One doctor described this type of problematic client during an interview:

> There are some breeds and some individual animals—this is a funny thing—that just won't fight. It's like they just give up. It doesn't matter what you do for them, they just don't get better—like Afghans and greyhounds. I don't know if it is a spiritual problem or if some animals just can't handle being

sick. I had almost rather like to see them spit and fight a little bit. They are at least fighting. But the animals that just lay there . . . might just have a broken leg but they are never going to get up and walk. This doesn't happen very often; most animals will fight injury.

One of the cases I encountered during my fieldwork in the hospital poignantly brought home for me the intense disappointment generated by medically problematic patients who fail to respond to treatment. Having been admitted as an emergency after being hit by a truck and badly injured, a large, gentle collie came to be the focus of special concern and attention in the hospital. For weeks we all followed Muddy's condition, rejoicing when his temperature declined or when he ate and worrying when he appeared listless or in pain. Rather than confine him in one of the crates reserved for severely injured animals and surgical cases, the doctor handling Muddy's case decided to set up bedding near a wall in the surgical preparation area where Muddy could be exposed to the daily activity of the clinic and be more carefully watched by doting doctors, technicians, and researchers. After surviving two operations on his severely damaged rear leg, Muddy appeared to rally. Then a few nights later, while attempting to stand, he redamaged his leg beyond repair. Muddy's stricken owners chose to have him euthanized. For days after this unfortunate and unexpected passing the atmosphere of the hospital was uncharacteristically restrained. The veterinarian responsible for Muddy's case was noticeably shaken by her experience with her medically problematic patient. I quote from field notes:

I am getting ready to leave for the day and notice Nancy. I know that she had been in charge of Muddy and had put him down on Thursday night. I say, "I was very sorry to hear about Muddy. I was here for the puppy class on Thursday night and Katy [a tech] told me what had happened. I went back and said goodbye to him. I was kind of shaken. I'm sure you were, too." Nancy says, "Yes, we're all pretty depressed about it. You try to keep yourself distanced from it but Muddy was different. He had been here for so long and people were so good taking care of him." I glance over at Muddy's spot on the floor. "Yeah, he was always lying there in the middle of everything. It's not going to be the same without him here." Nancy agrees, "Yes, I purposefully did that. I thought it would be good if he had the stimulation. Much better than being isolated in a cage. We did all we could but he was in a lot of pain at the end." I say, "Yeah, when I went back there to say goodbye the other night he wasn't as responsive as he had been before. I hear the owners didn't come in for the final act." Nancy nods, "Yes, they were so upset that they thought that it would just make it harder for him. I can understand that." I feel tears welling up in my eyes. "I guess the end of his life wasn't that bad. He had a lot of people caring for him and didn't really seem to be in that much pain. He actually seemed pretty happy at times. It's a terribly sad thing." Nancy is obviously saddened by the whole situation. As we talk she stares down at the floor and chokes back tears.

Owner Responsibility for Problematic Patients

As the (presumably) more responsible member of the animal-human "with," veterinary clients typically were held accountable for the problems their pets presented during clinical encounters. Owners whose animals were ill-groomed, malnourished, or significantly overweight or showed other indications of neglect were viewed with some distaste by the veterinarians and the support staff. When encountering clients who were apparently neglecting their animals, the doctors would commonly take an educative approach; owners frequently were instructed about such matters as feeding, grooming, parasite control, and other commonplace features of pet ownership.

Interestingly, the veterinarians rarely defined clients' failures with regard to their animals' well-being as the consequence of purposive cruelty or disregard. Instead, neglectful owners typically were seen as ignorant rather than cruel. They had chosen dog breeds or animals species that were inappropriate for their situation and/or personality, they failed to adequately teach their dogs about their subordinate status in the family "pack," they over- or underfed because of misplaced love or inattention to nutritional needs, and they were not ongoingly on the lookout for signs of infirmity or discomfort. A vet told me about one such ignorant client he saw regularly:

> There are some people who are just plain difficult, and I don't even know why they go to the vet sometime. I had one Saturday. Over the years I have gotten to know her. She is just a difficult person. She likes me more than she likes any of the other vets, but she has a rotten disposition—a rotten attitude. She acts like her dog is the kindest, nicest thing, and then when it comes out at the end of the visit she will say, "Well, I can't do that. He will bite me." The dog has dry eye and needs all kind of medication in it. And there happens to be one medication—it's a little expensive but it might actually cure it rather than just have to put stuff in over and over again. But I

knew she wouldn't want it because it was expensive. So I said, "Well, why don't we try these other things first, see how you do with them and see if they work. If you are able to get the drops in we can go with the more expensive thing which may give you a cure in the long run." She said, "Well, I can't even do that." Well, sorry. Get a fish.

Especially in their attempts to understand patients who were problematic because of their skittishness or aggressiveness, the veterinarians sometimes expressed the opinion that the animal's personality was a reflection of the owner's personality or a consequence of the interpersonal relationships and "atmosphere" in the home. For example, one vet offered this sort of explanation and spoke of the tactics he used to deal with such problems during a clinical visit:

Over the years I have seen households go through several pets and there are certain households that always have skittery, aggressive animals while other households always have nice, calm, quiet, easy animals. [Tense animals tend to come from] a household where there is a lot of tension somehow—open, verbal fighting or just a lot of loud voices all the time. Just not an easy, soft way of living. I think that really makes a difference. It's not necessarily the relationship with the dog, it's the relationship between the [human] individuals. The dog is picking up on that. Certainly I believe that if the owner is too permissive with the dog—it depends on the dog and the breed, but dogs are pragmatic and they are going to try to take advantage of the situation. But the people in the household—when you have a mother that is always screaming at the kids, or a husband that is screaming at everybody, or just comes home and is irritated all night long, or just a situation where there is unspoken tension, animals will pick up on that. If I see a client that is really uptight in coming into an office visit, it is not infrequent that the animal is uptight too. They are reading their owner. If I can just talk to the owner for a few minutes about something else—the weather or anything just to divert them a little bit—you can see the animal soften up too. Doesn't always work but a lot of times it does help.

Ideally, owners of potentially dangerous animals will inform the veterinarian of this and take steps to control their pets. Owners who are remiss in this responsibility commonly were defined as bad clients. Here is a story about a client who prompted atypical conflict by failing to adequately warn one of the vets:

Keith overhears some of the conversation [between Debra and me concerning passive clients with dangerous animals] and tells a related story. "One time I heard Don really laying into someone. I rarely hear things like that from him, but the client came in with a big German shepherd. Don asks the guy if he is "okay." The client said yes and Don went down to do his front nails and the dog snapped at his face. He says, "I thought you said he was okay!" "Well, he is okay but he does bite sometimes." Don is pissed—"Hey, look! When I ask the question it's for a good reason!"

In a similar vein, another vet talked about clients who give adequate warning about the potential danger their dogs pose and those who don't:

Clients are funny. Some clients are just hoping that their dog won't be a jerk. It's not that they don't want to warn you, it's that they don't want to admit that their dog can be a real jerk. Maybe they aren't that way at home. Oftentimes it's just wishful thinking on the clients' part. Or they don't really know what to do with the behavior. You walk into the room and the dog starts growling at you and the client just sort of sits there. You ask them if he is friendly and they say, "Yeah, usually." Well, he's not now and you aren't doing anything about it! Sometimes you can just approach a dog in that situation and reassure them and it's okay. Cornered in a little room like that, dogs get really edgy. Then you get the dogs that are DOO DOO DOO! [crazy sound] They just don't care. I just don't take a lot of chances with dog bites, and I don't put my face right up to theirs. But I really appreciate the client that says "my dog will bite you." Or when you say, "Is your dog friendly?" he will say, "Usually at home he is good, but he gets nervous here and I really don't know." That's great. Most of the time clients that don't do that—it's not intentional, they just don't know. They are just not tuned in. Or they don't like the behavior and are trying to deny it.[22]

While veterinarians afford some leeway to owners whose association with problematic patients is seen as largely a matter of the owners' relative ignorance, vets do not view as charitably clients who appear to neglect their animals. Love for animals is the major factor that draws veterinarians, and veterinary technicians to their occupations and failure to adequately care for one's pets typically is seen as demonstrating a kind of moral deficiency. Here is a woman vet's description of a bad client whose negligence is compounded by his manipulativeness:

I had [a bad client] today. It's this old dog and she has been incontinent for a year and they keep her outside. So they brought her in and said, "I think she has maggots on her. I don't know, we clean her up and stuff but I think she had maggots on her." I take her in back and her whole underside is eaten up, she has holes all over her, maggots are crawling in and out. It's not something that happened yesterday. Then I look on the history and it says, "will get maggots, have to watch." So the guy clearly hasn't been taking care of her. I call him up—I'm already kind of mad because I know he is not taking care of her. She's fifteen and he's hoping she'll die tomorrow but he doesn't want to put her to sleep. So I say, "She's infested with maggots and if we are going to pull her through this she is going to need constant care." And he said, "Oh no! If it is going to mean really big surgery put her down, put her down." And I hear his wife start crying in the background saying, "Oh what's wrong, did we do something wrong?" And he says, like, "No, just shut up." So I am like doubly mad at this guy because he is just using me to put this dog to sleep. He has probably wanted to put the dog to sleep but can't because of his wife so he has just neglected it. He wouldn't let me talk to his wife. He said, "No, if you think it is going to be a really big deal just put her to sleep." I said, "No, it's not a big deal. We already have her under, but it has to be taken care of. "NO, no, no!" So he's a bad client. He's neglectful and he's manipulative.

It is especially in those cases where the owner's negligence threatens an animal's life that veterinarians view the client with considerable distaste. Such a response is described in my notes:

I go back into the pharmacy and exchange a few pleasantries with Debra. She catches me up. "You should have been here on Saturday. We did a C-section on a golden. She was in terrible shape. The owners just weren't paying attention." [I ask what was wrong with the dog.] "It's hard to say. She wasn't up on her shots and it may have been a viral infection. When I opened her up her abdomen was full of fluid and her intestines were inflamed. She had had diarrhea and was vomiting for two weeks! She had eleven pups in her. She had delivered six at home and was straining for hours. She was very weak when they finally brought her in. We did the C-section and saved two of the pups; one was born dead. She hung on for a day but was just too weak." Martha chimes in. "She didn't smell too good. She was full of black water. Linda and I worked on the two puppies but we just couldn't get them to breathe on their own. We worked on them for over an hour, but the time comes when you just have to make the decision. She was such a sweet dog, too. We all felt really bad. We couldn't believe that the owners would just let her go like that."

Killing With Kindness

Death is a central and omnipresent feature in medical settings. Typically, death is viewed as an enemy to be feared, fought against, and, if all goes well, defeated.[23] However, in some situations prolonging life may simply prolong a patient's agony.[24] This problematic consequence gives rise to heated debates regarding the appropriateness of euthanasia and situations in which medical practitioners are justified in actively providing or passively allowing a pain-ridden and/or terminally ill patient to experience a "peaceful" or "easy" death.[25]

In human medical settings the debate over euthanasia generally focuses around whether the *sanctity* of life should or should not be valued over the *quality* of life. Giving primacy to the former value leads to a rejection of "mercy killing" while the quality of life position acts as a foundation for medical personnel allowing or actively assisting with euthanasia in certain circumstances.

Though it is a matter of considerable concern in certain veterinary and animal rights circles,[26] the euthanasia of dogs and other companion animals typically is regarded as far less controversial in the larger society than is the mercy killing of humans. This relative lack of concern is grounded on the common cultural definition discussed in previous chapters—the view that dogs and other animals are objects rather than sentient individual beings.[27]

The emotional intensity of the relationship that often develops between people and their animal companions commonly prompts human caretakers to be ambivalent about, or reject entirely, the definition of their animals as mindless, objectified pieces of property.[28] Instead, as we have seen, they view the dogs and other companion animals with whom they share their everyday lives as unique, emotional, reciprocating, and thoughtful "friends" or "family members." Given these close ties between people and their pets, caretakers are confronted with painful choices when forced to make decisions regarding the provision of medical care and if, when, and how to manage their animals' deaths.[29] In turn, as a central party in decisions about the medical management and eventual death of companion animals, veterinarians must also regularly confront these issues. For the veterinarian this is more than simply a matter of rational occupational practice. The mistreatment, maltreatment, and especially death of animals commonly are, for the veterinarian, matters of considerable moral and emotional weight.[30]

Somewhere between 2 and 4 percent of veterinarians' clinical encounters involve euthanasia.[31] This represents a massive, voluntary termination of companion animal lives. Given the most reliable national data, somewhere between 1.8 and 3.6 million dogs and cats are euthanized yearly in the course of routine veterinary practice.[32]

In comparison to the typical patterns of "death work" in which physicians are involved, that of veterinarians displays unique aspects. Practitioners and clients overtly recognize that "dispensing death" is a part of veterinary work while physicians and other human medical personnel, confined by numerous legal and moral restraints, totally reject euthanasia as a practice alternative, discuss it reluctantly (if at all) among themselves or with those who purchase their services, and/or engage in active euthanasia secretively and often ambivalently. Consequently, while veterinarians are usually present during and directly involved in their patients' deaths, physicians are rarely in attendance when their patients die.[33]

Judging Legitimacy and Negotiating Death

As we have seen, veterinary interactions typically involve overt negotiation between the doctor and the client around the diagnosis and treatment of the animal-patient. In the end, however, the animal's owner, as the purchaser of the veterinarian's services, has the final say as to the fate of the object/being which/who is his or her property. It is in the case of the euthanasia decision that the control exercised by the client creates the most troublesome ethical dilemma for the doctor. As the person possessing the most expertise and ultimately the one who causes death, the veterinarian has various alternatives when interacting with clients who have made, or are in the process of making, the decision to euthanize their animals.[34] The doctor can offer counter arguments in an attempt to dissuade the client, consent to the client's request, or send the client elsewhere. To a major extent, the course the veterinarian chooses depends on his or her evaluation of the worthiness of the rationale offered by the client in support of euthanasia. In general, these judgements range from reasons the veterinarian sees as legitimate and therefore supports, to those seen as illegitimate and, to a considerable degree, reflective of a moral failure on the part of the owner.[35]

From the veterinarian's perspective, the most legitimate reasons for euthanizing a pet revolve around the animal's quality of life. In the clinic patients who were old and infirm or suffering pain because of severe illness or injury were seen as the most legitimate candidates for euthanasia.[36] One vet emphasized quality of life issues when he described his discussions with clients contemplating euthanasia. Notice the distinction he makes between legitimate and illegitimate reasons:

> I always tell people that dogs really live for two things—their bodies and their love for their owner. So if the animal isn't eating and having that pleasure or they don't recognize their owner—if one or both of those things takes place—then it is time to consider euthanasia. You would be surprised how people come to the decision. Some people will bring in a dog that looks like it has gone through a lawn mower—really a mess—and they will say, "You have to do something. I'll pay anything." Other people will bring in a dog that has been hit by a car or something and it just has a little limp and they'll say, "It's in pain. Put it out of its misery."

In contrast to rationales emphasizing the illness, infirmity, or pain experienced by the animal, the other category of reasons typically offered for euthanasia focuses on the *owner's quality of life*. As such, veterinarians tend to view these justifications to be significantly less legitimate. Behavioral problems, especially canine aggressiveness, are one of the major issues for which clients seek veterinary assistance.[37] Despite the fact that the vast majority of behavioral problems owners experience with their dogs could be remedied fairly easily through minimal training,[38] the veterinarians tended to view this proffered reason to be moderately legitimate given the limited time, energy, and knowledge of most clients. One interviewee presented her acceptance of such a rationale based on her evaluation of the animal's quality of life:

> I can accept putting an animal down for behavioral problems as long as I think you have given it a good shot at trying to rectify the situation. I can sympathize with clients who don't have the facilities to handle a dangerous animal. If the animal is not going to really be an acceptable pet for someone else, the quality of life for an animal like that is not going to be high. I don't have much trouble with euthanasia when I think it is a quality of life question. If the animal's quality of life is not going to be good—this is a hard thing to hear myself say—I think they are better off not being around than being stuck in a cage for the rest of their life.

Considerably further down on the legitimacy scale are euthanasia decisions clients make based primarily on economic considerations. While the veterinarians typically disapproved of crass monetary rationales, they tended to be somewhat resigned to decisions made on economic grounds, emphasizing the balancing of the client's interests and those of the animal. With some show of distaste, one vet described a case in which a woman chose to euthanize her cat based on financial considerations:

> I had one the other day. It was a sick cat and I suggested that we keep it in the hospital for a day because it was so sick, an old cat. I thought we could do a CBC, send a profile off and have that all back the next day, and the cat would do better if it were in the hospital with injectable antibiotics and fluids under the skin. She said, "How much is it? We are more attached to the dog than we are to the cat." So I gave her an estimate of 70 or 80 dollars for over-night. . . . "That's too much. Put it to sleep."

From the vet's perspective, the least justifiable reason for euthaniz-ing an animal—especially one that is healthy—is for the simple con-venience of the owner. Clients who employ this category of rationales typically are judged to be morally suspect. They are perceived as defin-ing the animal as a piece of property rather than as a sentient being with feelings and interests:

> The ones I really can't stand are the clients who come in here and they want to euth the animal for all kinds of ridiculous reasons—they are moving to a smaller apartment, or they just got a new couch and the cat doesn't match the color, or the dog has grown up and isn't as cute anymore. It's like it's this piece of trash that they just want to throw away.

As the level of perceived legitimacy of the client's reason for request-ing euthanasia declines, the veterinarian's ethical dilemma concerning whether or not to accede to the owner's wishes becomes more pro-nounced. In some circumstances veterinarians try to convince people to change their minds or simply refuse to euthanize the animal.[39] One veterinarian described an encounter in which he successfully steered clients away from euthanasia:

> Just today I had these people come in with this cat. It was this argumentative mother and daughter and they said that the cat had had a stroke. The cat has vestibular disease, head tilt, falling to the side, there's no ear disease. It has idiopathic vestibular disease. With no treatment it will get over it in a couple of days. They said, "It's had a stroke. Put it to sleep." I said, "Well, let me show you. It's moving its tail. It's alert and knows where it is. Watch me move its paws. It is totally proprioceptive. It's doing fine and I would really like to not put it to sleep. Give it a couple of days and it will get better." They really didn't want to hear it, but I was able to talk them into it. I said, "It's your cat,

but I would really like to wait a few days and see if there is any improvement." She says, "Well, if you can tell me she is probably going to get better, then I'll do it." I said, "She's uncomfortable, she's not in pain." People sometimes try to corner me into saying that the animal is suffering.

When they did go along with the client's request despite their disapproval of the decision, the veterinarians with whom I worked would sometimes neutralize the guilt associated with the decision by making reference to the "fact" that they were paid by the client to perform a service. At other times they would call on the standard rationale they also used to support cropping the ears and docking the tails of certain breeds of dogs: "If we don't do it they will just go to someone else or do it themselves."

It is rare that the exchange between the veterinarian and the client around a pet's euthanasia involves the latter requesting the procedure and the former complying with the client's wishes. More commonly the client approaches the emotion-laden decision hesitantly and with intense feelings of ambivalence and comes to the vet for his or her medically informed advice. In this role of counselor[40] the veterinarian assesses the animal's situation, judges the client's position, determines whether further medical intervention is feasible, and, commonly, "steers" the client toward or away from euthanasia.[41] One vet described the exchange as a complex mix of making medical judgements, evaluating the client, making a decision, and, ultimately, taking responsibility for the decision:

> When [clients] ask me [about euthanasia] in a medical context I try to assess what the prognosis is for this animal having a comfortable life—how long he is going to live, how comfortable we can make him for the time he is going to be alive. I try to get as much medical information as I can in order to make those judgements. People ask, "Well, what would you do?" I'll tell them if I think the animal is comfortable and has some comfortable time left. [In that case] I'll try to encourage people to give them a little more time if they can financially swing it. I had a client the other day ask for advice, "Is it time?" And I said, "If he is still functioning like a dog and if we can make him a little more comfortable on a medication that is not going to make him really sick, let's try this and see if it works. If it doesn't we will deal with it in three or four weeks." Most clients are willing to do that. If I know they *want* to put the animal to sleep—you can read them sometimes if you open up to them and feel where they are at—you can tell when they want you to say, "I think it is time." Sometimes they need you to say that but they can't directly ask

you. You can tell by the look in their eyes and their emotional state that they want someone to say, "I think it is time." That's what you say to those people. It's funny, I'm helping the animals, but in some ways you are counseling the owners as much as you are helping the animal. I think they are very grateful and relieved. I don't mind taking that responsibility.

No matter how the veterinarian evaluates the legitimacy of client requests for euthanasia or what the eventual outcome of the negotiation with owners, the doctor's ability to make life or death decisions is a psychological burden. One doctor talked about his ambivalence with euthanasia decisions and the conflict that some of these decisions generated within the hospital:

Sometimes [the decision to euthanize an animal] is clearcut and it is easy and straightforward. I know that I am helping the animal and am helping the people and haven't invested a lot emotionally into it. It's more easy to deal with those cases. It was a very hard thing to learn how to deal with. Most of the time I agree with what the people are doing but sometimes you don't. I'm not a very judgmental person so it is easier for me to deal with it. Some of our employees are very judgmental and they are unable to see the entire situation. They think the people are cruel and they are putting the dog or the cat to sleep for no reason; they shouldn't be doing it and they are an awful person. I realize there are a lot of situations that people just find unbearable. People handle things in different ways. Some people, if they have to get rid of a dog, would rather have it put to sleep than place it with someone else because they wouldn't necessarily know what had happened to the dog. Sometimes if it is a young healthy animal that would be easily placed and could find a great home, then I try to talk them out of it. In other situations where the animal is like twelve or thirteen years old, has some medical problems, and just—it's a sad thing to put the animal to sleep because they might be moving into a smaller house or elderly housing where they couldn't take the dog. But it may give everybody peace of mind just to put the dog to sleep because it is an older dog. Placing the dog with someone else who is going to be attached to it for just a year and then have it die is difficult. It may be a difficult adjustment for the dog if they are arthritic and have some other problems going on. Some of the employees don't see that—that there are other sides to it—so they get real huffy about it. Sometimes I find myself having to justify what is going on to them.

The Euthanasia Encounter

The following description from my field notes reveals the basic elements of the encounter between the client and the veterinarian surrounding the euthanasia of a companion animal:

I go into one of the exam rooms where a youngish woman is waiting with a large old black dog and her three- or four-year-old daughter. As I come into the room the daughter looks at me brightly and says, "My dog is going to die." I have no idea how to respond so I say nothing, squat down, and pet the dog. I observe to the owner that she must have some Newfoundland in her. I look up and see that the woman is starting to cry. Feeling embarrassed and sad I quickly and quietly retreat back out into the pharmacy. [The technician] is showing the file to Keith and informs him, "They're in room 3. The kid is all psyched up." [She says this with a disapproving tone.] I accompany Keith when he goes back into the exam room a few minutes later. Keith asks, "What can we do for you? [I am interested to note that his tone is friendly and rather upbeat.] You want to put her to sleep?" The woman responds, "She's getting so old. She just can't get up by herself anymore. She's incontinent and she has this large growth on her side. [At this she reaches down and parts the dog's hair to show the fatty growth. The dog grins happily and rolls over on her back to be scratched.] But she was okay yesterday when she found deer droppings to roll in." Keith says, "So she has pain getting up in the morning? It's hard when we get this old." [This last observation is directed mostly to the dog.] The tech comes in with electric clippers and a syringe filled with the characteristically bright blue euthanasia solution. Keith picks the old dog up and puts her on the exam table. She lies on her stomach with her head facing out into the room. Keith asks, "Have you ever done this before? I'm just going to give her an overdose of anesthetic—ten times the normal amount. She will just go to sleep." He shaves the dog's foreleg and the tech holds the animal's leg with her thumb, stopping the blood flow and making the vein protrude. Keith asks the woman to move to the end of the table. "Come over here [to her head] so she can see you. Just stand there and pet her." The woman moves to the dog's head and pets her gently. The daughter also stands in front of the dog. The little girl is now crying and the mother looks down at her and says reprovingly, "You *wanted* me to bring you." Keith gently slides the needle into the dog's vein and slowly depresses the plunger. The dog's head stays up for most of the injection then drops to the table. Her eyes remain open. The woman and her daughter are now both sobbing. Keith checks the dog's heartbeat with his stethoscope, makes a grim/sad face to woman, and we all leave them alone with the body. As we leave, I quietly say, "I am very sorry" to the woman. I go back into the lounge feeling sad and somewhat angry. It didn't seem to me that the poor dog was all that sick.

Such "orchestrations of death"[42] represent, for veterinarians, the most time consuming[43] and emotionally wearing clinical exchanges in which they are routinely involved. Made aware of the upcoming euthanasia by a notation on the clinical record provided by the receptionist, the doctor typically offered some form of neutral opening statement upon entering the examination room. He or she would, for example, make an observation about the animal's physical condition, ask the client questions about the patient's age, or make some other attempt to "break the ice." Usually after some brief discussion of the animal's negative prognosis or the signs and symptoms that prompted the client to make this final decision, the veterinarian would ask clients whether or not they wished to stay for the euthanasia.[44]

Most of the clients I observed during my fieldwork chose to stay.[45] From the veterinarian's perspective, the presence of the client was potentially problematic. The euthanasia was not always an "aesthetic death"[46]—the veterinarian could "miss the vein," the patient could struggle or cry out when the hypodermic needle was inserted or might urinate or defecate while dying. As a consequence, the presence of the client increased the veterinarian's stress. This was particularly the case for those just beginning their practice careers. As one experienced vet observed:

> When they first start working, a lot of the young kids don't like to euthanize an animal with the client there. They're afraid they won't get the vein and will do a subcute with the pentobarbital and the animal will show pain. It's a lot of stress anyway. They don't anticipate having to deal with the client's emotion. You don't learn anything in school about that.

When the client wished to be present, the veterinarian would shape the client's expectations of what was to follow by explaining the euthanasia procedure. He or she usually explained that the animal was to be injected with an overdose of pentobarbital, that the animal would feel no pain other than the prick of the needle, and the patient would be dead when its eyes closed though there might be some continued movement or apparent (agonal) breathing. For example:

> [The client] opens the door of the exam room. "We're ready." Deborah has drawn up the pale lavender pentobarbital solution and comes in after calling [the tech] to come hold the vein. She has him go get the electric clippers on the counter. She explains, "Have you ever done this before? I am going to shave his arm and then I will be giving him an injection of an anesthetic. The only pain he will feel will be the prick of the needle—it will be like drawing blood. Then he will just go to sleep. He may seem to breath or make some movements, but they are just electrical messages to the muscles."

Either prior to or immediately following the description of the procedure, the vet would ask clients if they wanted a few minutes alone with their animal. Most said they did and used this time to bid farewell. Of all the interactions between people and their animals I observed during my time in the clinic, these sorrowful moments were the most emotionally difficult. My field notes record an instance of my eavesdropping on such an exchange and the feelings generated by my overhearing the leave-taking between an older couple and their dog:

> I am not real happy with this, but I am committed to tapping into this experience. [The tech] brings the dog—a small grey terrier—into examination room 4 and gently hands it to the man and his wife. I go into the adjoining room to listen and watch what I can through the half-closed door. I am very uncomfortable with doing this. I feel like I am spying on an intimate and painful moment in these people's lives. The man says, "He doesn't look like he is in any pain." The wife agrees. They both pet the dog, hug him, call him by name. They are both crying. The man keeps repeating, "Be a good puppy. We love you."

After injecting the patient with the euthanasia solution and checking his or her vital signs, the veterinarian would, once again, typically ask if clients wanted a few more minutes with the animal's remains. Again, most owners who attended the euthanasia wanted some time with the body. Having previously asked clients what they wanted to do with their animals' remains, vets frequently used this time to prepare for the disposition of the body.[47]

Coping with Euthanasia

Regularly beset with the pain, illness, and fear of animals and the anxiety and grief of their owners, the veterinarians, of necessity, had to find ways of coping with the ongoing emotionality of their occupational experience. One major protective mechanism employed was to emotionally separate themselves from euthanasias and other painful situations they encountered. As is common in medical settings generally,[48] the vets often employed humor as a protective device. They would, for example, sometimes half-jokingly refer to themselves as "Dr. Death" or "Dr. Doom" when preparing to go into an examination room to perform a euthanasia or after having been responsible for a series of deaths in the course of a single work day.[49]

Whether through humor or the use of some other means of distancing themselves from the painful emotions resulting from routinely dealing in death, the veterinarians all saw at least some degree of emotional separation as being essential to their psychological well-being. One doctor observed during an interview:

> I find that emotionally I just have to insulate myself from a lot of [client pain over euthanasia]. If I were wrapped up in every case I would just be a mess. I'm not cold, but I *am* detached. I try to give the people what they need, be calm about it, and tell them not to feel guilty.

When I asked another vet if euthanasia still affected him at all, he uncharacteristically spoke rather coldly of how he focused on veterinary practice as a "business" and defined euthanasia as simply an aspect of his job:

> No. There are so many animals out there and there are so many mismatched animals and people that some animals don't deserve to be with some people and some people don't deserve to have some animals. I don't personally feel it is my place to play god and decide which animals deserve to live and die. This is a business. Euthanasia is what I'm paid to do and I don't have any problem with that. . . . When someone brings in an animal [to be euthanized] I don't usually ask them, "Well, why are you doing this?" When people ask me for advice I tell them that animals are here to give us pleasure. They serve us. Secondarily we serve them; we take care of them. When that service leaves, [you can either] place the dog or euth it. There shouldn't be an antagonistic situation at home because you hate the dog, the cats are destroying the furniture, et cetera. No, I don't have a problem with euthanasias.

The veterinarians' relationships with clients and patients were central to how emotionally problematic they (and the clinic staff) found euthanasias to be. "Stranger" animals were typically put to death rather perfunctorily as when unwanted and unplaceable dogs were brought to the back-stage area of the clinic by the town animal control officer. There was also little emotion felt or displayed as physically unattractive or intractable animals were euthanized when their owners were not present.

The veterinarian's definition of the client was another factor shaping the emotion he or she felt when euthanizing a dog or other companion animal. Far less was felt when the owner was demanding, overly concerned with the expense of treatment, or had other characteristics of a "bad" client. One doctor emphasized his relationship with the client and told of a recent case when I asked him to talk about the difference between euthanasias that were, or were not, emotionally problematic:

> I think it is usually where I know the client more and I know what is going into the decision. I put a cat down last week. It was an older woman that I have been dealing with for umpteen years and she has taken in older animals. She is a private duty nurse and she gets really attached to her patients and when they get ready to die she takes their animals for them. . . . [Soon after her husband] died all of her dogs died one at a time. Through every one of these she was really upset. Then I just put one cat to sleep about two weeks ago because it had a huge abdominal mass—a kidney tumor. And then I put another one to sleep last week because it had a huge tumor in the mouth. This was just like more than this poor woman could handle. I was really upset about that.

Since the veterinarian's emotional experience is closely entwined with that of the bereaved owner, he or she has a vested interest in fostering the healing process. In the clinic clients anticipating euthanizing their animals were provided with informative pamphlets, offered helpful books and videotapes, and advised by the doctors. Following euthanasia, clinic personnel also did what they could to ease the client's pain. Bereaved owners were provided the time and privacy to bid their animals farewell, and doctors and staff members routinely treated them with solicitation and sympathy. For regular clients the clinic also took an important symbolic step to lend closure to the owner's loss experience and speed the healing process. The doctor who had euthanized an animal would send a donation in the pet's name to a local veterinary school. The school, in turn, would write to owners informing them of the donation and offering condolences for their loss. Upon receiving the letter from the veterinary school, owners commonly sent grateful and heart-touching letters to the doctor who had euthanized their animal. Here are two examples of letters posted on the staff bulletin board:

> Dear Dr. _____,
> Thank you very much for your kind, thoughtful gift in memory of our beloved Bear. We received a very touching letter from [the University] which moved us to tears. They say, "Time heals all wounds," but we still find it difficult to mention Bear. We realize how much you must miss your beloved dog too. We appreciate your thoughtfulness greatly with hopes research will

someday help many animals with problems. Thank you again for caring for our Bear. He left us with so many beautiful memories.

Dear Dr. _____,

I have been searching for the right words to show my appreciation for all you did for my dog, Suki. A simple "thank you" doesn't seem quite enough. Your caring, kindness, generosity and support meant so much. His life was a struggle from the start—and for a "first time mom" not what I hoped for or expected. Yet, you helped make difficult times and decisions bearable. I always felt he was in technically skilled and loving hands when I left him with you.

My loss was further comforted by a wonderful letter I received from [the University] regarding a donation the hospital made in his name. What a lovely and meaningful gesture! I was very touched. I hope others are helped.

I miss Suki terribly and know that only time will help to heal the pain. When I feel able, I'm sure I'll find another puppy to care for and you'll be seeing me again. Until then, please know how grateful I am for everything you've done.

These letters and the many like them clearly demonstrated the intensity of the relationships clients had with their animal companions[50] and the appreciation elicited by the veterinarian's display of understanding concern. For the vet, in turn, the memorial donation and subsequent appreciative interactions with clients helped to bring closure to, and ease the personal sadness attendant upon, causing the death of a regular patient.

The veterinarian's death work, then, precipitates two troublesome and related dilemmas. The practitioner must find means of dealing with the "moral stress"[51] precipitated by the conflict between allegiance to an ethic of care and routinely being called upon to perform and rationalize euthanasia. Further, the episodic nature of a mixed practice requires the veterinarian to move through clinic encounters involving joy, sorrow, anxiety, and pain as he or she moves from appointment to appointment. This alternation of routine, painful, and joyful interactions requires the veterinarian ongoingly to engage in "emotional labor."[52] He or she must take care to manage his or her emotional displays when interacting with clients. For the doctors with whom I worked, the emotional management required in daily veterinary practice was regarded as one of the most burdensome aspects of the job:

It's an easy profession in which to get burnt out. You have to change personalities so many times. You put an old dog to sleep that you have seen for years
and then you walk into the next room and this client has a little puppy that
they just got and they are really high and you have to be real happy. And
you're going along with fifteen-minute appointments and these people come
in and *they* are ready to put *their* old dog to sleep. And to be honest, you're at
the point where it is just another thing—just another fifteen-minute appointment. And you have to stop and slow down and be there for the people and
sometimes that's tough.

This chapter has focused primarily on the day-to-day occupational
experiences of veterinarians as they deal with both animal patients and
human clients. As we have seen, the relatively commonsensical categories used to define clients and patients are incorporated in the collection of stories that constitute the ongoing lore of the clinic. The collective lore of all medical settings is composed of these sorts of stories
that incorporate fairly clear ethical principles as well as of identifying
social types and specifying certain techniques that have been found to
be more-or-less effective in handling both unique and commonplace
problems. The local stories help to ground and justify the difficult decisions one is forced to make in all medical settings.[53]

Like essentially all jobs, veterinary work is predominantly a series
of routine events. While all the veterinarians with whom I worked saw
their occupational routine as rewarding in its predictability, it was the
unique happenings—the unusual cases, the "interesting" surgical pro-
cedures—that added spice to the daily round of routine events. Unique
cases were valued because they provided veterinarians with more experience, allowed them to make use of and hone their technical skills,
and offered opportunities to successfully solve diagnostic problems.

The rewards of veterinary practice go beyond the ability to use technical abilities, solve diagnostic problems, learn new techniques, and encounter unusual medical situations, however. Clinical practice is, as we
have seen, an intensely social activity made even more powerful by the
emotional connection that commonly exists between owner and animal. To be a veterinarian means not only to deal with problematic patients or interact with sometimes annoying, ignorant, or belligerent clients. Veterinary practice also entails healing sick and injured animals
and being the recipient of fervent appreciation offered by clients who

recognize that their pets have been cared for with compassion and skill.

It is in those situations focused around the euthanasia of a dog or another companion animal that the veterinarian's compassion is most apparent. In our society the companion animal to whom the veterinarian ministers often is regarded ambivalently as either a socially defined "person" with whom one has a relationship or as an object that one possesses.[54] As is the case with ostensibly human actors such as the aged or terminally ill who are similarly relegated to this marginal realm between person and nonperson, the decision to euthanize a companion animal and the feelings associated with this decision depend on a kind of social calculus. In addition to the being's defined social worth— especially as sentient being or possessed object—his/her/its perceived health, available treatment alternatives, and the impact of survival on those on whom he/she/it depends are elements of this calculation. While the euthanasia of severely damaged neonates, the comatose, those in extreme pain, and terminally ill humans generates considerable social controversy in our society, the purposive killing of nonhuman animals is a matter of less concern given available cultural definitions by which they may be officially denied the status of personhood. Conventionally, nonhuman animals, lacking language, are presumed to lack the ability to construct concepts. Having no concepts they do not possess a sense of self and, therefore, are unaware of the potential misfortune of self-loss.[55] As sentient beings they can suffer, but they cannot conceive of or fear death.

People who live with dogs and other companion animals, and the veterinarians who attend to their physical well-being, however, commonly regard companion animals as virtual persons, as individual beings with whom one may enjoy authentic social relationships bounded by shared histories and encompassing direct knowledge of an animal's unique personal attributes.[56] In particular, owners typically see their dogs and other pets as friends or family members whose pain and illnesses are matters of regret and whose natural or imposed deaths they experience as significant misfortunes that precipitate intense remorse.

Some owners, however, relate to their animals as objects to be possessed. While these "objects" may have some measure of value as pieces of property, their disabilities, possible deaths, and euthanasias are experienced as events with little emotional weight. As objects the animals can be disposed of, and similar species/models can easily be acquired.

On their part, veterinarians make similar distinctions among their patients. Some are generic animals/patients/cases. These are "put down" routinely and with little show or experience of regret. Typically, these executions are accomplished rather off-handedly and sometimes are accompanied by macabre humorous banter. In contrast, regular patients with whom veterinarians have developed relationships are "put to sleep" gently, and their passing exacts emotional costs that must be paid as part of the dues of clinical practice.

We see in the daily work of veterinarians and especially in their interactions with clients surrounding the act of euthanasia a rich and striking example of the creation of personhood as a social accomplishment and the emotional elements of the significant relationships we have with beings relegated to this valued position. As in the previous chapters, we have seen here in the experience of the veterinarians and their clients that personhood as an elemental social designation may be acquired or forfeited, given or taken away. Personhood is a social identity that determines how beings are treated, the rights and freedoms they possess, and even whether and under what conditions they are allowed to live.

Ambivalence, conflicting definitions, emotional connections, and struggles for control exert significant pressure on the occupational lives of veterinarians as they work with dogs and other animal patients and attempt to negotiate their interactions with the human clients who purchase their services. In the social situations that revolve around people routinely interacting with dogs, however, the ambivalence, control problems, and emotionality experienced by veterinarians are typical rather than unique. We turn now to another setting in which these issues are of paramount importance. For those occupationally involved in training guide dogs, ambivalent definitions and related control tactics are also matters to be dealt with on a daily basis.

5

The Guide Dog Trainer
Understanding and Teaching Dogs

or many of us, the interactions between guide dogs and those who train them and between blind owners and their guides represent the ultimate in canine-human social exchanges. It is, at the same time, important to realize that the guide dog training setting is fairly unique and that trainer and owner interactions with guide dogs are relatively rare. There are currently fewer than twenty guide dog training programs in the United States[1] employing what the trainers with whom I worked estimated to be fewer than two hundred trainers. Further (or, perhaps, consequently), guide dogs are employed as mobility aids by only a small proportion of blind people. As of the mid-1980s only from 1 to 3 percent of visually handicapped people owned or had interest in using guide dogs.[2]

As I pointed out in the earlier methodological discussion, the Devoted Companions program in which I participated was relatively small and was unusual in that trainers provided instruction to individual guide dog recipients in their home communities. This is in contrast to the common "live-in" model in which cohorts of potential owners are brought into the training facility, matched with dogs, and, over the course of a few weeks, instructed in their use.[3] When I was there, the program had around seventy puppies that were being raised by "foster families" as potential trainees. These puppies lived with the families for eighteen months before being evaluated on their suitability as guides. Dogs that were judged by the staff to have the appropriate health and temperament were then assigned to one of the six full-time trainers who worked with them for between six and eight months. Each trainer was responsible for six or seven dogs at a time. When dogs were deemed to have acquired the necessary skills, they were matched with blind applicants. Trainers then took the dogs to the chosen owners and for about three weeks worked with the new owners and their dogs in the communities in which the "teams" would operate daily. Each trainer went on from eight to ten such "placements" a year.

Becoming a Guide Dog Trainer

The trainers at Devoted Companions all had a basic love for dogs, had grown up with dogs, and shared their homes with dogs. For some, the dog-focused life occasionally presented a bit of a problem. As one trainer put it:

> I just sometimes get tired of dogs. I work with them all day and then when I go home there are all these dogs around frantically trying to get my attention. Sometimes I feel like I just can't stand to see another wagging tail.

Most of the trainers had moved into the job somewhat indirectly. The most common routes were through having the experience of fostering potential guide dog puppies when they were younger or having been involved in some sort of dog-related job such as working in a boarding kennel or doing professional obedience training prior to moving into guide dog training. One interviewee described the former route:

> Way back in '74 my parents decided to join a foster family program. Apparently, they had read about it in the paper and, unbeknownst to me, this was going to become my puppy, my project. I raised my first pup, and her name was Yuma, a big beautiful dog for a female. The only thing I got [from the program] when she graduated, was just a little snapshot of her posed with her harness on. . . . That's the last I heard of her. But it was a big deal, as you can imagine, separating yourself from the puppy. . . . When I graduated from high

school I became involved with my second dog through a 4-H Foster Puppy Club. After high school, I went into the retail business. I managed a [clothing store] for a couple of years and did not like that at all. . . . I did that till '81. Then I started thinking, "Well, what am I going to do with my life?" and I remembered seeing a movie about the training of guide dogs. I didn't remember what the movie was called or anything, but I remember looking at the screen and the trainer was blindfolded on this busy street with his dog. His dog's at the curb and he's asking the dog to go but the dog wouldn't move. And I'm just saying, "Wow, this is great!" I was already half in the program, you know, doing the foster puppy stuff and I said, "I can do this." . . . [So eventually I said], "Let's see if they still have the foster puppy thing going on up at Devoted Companions." . . . I went to a few meetings, and I met [some of the staff] and asked them, "What kind of opportunities do you have for a guy who wanted to do this for a career?" . . . I didn't know a thing about training the dogs or what was expected or anything, but my interest was there. . . . They said, "Well, there's no openings at the moment, but let's take your name, so on and so forth, and we'll get back to you." So it had been quite a while since I'd heard from them and I finally sat down and wrote a letter and told them what I had done in the previous years as far as raising foster puppies, and so on and so forth. . . . I sent that in and got the official rejection letter. "We still don't have any openings but your letter will remain on file, blah, blah, blah. You may call me anytime, Sincerely." So I basically made a pest out of myself over the next six months, a mild pest. . . . Finally they said, "Yeah, come in for an interview."

Another trainer told of moving into the job through a more focused dog-related path:

I was going to [the state university]. I was in the pre-vet program there. At the time, there were not a lot of vet schools around—there still aren't—and I was in classes with guys who were seniors, who had 4.0s all through school and had dads who were vets and had lots of money within the family and who still ended up working in [department stores]. And I said, "Something is wrong here. I have to think about changing what I'm doing." But I've always liked working with dogs and I've always enjoyed working in and around animals. So, I went to another school to learn about dog training and dog behavior. . . . I learned a lot there from my instructor. I did a lot of dog psychology classes, obedience training, security dog training, worked with the police, kennel management. I worked at several kennels after I had left there. I was a kennel manager at one. Then the school called me back and wanted me to work for them, which I did. Then I left there after several years to start my own business doing dog training. We had that for five years and the girl who was the [kennel] manager [at Devoted Companions] and I did a seminar together about dog behavior for dog professionals throughout [the state]. We got to know each other, and she said, "You know, we need someone to do some work at [the program]. Are you interested in coming down?" I was like, "Well, I have my business, but it sounds kind of interesting, so let me come down and try." And I just got more and more involved in Devoted Companions. I sold my business to my partner and I came on here full time. . . . It'll be almost ten years now.

Regardless of the experience or training they had prior to coming to work at Devoted Companions, all of the trainers agreed that what they called "dog understanding" was the most essential attribute of a successful guide dog trainer. This understanding involved knowing species characteristics ("how dogs think" as one trainer put it), the attributes of the individual breed with which one was working, and—most importantly—recognizing the unique characteristics of the individual dog being trained. Knowing that the particular dog tended to be willing or lazy, headstrong or pliant, nervous or calm, smart or dim, and so forth was central to constructing a viable training relationship with him or her and thereby achieving the goal of producing an effective guide. In a field conversation one trainer emphasized having a general understanding of dogs and the central importance of an individualistic approach while gently criticizing more mechanically production-oriented guide dog programs:

> You have to modify your approach so that it is appropriate for each dog. That means that we aren't like a lot of the guide dog schools. They tend to work on a cookie-cutter model. They just want a dog that goes about doing what it is taught. There are two different approaches. I can't stand to watch some of the trainers [in other programs] work. I think [the trainers here] are especially good trainers because they have an understanding of dogs and how they think. They adjust what they do for the particular dog. Others want the dog to be a machine. They give a correction when the dog has no idea what is going on and when it doesn't understand what it is being corrected for. Hey, it's just a dog!

Another trainer, who described guide dog work as a creative "art," spoke of dog understanding as an attribute that differentiated the mechanical approach of "trainers" from the flexible and individualized approach employed by "instructors":

> A dog trainer is a person that will have a very regimented training technique. If the dog does it right it gets praised, if it's wrong it gets corrected. It's either right or wrong; there's no in-between. An instructor is more humanitarian. In-

structors can read a dog's good day or a dog's bad day and know when to put a little pressure on or when to take pressure off. It's very easy for a person to say, "Well, you want to have a dog that's always consistent, and so you always handle the dog the same way, and the correction is always X number of foot pounds of force on the leash." It shouldn't be that way. . . . [Knowing a dog's unique] personality is what separates the men from the boys, the successful trainers from the hacks.

The Problems and Rewards of the Job

Like most jobs, guide dog training centers around routine. An interviewee described a typical day:

> I usually have about six dogs. In the morning I take them all out. I usually pair them and see which ones do really well together, mixing the personalities so I don't get two dominant dogs together, and I'll take them out for a run. I'll take them out for a free run, exercise and play with them, then load them up in the van. After they're all exercised and whatnot, I'll usually take them out and work them in an area that I feel would be most beneficial for all of them. I'm usually out till maybe two in the afternoon and start heading back here about 2:30. Now, depending upon the day, when I get back I like to do my obedience and fetch in the afternoon. . . . I try to get all my dogs well-groomed at least once a week and [get their] nails done. Right now I'm doing it on Fridays. So I'll come back a little bit earlier on Fridays and I'll brush everybody, clip toe nails, and like that. It not only helps the kennel staff, but we can go over the dogs and see if there are any hot spots developing or raw spots, or whatever. And it keeps them well-groomed and it's kind of a bond between you and the dog when you do the grooming. . . . Most of the dogs are fed twice a day. . . . All of the dogs get something in the morning and the kennel staff will usually do that. [The trainers] are responsible for feeding our dogs in the afternoon. We can monitor who eats what and how they are doing. . . . That's pretty much our day. Sometimes you get little kinks thrown in, like photo shoots in the afternoon and trips to [placements].

Given this description, it was interesting that all of the trainers said that being free of routine was one of the major rewards of the job. The other characteristic of the work that the trainers found most appealing was freedom from overt supervision by superiors:

> None of us are in this for money, that's for sure. Most of it is working with the dogs, and you can be very flexible. We have very little kind of supervision. . . . I mean, if we feel that we need to go [somewhere], we go there. Like our boss would never know if I went to the mall and ended up shopping all day long and my dogs never got out of the van. No one would ever know

that. But none of us would ever think of doing that. You work here and that's not right. I think we're all pretty disciplined in ways like that.

This flexibility and freedom from control was especially appealing to the trainers who had worked in other programs in which the pressure of having dogs available at a specific time for an incoming cohort forced a more regimented production approach:

> I love this job because you do everything yourself. You decide where to take the dogs, what they need, what to work on, you know. It's just completely up to the trainer and what they need to do. Whereas at [the other program where I worked it] was much more structured. You came in, you did route 1, route 2, route 3, you know, specific routes. Everything was very much prescribed, everything. But the dogs were trained in twelve weeks, too—from the day they came in to the day they went into classes, twelve weeks. So you didn't have time to relax them or, you know, take an extra day doing whatever. It was very, very quick.

Since the basic work of training took place on public streets, trainers regularly encountered the same sorts of problems about which the guide dog users spoke in Chapter 3. They frequently had to put up with misguided concern, unwanted attention, and, occasionally, fearful responses from members of the public. One afternoon I accompanied two trainers to a relatively deserted suburban residential area where they were going to do "traffic work" with their dogs. Teaching the dogs that they should be watchful for approaching vehicles and exercise "intelligent disobedience" if commanded to move ahead when it was unsafe was a central element of this phase of the training. The trainers worked as a team with one on the street with a dog and the other in the program van. When the trainer on the street approached a "down" curb the dog would stop. As the dog was commanded to cross the street the trainer in the van would roar up to the dog and the other trainer would exert a sharp correction if the dog started to go forward. My comment that this would look like harassment to the untrained eye prompted the trainer I was with to tell the following story:

> We have to look out for the police. They sometimes think we are harassing blind people. Once when we were doing traffic training in [town]—this was before we had the signs for the vans [a magnetic sign reading DEVOTED COMPANIONS, TRAFFIC TRAINING is stuck on the side of the van]—I was driving and I pulled up in front of Dick and his dog and suddenly there were all

these lights. This big burly cop comes running up to the van and starts screaming at me. "Don't you know that you are supposed to stop when you see a blind person with a dog!" I explained to him that we were doing traffic training. When Dick comes up the cops says, "Is she with you?" and Dick just smiles. I could have killed him.

Seeing someone accompanied by a guide dog in harness prompts most people to assume that the person is blind. Upon encountering trainers working their dogs on city streets people tended to treat them as handicapped. This meant that trainers often were either pointedly avoided or subjected to unwanted assistance. I quote from field notes recorded early in my time in the field:

> It is interesting to see how people react to us and the dog. Some people see us coming and give wide berth. Others—usually young males—seem to purposefully move in front of the dog. At one point we are stopped at the exit of a parking garage and Judy motions the car there to go on. The car, an American junker, stays stopped and just as we started across the car lurches forward, its bumper tapping me lightly on the leg. We get across and I look back at the driver, frowning. The young man driving the car looks at me, shrugs, and laughs. People walking the same way we are tend not to go around us on the street or on stairs. They just slow down and stay behind. Mothers point the dog out to their children. Judy observes that it is interesting to listen to people talk in these situations since they almost always start talking about their own dogs. . . . After a few tries we all get through the revolving door into the mall and as we approach and haltingly get on the escalator a few people are watching. The security guard tries to be helpful, clearly thinking Judy is blind. "There is an elevator just over there you could use." We ignore him—actually, everyone is generally ignored. . . . The incident with the car prompts me to ask, "Do you often get hassled on the street?" Judy replies, "No, almost never. I actually feel pretty safe going almost anywhere because of the dog. I can truly say that I even feel safe on most city streets. The most common problem I have on the street is with people trying to help me. People tell me when it is okay to go across and take my arm to help me across the street even when no traffic is coming. Once in New York this woman even grabbed the harness handle out of my hand and started across the street with the dog. HEY, WHAT'S GOING ON? They think I'm blind."

In addition to the unwanted and unnecessary assistance precipitated by being with the dog, trainers, like guide dog users, have to put up with a certain amount of well-meaning public attention. Because they are representatives of the program, trainers typically deflect this attention quickly but courteously. I quote again from field notes:

Mike and I approach a group of older women on the street. They loudly express their opinions about how pretty the dog is. One says, "Oh, he's *so* cute. Is he training to be a guide dog? Can I pet him?" Mike coolly replies, "We ask people not to pet the dogs while they are working." Somewhat embarrassed she says, "Oh, okay. He is beautiful though." "Thank you." . . . Later we are standing at a curb. When the light turns, Mike and the dog start across the street. A young guy crossing with us observes, "It is amazing how smart they are. They can even tell the difference between a red light and a green light." Mike just smiles.

Working with the Blind: Constructing the Team

Love for dogs and the desire to have a job that focuses on them are the major factors that draw guide dog trainers to the occupation. However, like the veterinarians discussed in the previous chapter, trainers soon learn that working with people is a major part of their job. One interviewee spoke of his dominant interest in training dogs and his eventual realization that teaching blind owners was a task of equal importance:

> When I first got involved with Devoted Companions, I went to [the director of training] and said, "I imagine there's been a mistake here. I like dogs, I really like dogs, but I'm not that wild about people, for my own reasons, my own personality. . . . For whatever reasons, I'd prefer to work with animals."
> . . . When I was first interviewed for the job, they knew I really enjoyed working with dogs and was really excited about their behaviors. [The director] said, "Well, that's good, but how are you with people?" At the time, I wasn't even sure why this was such a concern. But, it's a big part of the job. . . . But the reality is that the fact that I might be able to get a dog to function as a guide, and get it to take me around the block blindfolded, is of really no consequence to anybody. . . . The only way that I have really done anything that's worth earning a paycheck is if I can teach a person, a blind person, how to do the same thing. And, that's a completely different job. . . . Ultimately, my job is to try to make [blind] people trainers in a very short period of time and make them [understand dog behavior]. . . . [I tell them that their dog] will continue to be trained every day. I'm no longer the trainer here. *They* are going to become this dog's trainer. . . . It's really simple.

The central importance of working with the visually impaired meant that understanding blind people was an occupational necessity. None of the trainers with whom I worked had had formal training in this element of the job. In essence, their education in working with blind recipients came from direct experience. The younger trainers who had worked only at Devoted Companions emphasized the importance of what they had learned about these matters from more experienced trainers during their three-year apprenticeship.

Categorizing both dogs and recipients was a necessary adjunct to matching dogs with owners. Dog-person teams were constructed after taking into account certain basic features. Dogs were judged primarily on their size, energy level, preferred walking pace, and whether they were headstrong ("hard") or compliant ("soft"). Recipients, in turn, were evaluated on their level of physical ability, the amount of vision they had, and the kinds of areas in which they would be working with the dogs (especially whether they lived and worked in urban or suburban/rural settings). One trainer emphasized the importance of taking both physical and personality variables into account when matching dogs and recipients:

> The three factors that I have to start with to make a successful match are the pace of the person and the dog, the amount of pull the dog is going to give and the amount of pull the person can withstand under good circumstances and not good circumstances, and the amount of correction that the dog needs versus the amount of correction that the person is able to give the dog. . . . Then you get into balance, reaction time of the person, voice, experience. There may be times when you have a very soft dog that is slowly maturing and is easily upset if it's mishandled. So you need to give that dog to an experienced person or a person with great coordination and flexibility in their ability to handle a dog. So they would give the dog the time to blossom and make minimal mistakes and the dog would be able to gain trust in the person. Then later on, once they have their working relationship, either of them can make mistakes and the other will compensate. . . . It can also come down to what type of dog the person likes. If you have a personality conflict or even if the person says, "Well, I want a big dog," and you don't give him a big dog, right away there's dislike and everything goes right down the tubes. . . . A person that lives in a metropolitan area may need that large dog to impose the general public. And if they don't get it, they may not feel confident in their dog's ability to be able to service them. . . . So personalities are very, very important. . . . Sometimes you'll give a person that is very reserved and lacking in confidence a dog that's a little on the bubbly side, because it helps to bring that person out and have them enjoy themselves and feel better about themselves.[4]

Evaluations of recipients' desires, expectations, and personalities were, then, as important as judging their physical abilities when constructing the dog-person team. When asked what he saw to be the major things that blind recipients wanted to gain from having a guide dog, one trainer made the distinction between understanding the dog as primarily a functional mobility aid and viewing it as a friend and companion. Those who had a social rather than functional orientation were judged to be better guide dog users:

> I've met a number of blind people who are lousy guide dog users. They would be better with a cane; they have really no interest in the dog. These are usually people that have strictly an interest in mobility—how to get from point A to point B—but when they get there or get home, they don't want to have anything to do with the responsibility of the care and maintenance of a dog. It is a tremendous amount of work. It's much easier when you get home to fold up that cane and put it in the corner. But to have to get home and feed and groom and care for a dog and make sure it's not barking and it's healthy, that's a great deal of work. So you get blind people that sometimes will apply to us for mobility aid only, and very often those are not the ones that I think the situation with dogs works well. . . . Then you get people who just absolutely adore to have a dog, to have a friend that they can reach down and find all the time. . . . They want a guide dog not only for mobility but also as a social ice breaker, a way to meet people. People are much more apt to approach a blind person with a dog rather than [someone] with a cane.

The Trainer's View of the Dog

Most essentially, the guide dog trainer's task is to define the dog's behavior as "intelligible"[5] and employ this understanding as the foundation of an effective training relationship.[6] Whether they spoke primarily of dogs as organisms shaped by behavioristic principles or as, at some level, thoughtful, manipulative, calculating, emotional beings with unique personalities, all the trainers saw dogs as relatively simple creatures. At some point, all of the trainers expressed a measure of distaste for the popular image of the guide dog as a "superdog"—"the noble leader of the blind who can do no wrong," as one trainer succinctly put it. While recognizing the public relations and fund-raising advantages of this portrayal, they believed that this "deification" of guide dogs did them a disservice and eventually reflected badly on training programs since, when dogs made newsworthy errors resulting in the death or injury of their owners, primary blame was directed at the training program that was presumed to have turned out an inadequately trained service dog.

Linked to the public relations imagery of the guide dog as "superdog," was the popular presentation of the service animal as engaging in a "natural activity" that made use of his or her basic canine instincts and abilities. One trainer put it this way (notice the biobehaviorist imagery):

> People in the guide dog field say [that] they're capitalizing on the natural pack drives of the dog and the dog's willingness to please. I don't buy any of that. . . . I look at the dog's natural drives, in just three areas: in defense, in prey, and pack. . . . Within the pack . . . [there is] a pack leader and some subordinate behaviors in animals below that. With a guide dog I don't think you can really say that you can capitalize on the pack drives because at one moment we're asking the dog to be a subordinate animal when it's told to lay down underneath the table and be quiet, it's corrected for obedience and stillness and all the functions it's going to have to perform at the subordinate level. And the next minute, literally the next minute, the dog is asked to guide and make independent decisions without the approval or consultation of the pack leader. That makes no sense. It's a perverted relationship, I think, for an animal. You certainly can't capitalize on any prey behavior, if there's any chase or any instincts to pounce or any stimulation movement, those will all have to be suppressed. Defense is unacceptable as well. Protectiveness, territorial barking, behaviors that are known to be defensive behavior, certainly aren't desirable at all. What we're really looking for [is] dogs that have extinguishable drives, drives that are available to the dog but are extinguishable without completely eliminating the dog's ability to continue to function as some kind of an animal.

All the trainers also spoke of the basic skills and materials necessary to successfully produce a serviceable guide dog. On their part, trainers needed to possess what was often referred to as "dog understanding," a knowledge of dog behavior and canine ethology combined with the ability to "read" the dog so as to understand how he or she was experiencing the specifics of the training situation and interaction. To become effective guides, dogs, on the other hand, had to possess some degree of basic intelligence combined with a "willingness" to learn while putting aside his or her "natural" interests:

> I mean, we have dogs that I am convinced are retarded. They're just dumb; they're not right. They just don't pick this stuff up. And [then there are] other dogs who are just very bright, [who] pick things up just very, very

quickly. . . . Willingness obviously is [another] trait that has to be there. The dog has to be willing to learn these things and willing to work for you. Because without the willingness, then there's nothing. The dog has no need to work. . . . It's a very unnatural thing. None of the things that we do with dogs fits their natural instincts.

Hard vs. Soft Dogs

One of the most elemental distinctions trainers made among dogs was to define some as "hard" and others as "soft."[7] This differentiation largely had to do with the trainer's estimation of the dog's sensitivity and how well he or she could handle the stress inherent in the training process.[8] Hard dogs were tougher, had high energy levels, and were more challenging for the trainer ("you have to keep on top of the dog all the time"), while soft dogs were "sensitive, low key, and quiet." One trainer talked about this distinction as having to do with the dog's "frame of reference"; notice how the interviewee gives voice to the hypothetical dogs' thoughts:

> Now I kind of look at it in terms of there being two very distinct types of dogs—one has a very internal frame of reference and another [has] a very external frame of reference. One dog having the ability to look at a situation and say, "I've seen something like this before. Yeah, there's that, there's that, I'm okay with that," and be okay with himself. Another dog that walks into the same situation and says, "I recognize that and I recognize that, but what else is out there that's going to get me? What's this, what's that?" Those are dogs with a very external frame of reference; those would be the ones that, I think, show more levels of suspicion. . . . I think the better dogs are ones that sometimes we call harder dogs. They tend to be the ones that are more internally-referenced. They're okay with themselves and they can look at a situation and recognize a couple of familiar things and be okay.

Another trainer described the hard and soft categories and added a middle type of dog that combined elements of both and, therefore, represented the ideal trainee:

> A hard dog would be a dog that is very independent, very energetic, and would bounce back very quickly after it's dominated. . . . [But] it's unfair to really categorize animals into specific groups, because you have an intermingling of personality traits. . . . It's very hard to categorize if you really want to be fair with the dog as far as handling it, or talking about it.
>
> [Keeping that in mind, what—in contrast—would a soft dog be?]

A soft dog would be a dog that is very sensitive to its environment as far as noise or the person that's dealing with it. . . . Soft in respect that it's sensitive to noises and easily impressed by its environment.

[If you had the ideal guide dog, what characteristics would it have?]

The ideal guide dog would be a mixture of all the traits. Soft enough and sensitive enough so that it would be willing to please. With a minimum of force—whether verbal or physical—you could get the dog to behave or to control itself and respond to what you wanted it to do. But not so hard that it was totally oblivious to either its handler or the outside environment. I want [the dog] to be cautious of objects and sensitive enough so that it's careful about its work, yet hard enough so that when I make a mistake, or the blind person makes a mistake, the dog isn't upset by it. It just rolls off its back and it says, "Yeah, so what." And with a minimum of praise, the dog says "Yeah, it's fine. Who cares" and goes on about its work. That's the ideal dog.

As evident in this trainer's description of the "ideal" trainee, some trainers saw themselves as being better with one type of dog than they were with the other. One interviewee spoke of her liking for soft dogs:

I prefer the soft dogs, the sensitive dogs, the more low-key dogs, the quiet dogs, [but] dogs who have enough zip and enough enthusiasm to get out there and to do it. I don't like the high-drive dogs. Super high energy, just got to go, go, go, all of the time. . . . I like the dogs who are okay with them-selves, who have enough drive to get up and go out and do work, but also when you come into a store or a restaurant, have enough self control [to say], "Okay, we can lay down now and behave ourselves and be quiet." I have a lot of those kinds of dogs. Those kinds of dogs are assigned to me. I get the more sensitive dogs who need boosting. . . . Their confidence level has to be built up. They're very soft dogs.

Another trainer talked about the disjunction between the kind of dog with which he liked to work and the kind of dog he saw as making the best guide:

Oddly enough, the personality that I do lousy with is the soft ones. The [best dogs are] real aloof dogs that don't really like people at all, are better in their nerves, are okay with themselves, and generally harder dogs. So, what I like in a dog is, unfortunately, a dog that doesn't work real well for me. The dogs I have are very soft. . . . I've got to have that in a dog. . . . For some reason in my personality, I need something a little dependent, not clingy, but some-thing that says, "I'm real happy you're here."

Understandably then, a dog's hardness or softness played a signifi-cant role in how the trainer interacted with him or her. Hard dogs were treated with a firm hand, soft dogs were handled with kid gloves. One interviewee, who presented himself as a generalist, made a distinction in terms of the dog's willingness to trust or forgive within the training relationship:

> [People] may think it's easier to train a hard-type dog, because it's more for-giving. It doesn't internalize and it doesn't take it to heart if you're maybe having a bad day and gave an unfair correction. With a soft dog, no matter how big you are, you're not going to make that up. It's going to be very, very difficult to get that soft dog to trust you again if you blow it. I think I'm open-minded enough to be able to try to accommodate dogs with different types of personalities.

Another trainer used a gaming analogy in speaking of how he worked with the soft dogs with whom he believed he was most effective:

> I will tend to be a soft trainer myself. I tend to let the dog get away with a little bit too much and be a little bit on the out-of-control side. This way I feel that I know my dogs at their worst. . . . Sometimes I compare it to poker. I want the dog to show me its hand, what it's got, before I show the dog my hand. Because I always have the better hand. But I don't want the dog to know that until later. You're experimenting all the time when you're training and the trick is to only experiment to the level that you get the response you want so the dog learns what's expected of it and [doesn't] get confused be-tween what it's learning and my teaching. When you're using discipline to teach, I want the dog to learn what the problem is . . . and not that I'm the bad guy.

Emotionality

It is clear in the above that a dog's emotional experience is an important element shaping how trainers define and interact with their trainees. Like the everyday dog owners in Chapter 2, all of the interviewees perceived dog emotions as being rather basic in comparison to those experienced by people:

> I don't know if [dogs] experience [emotions] in the way that we do. I think that they, most certainly, are in conflict at times during training . . . , but I don't think that they think . . . [or] that they have the emotions that we have—that we're happy and think we're happy, and we know why we're happy, or depressed and we know why we're depressed, or we think we know why we're depressed. . . . I don't think that they have the depth that we do as far as emotions.

Another trainer talked of dogs' embeddedness in the here-and-now and what humans define as their emotional displays as being a simple reading of the specific situation. Employing obvious behaviorist doubt, he overtly discounted a dog's ability to be reliably empathetic or feel guilt:

[Do you think dogs feel sad or depressed?]

I've heard that a lot, when another dog or a family member has died, or something. I guess I've seen those behaviors and I've never really given them a whole lot of thought. In those cases, you do see a dog and you go, "Yeah, it does look sad." I guess they do show emotions in those areas, but I don't know if that's the same type of sadness you or I feel, because we've put so much more into that, so much more in the past, and so much more of what this event is going to do in the future. [Dogs] are living in the present. I think they more make association that something's not right and something is different and you may see a response that appears that the dog is very sad or unhappy. But I don't know if it's the same type of emotion that we would have. . . . You hear people go on and on about, "Gee, I wasn't feeling well, and my dog knew that." I think they're just very good mirrors of our personalities and what we're feeling. I don't think it's at all like that. I think I've proven it to myself. I've been in miserable moods and been able to make my dog look like it was the greatest day in the world.

[Do you think dogs feel guilt?]

I think that would require that they're able to think about what they've done in the past and be concerned about how it affected you, and I don't think that's possible. I think they primarily are concerned about how [things] affect them and what is going on right now.

In contrast, another trainer saw dogs as experiencing the emotion of guilt, though he did acknowledge that it was often hard to differentiate between when a dog was feeling guilty and when it was simply afraid:

Oh, yes. I feel [dogs] feel emotion—happiness and sadness, guilt. Absolutely.

[Why would a dog feel guilty?]

When a dog has been trained to do something specific and fails—like, for example, dirtying in the house. A dog that's housebroken, I think, will feel bad, will feel guilty, when it's gone and had an accident because it didn't feel well, or it didn't get out of the house in time. I believe they can feel guilt. . . . But, on the other hand, it could be really hard to tell the difference between guilt and fear. We'll never know that.

Of course, feeling fear would mean that the animal was aware of some sort of violation and anticipated that there was a potential future in which there would be resultant consequences.

Dogs as Thoughtful

As we saw in Chapter 2, understanding dogs as involved at some simple level in a mental life that entails devising plans of action based on thoughtful evaluations of immediate situations is commonplace in owners' everyday perceptions of their canine companions. This was the issue about which the guide dog trainers appeared to hold the most ambivalent views. Based on their routine experience with trainees in the field and their everyday interactions with their own companion dogs, the trainers expressed clear notions of dogs as minded beings. On the other hand (and often at the same time), based on the behaviorist orientation central to training ideology, they often offered analyses of apparent canine thinking as actually being conditioned responses to past reinforcements or punishments. One interviewee succinctly presented this latter orientation:

> My dogs do not think. They respond to certain stimuli. They respond to the way they've been taught, whether it's good or whether it's bad. It's up to [the trainer] to just reinforce those things.

At one point in an interview another trainer described the *hypothetical* dog similarly, as a kind of automaton behaving according to the trained-in program:

> I think the dog has no concept or understanding that when I brush this person up against a hedge it's not going to hurt, but if I run them into a pole, they're going to clonk their head and it's going to hurt real bad. The reason the dog avoids running a person into either of those things is because they know through training and through experience, and also through repetition that we have done within the training. After the learning stage, after we [have] taught them when and how to move over and we start to come in with the reinforcements, they start to avoid running you into things and avoid obstacles just because that is the way that they're going to avoid a leash correction.

Later in this same interview, however, when asked directly whether she saw dogs as "having minds," this trainer offered a very different perspective supported by an example of a *specific* dog figuring out the solution to a problem in the field:

> I think [dogs think]. And in the type of work that we do you can see it happening. For example, I was in Williamson this morning and there was a tractor-trailer kind of thing parked on the sidewalk doing something at one of the schools. It's interesting to watch the dog think a problem through because there is this tractor-trailer here, and it had a hose going up onto the roof, and then there was a tree here, and the dog could go in a certain distance before it came to that tree, but couldn't go through because it was an overhead and I would have clonked my head on it. So it gave the dog several choices, to either go this way and stop to indicate the overhead, swing way onto the lawn around the other side of the tree and come out, or turn me 180 degrees around and take me to the curb to go out into the street and walk around. What actually happened was the dog started to go in, came to the tree and stopped. You could see the dog, I mean, he's looking around and he was looking to see where I could go and see what his options were and it was interesting to see what the dog would do. This is an experienced dog that I had, so I pretty much put the responsibility on him, and he chose to spin me right around and take me away from all of those things, and out around and around. . . . So I think they do think things through.

A central element of the image offered to the public is that a well-trained guide dog will, in certain circumstances, exercise "intelligent disobedience."[9] In the typical example, the blind person is standing at a busy street corner and, unaware of the danger of oncoming traffic, orders the dog to cross. Sizing up the situation and recognizing the danger, the loyal guide dog exercises intelligent disobedience, *choosing* to disregard the command in order to protect his or her owner. While recognizing the public relations value of this feature of the "superdog" portrayal, all of the trainers had spent countless hours doing "traffic work" and most tended to question whether intelligent disobedience was the consequence of thoughtful calculation. They typically saw intelligent obedience as either a conditioned response or an indication of the dog's basic instinct for self-preservation. One of the more experienced trainers presented the conditioning explanation when asked about intelligent disobedience:

> One of the things that's reported here and [in] other schools is the example [of] intelligent disobedience. You hear a lot [that] in traffic the dog knows it shouldn't go forward because a person can get hurt. Well, how does the dog know a person can get hurt, when they don't know that they can get hurt

from the car? Cars never hurt them, not in this program, we don't bump the dog with the cars. The dog has no idea that the car can hurt them. But it's been taught through training that they have to respond to that car, when it comes within a given distance, in a certain way. And if it doesn't respond through training, it's reprimanded and corrected. . . . So I don't know if you could call that intelligent disobedience. I think you can call it obedience. The dog understands *through conditioning* that it has to respond to that vehicle in set manner and there are consequences for that manner, good or bad, depending upon what the dog does. I don't call that intelligent disobedience. It's great for p.r., but I don't think it's true.

Another trainer offered the more moderate self-preservation explanation of intelligent disobedience:

When the dog is asked to go forward and it denies the command because there's a car coming, [the public considers this] to be intelligent disobedience where the dog, supposedly, acted in the best interest of the human. These dogs have self-preservation instinct as well and they're not idiots. You watch a dog in the inner city. A dog that has no handler and is wandering around eating out of garbage cans crosses the street ten times better than most guide dogs. They're very good; they learn it on their own. They may have gotten bumped off a couple cars once or twice. [A well-trained guide dog] is a very responsible dog. You know, this is a dog that understands that it is not in its best interest to go forward right now because it's either going to get a leash correction or it's going to get itself run over. This is not at all intelligent disobedience.

Still another trainer went further in presenting a cognitive perspective that emphasized the *intelligence* shown by the dog displaying intelligent disobedience:

[Intelligent disobedience] is one of my favorite terms because it's a lot of what the guide dog is all about. It's problem solving in a respect. The dog is asked to do something, like cross the street at an unsafe time, and the dog has to process the information. . . . So the dog says, "Okay, I'm supposed to go forward because I've been trained to do that," but yet, the dog has to be intelligent enough and say, "No, a car is coming. It's not safe," and disobey. So, it has to think about what it's been told and be able to say, "No, now's not a good time. . . ." This is not really something that you can train for. If the dog doesn't have this certain intelligence, then you can't develop it. You can't develop intelligent disobedience.

Dogs as Manipulative

Human-with-human social exchanges are, most essentially, based on our ability to "take the role of the other" and from this imagined perspective attempt to discern how the other person understands the situation in which we are mutually involved. Since achieving our own goals typically involves prompting the other to behave in some particular way, we routinely construct our own behavior in order to manipulate him or her. Erving Goffman[10] presents these commonplace exchanges as theater pieces in which interactants perform in certain ways so as to define themselves and the immediate situation, thereby prompting others to behave in desired ways.

Even relatively simple and commonplace forms of manipulating one's co-actors—persuading someone to engage in sex or getting a busy sales clerk to assist with a purchase, for example—involve considerable insight and effort. One must define the current situation, determine a reasonable estimate of the other's definition of the situation, and choose a course of action premised on a prediction of how that action will shape the future of the exchange. Given the inherent complexity of manipulating the other, it was interesting to me that, when I asked the trainers about whether they thought dogs "were manipulative," they all answered in the affirmative and could offer specific examples when prompted. The most common examples involved situations in which trainees manipulated (or tried to manipulate) them. One interviewee described a "bright" but lazy dog:

> I think a lot of times [dogs are manipulative]. I have had several dogs do different things in order to avoid doing things. I had one dog that would come out and limp—very, very [obvious], you know—when I went to work the dog. I ended up looking at the feet, and everything else. There's nothing wrong. This dog is limping and I don't know why this dog is limping. I'll put it back in the van. He just didn't want to work that day. But then I get back here and he's running like a banshee, you know. No problem at all. And then, when I got on his case about limping—"Come on, let's go, we're going to go anyway"—his limp went away. It's incredible. . . . So they're pretty bright. They can figure out right quick what works and what doesn't. I think they can take things to their own advantage when they feel that it would benefit them.

In the context of dogs' manipulative abilities, interviewees commonly spoke of the training process itself as an exchange in which mutual manipulation played a central role. Giving the issue a type of behaviorist spin, trainers presented themselves as using punishments (leash corrections, verbal reprimands, etc.) and rewards (verbal encouragements, physical attention, etc.) to manipulate the dog's behavior. In turn, the dog's engaging in "correct" behavior was presented as a means by which the animal manipulated the trainer so as to acquire the desired reward. For example:

> Yes, I think [dogs] are the best at manipulating. I think they are terrific at being able to manipulate their handler and their person to gain their own reward. I don't know what kind of a thought process that is. I know they must be able to have a specific goal in mind, and they must be able to know what they think is necessary to be able to get there to that goal. And you can see it in dogs that have learned certain very basic obedience functions. [It] sits down [when you] get out a piece of food and they'll go through their entire repertoire to get to that piece of food. So, I think that they're not performing tricks for that food. Instead they're trying to manipulate their handlers, saying, "What button do I have to push for that reward to come?" . . . There are times when you watch the dog work with the handler [and you say], "Who's running the show, there? I mean, who's really pushing who, for what reward?" . . . So, I think they're the best at manipulating. I mean, they do it all day long.

Ambivalence and the Guide Dog Trainer

As I noted in Chapter 1, contradiction and ambiguity typify our social construction of animals. Most elementally, our ambivalence about animals derives from seeing them, on the one hand, as objects to be used, or, on the other hand, as individual beings with whom one may have an authentic social relationship. As both members of the society and workers in an occupation directly focused on shaping the behavior of animals to human ends, guide dog trainers hold mixed views of their canine trainees. While each trainer observed and interviewed tended to have an orientation that stressed either a behaviorist or a cognitivist perspective on dog training, all, at one time or another as I watched and spoke with them, evidenced some measure of ambivalence regarding their understanding of dogs. While this apparent conflict in their definitions of the dog-other held the potential for generating feelings of uncertainty, none of the trainers seemed to experience any ongoing problems in this regard. In the daily practical endeavor of training—getting *that* specific dog to learn the specific skills and how to use them effectively in specific situations—more abstracted definitions of the object/being undergoing training faded into the background. It was only when I confronted them directly with the apparent contradiction in field conversations or interviews that the potential problem moved to the perceptual foreground. Typically, in those situations the trainer simply accepted the contradiction ("Yeah, it does sound that way"), appeared somewhat puzzled by the ambiguity ("You know, I never really thought about that before"), or, rather mildly, attempted to recast their views so that apparent contradictions were resolved ("Well, I didn't really mean that. Instead. . . .").

When compared with the considerable discomfort and ambivalent feelings evidenced in those animal-human interaction settings studied by Mary Phillips,[11] Arnold Arluke,[12] and others, the guide dog trainers' relative lack of concern with the conflictual casting of the animal as either/both an object/tool or individual/being is interesting, but understandable. First, they are involved in occupations in which, unlike the laboratory workers studied by Phillips and Arluke, they exercise considerable autonomy. The trainers typically work independently and are simply required to turn out serviceable trainees in a reasonable period of time. Rarely, after having successfully navigated the hiring interview, are they overtly required to support a specific perspective or give testimony to a particular training ideology. Their work lives are structured predominantly by practical production considerations and rarely, if ever, are they required to symbolically demonstrate their legitimacy as trainers by voicing allegiance to the behaviorist perspective that tends to dominate in professional dog training circles.[13]

Further, the trainer's task is quite benign, relative to that of the laboratory technician or animal shelter worker. Teaching a dog to be an effective service animal is considerably different from providing basic care for large numbers of laboratory animals, preparing them for painful experimental manipulations, dispatching them when they are "used up," or euthanizing discarded pets. For the trainers, understanding the dogs as individuals and developing some measure of intimacy with them facilitates the achievement of their occupational goals. For laboratory technicians,[14] as well as slaughter-house workers,[15] animal shelter workers,[16] employees in factory farms,[17] and others whose interactions with animals center around pain and death, intimacy with the animal-as-subject promises considerable psychic trauma. Psychological protection and neutralization of personal guilt[18] require lab technicians, shelter workers, and the like to effectively cast the animal-other as an object. Those who are unable to do this routinely and effectively experience considerable guilt, remorse, and anxiety. Guide dog trainers rarely have to confront these sorts of trauma and, therefore, rarely have to fall back on a behavioristic ideological position that casts the animal as a "thing" to be used, manipulated, slaughtered, or disposed of.

Working in professions places people in situations where they routinely face certain ambiguities.[19] Successful professionals must find ways of navigating these inherent contradictions and coping with the uncertainties they may generate. For members of traditional professions—doctors, lawyers, scientists, and so forth—professional ideology provides an important perspective one may use to ease ambivalent feelings. Those in semi-professions, such as lab technicians or the dog trainers discussed in this chapter, also have an available ideological position—which they can employ in certain rare circumstances and ignore in most others—that aids them in understanding the animals with whom they work and how that work should proceed. Those further down the occupational ladder have no readily available professional ideology to trot out when ambivalence rears its uncomfortable head.

What is most interesting is that neither the laboratory technician, nor the guide dog trainer, nor the animal shelter worker is routinely torn by contradiction. Whether protected by official codes and perspectives or by the indigenous definitions provided by the local culture constructed by fellow workers, all are engaged routinely in the practical round of doing their jobs. In such practical worlds of social action, ongoing ambivalence is, like existential angst, cognitive dissonance, or postmodernist analysis, merely a cognitive luxury item. In the guide dog training program or other settings in which people routinely work with animals, ambivalence is, when one comes down to it, simply impractical.

6

Animal Abilities and Human-Animal Interaction

sometimes tell my students—only half jokingly—that the basic principle of sociology is, "Well, you know, it all depends." The point I am trying to make is that the interactional world which sociologists (presumably) are trying to understand is fluid and shifting. It is shaped primarily by the vagaries and uncertainties that come from the differing perspectives of social actors, the effects of different situations, and the ambivalences built into cultural definitions. As I have stressed throughout this book, one important issue of cultural ambivalence revolves around how nonhuman animals are regarded and, consequently, treated.[1]

In the larger culture, this ambivalence about the status of animals is understood and played out in a variety of ways. For the most part, animals are legally defined as pieces of property that people own, although most believe that as sentient beings animals should be protected from acts of overt cruelty.[2] The inequality of power that typifies human relationships with animals is central to Yi-Fu Tuan's[3] analysis of the ambivalent orientation we have for animals. Interactions with nonhuman creatures (and other elements of nature), he maintains, are characterized by the linked, but conflicting, feelings of dominance and affection. Humans dominate animals through breeding and castration, training, functional use (herding, hunting, and so forth), confining them in zoos, and sub-jecting them to the indignities of circuses and other performance situ-ations. By transforming animals into objects to be controlled, humans symbolically display and act out the dominance of culture over nature.[4] At the same time, however, the impersonality and affective impoverish-ment of modern life prompt people to focus consistently on animals as objects of affection.[5]

Of course, ambivalence is a vastly superior feeling to the massive guilt and remorse that would arise were we not to have the safe category of animal-as-thing and be forced to regard all animals as thinking, feel-ing, self-aware subjects. As Joy Williams put it recently:

> Humans don't want to enter into a pact with animals. They don't want ani-mals to reason. It would be an unnerving experience. It would bring about all manner of awkwardness and guilt. It would make our treatment of them seem, well, unreasonable. The fact that animals are voiceless is a relief to us, it frees us from feeling much empathy or sorrow.[6]

In the preceding chapters we have seen this cultural ambivalence confronted as dog owners see their animals alternatively as person-like companions or as items of property, as veterinarians confront conflicts about how to align their allegiances and deal with the constraints of their service occupation, and as trainers puzzle over whether their train-ees are objects to be manipulated through behaviorist practices or thinking individuals to be instructed about the intricacies of their as-signed tasks. While these definitional uncertainties precipitate prob-lems at certain times, for all of the groups of people presented in the previous chapters, the view that typically wins out is that canine com-panions, guides, patients, and trainees are thoughtful, emotional, and re-sponsive individuals who may rightfully be seen and treated as minded co-interactants.

In the following section of this concluding chapter I step back from the grounded world of people routinely associating with dogs and look somewhat more abstractly at the larger picture. Academic sociologists, philosophers, psychologists, animal behaviorists, and those of similar ilk have tended to discount the interactional abilities of nonhuman ani-mals. Even those animals with whom we choose to share our daily lives, they maintain, do not possess the mental abilities necessary to construct authentic relationships with us or link their perspectives and behaviors with ours so as to engage in authentic social interaction. To see animals otherwise is, in their view, merely an exercise in anthropomorphic delusion. As both a dog owner and a practicing sociologist, I have considerable trouble accepting this doctrinaire perspective. The task, then, is to marshal information that would lead to the reasonable conclusion that many nonhuman creatures do demonstrate—at least in rudimentary fashion—the requisite abilities to engage with us in the mutual exchanges that constitute social interaction. To this end, I will first examine the historical and contemporary groundings of the conventional view that animals are things that behave rather than beings who act. I will contrast this with information drawn from the work of cognitive ethologists and others that demonstrates that this traditional ideological discounting of animal abilities is open to considerable question.

While much of what follows continues to focus on canine capabilities and actions, a number of the examples used to counter conventional perspectives on the limitations of nonhuman animals will be drawn from studies of primates. Primates are "border animals" that define the boundary between "us" and "them." If we can broach this significant boundary, if we can demonstrate that animals of any kind can be reasonably seen as thinking, planning, having a sense of self, possessing a fantasy life, manipulating others for their own ends, and so forth, it is feasible to acknowledge that dogs and other companion animals also possess some measure of these abilities.

The picture that will emerge here is of animals as having identifiable emotional experiences, constructing and using mental representations in order to orient themselves to their surrounding physical and social environment, and communicating these "thoughts" to others. Having laid this foundation, I will explore the implications of this understanding of animal abilities as the grounds for constructing a sociology of human interactions with companion animals. Here I will examine the ability of animals, especially dogs and other nonhuman companions, to participate with people in authentic social interactions. I stress the significance of mutual gaze and mutual play, since it is in these linked activities that human-animal intersubjectivity and cooperative behavior are readily apparent.

Traditional Perspectives

The Cartesian Machine

The conventional view that animals behave rather than act has its roots in the seventeenth century writings of Rene Descartes. Bound by creationist dogma and entranced by the recent development of reliable clock mechanisms, Descartes regarded animals as mindless machines that, though having some measure of dexterity, were not motivated by thoughtful intent. Establishing the rationalist position that has come to be the orthodoxy of the traditional sciences (including, as we will see, the social sciences)—that the more clever the creature, the more valuable it is—Descartes based his argument on the "conversation test":

> For it is a very remarkable fact that there are none so depraved and stupid, without even excepting idiots, that they cannot arrange different words together, forming of them a statement by which they make known their thoughts; while, on the other hand, there is no other animal, however perfect and fortunately circumstanced it may be, which can do the same. It is not the want of organs that brings this to pass, for it is evident that magpies and parrots are able to utter words just like ourselves, and yet they cannot speak as we do, that is, so as to give evidence that they think of what they say.[7]

Lacking the ability to talk, animals could not think. Without thought, they did not experience emotion and were unencumbered by what Descartes saw as the elemental and most unique human possession—the soul.[8]

Descartes's views on these matters were in direct conflict with the perspective presented some four hundred years before by St. Thomas Aquinas who observed, "These powers [of thought and feeling] in man are not so very different from those in animals, only they are heightened."[9] Descartes's views were also rigorously attacked by some of his philosophical contemporaries—most notably Voltaire, who termed Descartes's pronouncements about animals "a pitiful . . . sorry thing to have said."[10]

The position taken by Voltaire, David Hume, and others that the mental facilities of animals were different from those of humans in degree rather than kind was a central idea presented by Charles Darwin in his *Descent of Man* published in 1871 and enlarged in *The Expression of Emotion in Man and Animals* published a year later.[11] The foundation of Darwin's view was of evolutionary continuity binding together living creatures moving along the path of inevitable change and progress. To a major degree, the evidence upon which Darwin based his position was drawn from anecdotal accounts offered by his many correspondents and from observations of his own cats and dogs. These observations and accounts convinced Darwin that animals have subjective experiences; they feel happiness and sorrow, sulk, seek revenge, are jealous and deceitful, sympathize with others, and even display a sense of humor. Granting that humans might have aptitudes that animals did not possess—principally, the ability to form general concepts and an understanding of the self—Darwin maintained that these qualities were "merely the incidental result" of human facility with language.

Behaviorism

While behaviorists drew much of their "understanding" from experimental manipulations of animals, the perspective they developed of both human and nonhuman animals posited that mental activity was not observable and was, therefore, an unnecessary component in accounting for behavior. In their attempt to legitimate psychology as a "hard" science,[12] behaviorists reverted to a Cartesian antimentalism. Behaviorists interested in the activities of nonhuman animals saw no need to conceive of cognition as intervening between stimulus and response. Behavior was either instinctive or the consequence of conditioned response, and attention to mental processes merely deflected attention away from the manipulation of the objective "variables of which behavior [was] a function."[13]

This "mechanomorphic" perspective[14] came to be accepted as the "common-sense of science"[15] and acted as the foundation of a methodological stance that ethnomethodologist D. Lawrence Wieder has called "behavioristic operationalism."[16] This approach is reductionist (behavior is reduced to the smallest possible units), individualist, emphasizes quantification, and, in essence, transforms the object of investigation into an automaton.[17]

Behaviorism as a perspective and behavioristic operationalism as a methodological orientation came to dominate ethological investigations of animals' behavior in natural settings.[18] When ethologists employed terms such as "think" or "feel" they were either condemned by their scientistic colleagues as being "sentimental,"[19] or were careful to tack on disclaimers such as:

> Note that the words "decision" and "choice" are not intended to imply anything about conscious thought, they are a shorthand way of saying that an animal is designed to follow certain rules.[20]

Ethologists involved in observation of animal social interactions in their natural settings often find it difficult to maintain an orthodox behaviorist orientation. Behaviorism is an inadequate grounds for the understandings required in constructing and maintaining day-to-day interactions with others. Wieder describes the practical problems encountered by chimpanzee researchers and others who hew to a behaviorist ideology:

> Living organisms are at once persuasive about the fact of their own conscious lives when met face-to-face, and, at the same time, descriptions of those lives as conscious are subject to ridicule by other scientists. Researchers thus find themselves compelled to describe their chimpanzee or dolphin associates as without consciousness and to contrive experiments that are reportable without referring to animals as subjects, while living along with those same animals as fellow subjects and, paradoxically, counting on this subject-to-subject relationship with them to conduct experiments that are reportable in behavioristic-operationalist terms.[21]

One response to the "grotesque anomalies"[22] posed by conventional behaviorism—I am conscious and no one else is, or my consciousness is an illusion—was the separation of the perspective into "hard" and "soft" versions. Cognitive ethologist Donald Griffin refers to these suborientations as "inclusive behaviorism" and "purposive behaviorism," respectively.[23] Inclusive behaviorist psychologists focused solely on contingencies of reinforcement, while their ethologist colleagues concerned themselves exclusively with the impact of natural selection on animal behavior. Purposive behaviorist ethologists, in contrast, continued to avoid the idea of "consciousness" but did acknowledge that animals, in all likelihood, were aware of the goals toward which their behavior was directed and could learn to adapt their behavior to changing situations.[24]

As a foundation for building an understanding of animal behavior, behaviorism was as limited as the sentimental anthropomorphism it replaced. In the field of psychology, introspective approaches, gestalt orientations, and other elements of the "cognitive revolution" have prompted a decline in adherence to pure behaviorism during the past two decades.[25] Increased ethological and psychological attention to planning, consciousness, will, purpose, and other subjective phenomena have expanded the theoretical contexts within which the activities of both human and nonhuman animals can be understood. In the field of ethology, this reaffirmation of the principle of evolutionary continuity and the acknowledgment of animals' ability to engage in some forms of minded activity heralded the rise of cognitive ethology—a perspective examined in some detail below.

Mead and Sociological Orthodoxy

George Herbert Mead frequently used animal behavior as a counterexample in discussing the supposedly unique character of human thought and social activity. His illustrative presentations of the limitations of squirrels, horses, elephants, foxes, canaries, cats, dogs, and various other nonhuman animals[26] were, in essence, neocartesian. He believed that the ability to *think* was dependent on the ability to *say*.[27] Commonly employing the example of a dog fight, Mead presented animals as engaged in what he called the "conversation of gestures."[28] This rudimentary exchange was thoughtless, meaningless, and non-self-conscious. That is, in the process of growling, attacking, retreating, and maneuvering, dogs were not indicating things to themselves prior to acting and were not exchanging conventionally shared symbols that could be employed apart from the immediate situation in which the encounter took place.[29] This "primitive social act"[30] did not entail self-indication on the part of the combatants; the growl, tooth-baring, and other aggressive gestures did not have the same effect on the gesturing dog as they did on the other.[31] Nonhuman "actors," he maintained, were unable to assume the perspective or role of the other and thereby anticipate the effect of their behavior on the other. While animal behavior was, according to Mead, rudimentarily purposive—directed at achieving certain ends and shaped by a simplistic future orientation[32]—it was "self-less" in the most basic sense. Animals did not possess a self because they did not have a sufficiently developed nervous system and could not employ shared symbols to participate in the interpretive acts of cooperation from which the self was derived.[33] In a basic, and typically convoluted, statement of his anthropocentric position, Mead observed:

> Gestures may be either conscious (significant) or unconscious (nonsignificant). The conversation of gestures is not significant below the human level, because it is not conscious, that is, not self-conscious (though it is conscious in the sense of involving feelings or sensations). An animal as opposed to a human form, in indicating something to, or bringing out a meaning for, another form, is not at the same time indicating or bringing out the same thing or meaning to or for himself; for the animal has no mind, no thought, and hence there is no meaning here in the significant or self-conscious sense. A gesture is not significant when the response of another organism to it does not indicate to the first organism what the second organism is responding to.[34]

Given this view of the essential limitations of nonhuman animals, the typical ways in which the dog owners, trainers, and veterinarians presented in this book see their animals are simply projections of their own experiences. Mead was very explicit on this point:

> We, of course, tend to endow our domestic animals with personality, but as we get insight into their conditions we see there is no place for this sort of importation of the social process into the conduct of the individual. They do not have the mechanism for it—language. So we say that they have no personality; they are not responsible for the social situation in which they find themselves. . . . We put personalities into the animals, but they do not belong to them; and ultimately we realize that those animals have no rights. . . . And yet the common attitude is that of giving them just such personalities as our own. We talk to them and in our talking to them we act as if they had the sort of inner world that we have.[35]

Mead's view of the basic neurological and social limitations of animals came to be a taken-for-granted assumption when sociologists occasionally passed lightly over the topic of animal-human interactions. Since animals were not full-fledged social actors from the Meadian point of view, their encounters with humans were one-way exchanges, lacking the intersubjectivity at the heart of true social interaction. People interacted with animals-as-objects. The dog owner babbling endearments to his or her canine companion is engaged in a form of happy self-delusion; he or she is simply taking the role of the animal and projecting human-like attributes onto it. Interpreting the behavior of the dog as authentic social responsiveness is the same form of anthropomorphic projection in which one engages when he or she talks to a computer,[36] automobile, or other inanimate object.[37]

In turn, conventional sociologists present social science as the exclusive study of humans since only humans, employing language, possess social abilities and culture. Animals are excluded from consideration since, "not being human, [they] can in no way be social or cultural beings as this would be a contradiction in terms."[38] The thoughtless, selfless nonhuman animal is, at best, presented by sociologists and other analysts of (human) behavior as perceiving rather than conceiving, as behaving rather than acting, as apprehending rather than comprehending. The animal exists only in the immediate situation.[39]

In the past few years this neocartesian assumption of the rigid qualitative barrier separating humans from nonhuman animals has increasingly come under attack. This assault has been spearheaded by ethologists, anthropologists, and others involved in ongoing, intimate interactions with animals. The presumption of human uniqueness is difficult to maintain when one is involved daily in watching animals interact with their colleagues in natural settings or when one is doing research directed at teaching selected species to acquire and manipulate conventional symbols that can, in turn, provide them with the ability to gain access to their intrasubjective experience. The behavioristic commonsense of science has increasingly begun to give way to the findings incorporated into a body of work that has come to be referred to as "cognitive ethology." This perspective persuasively presents animal mindedness as a far more convincing explanatory factor than are notions of stimulus and response, instinctive behavior, selfless primitive social acts, or the other models conventionally employed by social and behavioral scientists.

The Nonhuman Animal as Minded Actor

The cognitive revolution against the behaviorist perspective had as significant an impact upon the study of nonhuman animals as it did on views of the human psyche. Cognitive ethologists reaffirmed the

Darwinian assumption of continuity across species and began to devise a picture that overtly appreciated the complexity of the animal as typically engaged in activity shaped by some measure of thought. The dominant figures in twentieth century ethology—especially Niko Tinbergen[40] and Konrad Lorenz[41]—consistently employed an antimentalist perspective. Despite the fact that Lorenz's teacher, Jakob von Uexkull, had devised an orientation rooted in the Kantian tradition and emphasized the subjectivity (*umwelt*) of nonhuman animals, Lorenz, Tinbergen, and others saw the mental life of animals as an unwarranted assumption that had no place in the positivistic, increasingly mathematical enterprise in which they were engaged.[42] Ever suspicious of anthropomorphism, they routinely used quotes to set off "angry," "watchful," "teaching," and other descriptive words that could imply conscious intention on the part of the animals they were observing.[43]

The dominant figure in cognitive ethology, Donald R. Griffin,[44] his students, and those sympathetic to his perspective[45] actively attacked this antimentalist tradition. While acknowledging the relative ease of investigating animal behavior in domestic and laboratory settings, they emphasized that domestic animals were bred and trained to be docile and that the behavior of laboratory animals was markedly less social than when the same animals were going about their business in more normal circumstances. In turn, they stressed the importance of studying animal social behavior within natural settings.

The central proposition of cognitive ethology is that the assumption that nonhuman animals are aware (conscious) and, at least at times, engaged in thought is both reasonable and has explanatory utility. Most notably, intentionality is evident when the animal encounters problematic situations and consequently displays novel and adaptive behavior:

The fact that our own consciousness can be turned on and off with respect to particular activities tells us that in at least one species it is not true that certain behavior patterns are always carried out consciously while others never are. It is reasonable to guess that this is true also for other species. Well-learned behavior patterns may not require that same degree of conscious attention as those the animal is learning how to perform. This in turn means that conscious awareness is more likely when the activity is novel and challenging. . . . Thus it seems likely that a widely applicable, if not all inclusive, criterion of conscious awareness in animals is *versatile adaptability of behavior to changing circumstances and challenges*. . . . Consciously motivated behavior is more plausibly inferred when an animal behaves appropriately in a novel and perhaps surprising situation that requires specific actions not called for under ordinary circumstances.[46]

While maintaining that nonhuman animals have mental experiences and engage in conscious planning in certain circumstances, Griffin and other cognitive ethologists typically assume that the thought-world of animals is qualitatively different from that of humans. True to their Darwinian roots and echoing conventional sociological assumptions, cognitive ethologists stress the centrality of shared language symbols and tend to avoid the assumption that animals are self-aware, engage in metathought (thinking about thinking), or engage in other forms of complex intrasubjective activities.[47]

Animal Emotions

The nature of animals' emotional experience has been a matter of considerable interest to analysts of animal subjectivity since the classic work in this area by Darwin. Darwin was rather conservative in his discussion and did not necessarily consider animal expressions of emotion to be purposive. Darwin regarded the animal's expression as an *index* of its internal experience and did not assume that the creature was aware of or intentionally involved in communicating emotion.[48]

For the most part, contemporary investigators of animal behavior are equally reluctant to concede that nonhuman animals are consciously involved in the presentation of their emotions as an intentional display intended to shape the behavior of others. Some, however, especially those involved in primate language research, marshal data which indicate quite persuasively that, given the expressive tools, some animals do have the ability to reflect upon their emotions and communicate their feelings to others.

Many ethologists have been especially interested in displays of altruism as an indication of feeling-for-another. Cooperation is an essential element of ongoing interactions, and observers of animal social groups regularly present incidents in which animals acknowledge the presence of others, recognize mutual relationships (especially kinship and hierarchical relationships), engage in what appear to be caring and cooperative exchanges, and, in many cases, behave altruistically. Members of many species, for example, give warning cries when they become aware of predators or other sources of danger despite the fact that the cries may act to draw attention to and threaten the welfare of the one giving the warning.[49]

The literature on animal-human interactions is filled with accounts of situations in which dogs, dolphins, and other animals evidenced an awareness of the plight of humans and acted to assist them.[50] As we saw in Chapters 2 and 3, people who share their everyday lives with canine companions consistently express appreciation of their dogs' empathetic abilities and report incidents in which their animals acted in response to the emotions they were experiencing.[51]

The ability of animals to feel and express emotions is seen most strikingly in the research involving the teaching of primates to use modes of symbolic communication—a group of studies that will be discussed later in this chapter. Koko, a gorilla taught to use American Sign Language (ASL) by Francine Patterson,[52] would use the more than three hundred signs in her vocabulary to tell Patterson when she felt happy or sad, express regret that she had bitten her teacher three days before, and joke with and insult her human companions. While engaged in this latter type of interaction, Koko would typically grin broadly to indicate that she was aware she was being funny.

It is difficult to interpret these manifestations of emotion, especially when the expressions come from our closest nonhuman relatives, as not being similar to those offered as indications of subjective experience by our human co-interactants. Jane Goodall, who worked extensively with chimpanzees in the wild, expressed her conclusions about the emotional lives of the animals she studied in typically direct fashion:

> All those who have worked long and closely with chimpanzees have no hesitation in asserting that chimpanzees have emotions similar to those which in ourselves we label pleasure, joy, sorrow, boredom, and so on. . . . Some of the emotional states of the chimpanzee are so obviously similar to ours that even an inexperienced observer can interpret the behavior.[53]

In the everyday world of animal-human interaction, as we have seen, those who enjoy relationships with companion animals have no doubt about whether or not these animals experience and display authentic emotions. This commonsensical perspective could only be denied by those who maintain that "emotion" is merely a convenient category in "folk psychology"[54] or by someone, as J. R. Searle puts it, "in the grip of a philosophical theory."[55] My own information on how owners read, understand, and make use of their dogs' emotions is supported by a variety of recent data. For example, in a survey of over four thousand pet owners 88 percent responded that the love they received from their dogs was the major reward they found in the relationship.[56] In their studies of undergraduate students' views of dogs, Jeffrey Rasmussen and D. W. Rajecki found a strong tendency for their respondents to attribute emotions such as guilt, gratitude, and embarrassment to dogs.[57]

While what we humans think and speak of as emotions are social labels applied to psychological and physiological consequences of specific situations and interpretations, the feeling experiences themselves are more than the labels we apply to them. Feelings go beyond talking. Lacking the ability to label an emotion, as any proud parent of a newborn child will attest, does not negate the presence of the experience itself. On a practical level, it is difficult to deny that dogs "live in a world of emotion" as Leon Whitney puts it in his classic discussion of dog psychology.[58] As practical actors, owners and trainers, as we have seen, consistently use their dogs' expressions of emotion as a window into their experience and use this understanding as a guide to shaping their behavior.[59]

Acknowledging that nonhuman animals both feel and, to a greater or lesser degree, purposefully express these feelings has significant implications for our understanding of their subjective experience. We must consider that, as ethologists, dog owners, and trainers consistently report, dogs and other animals have desires and expectations—beliefs, if you will—and entertain propositions about future events. Otherwise, they would not experience and express satisfaction or disappointment, surprise or boredom. In short, we must consider the likelihood that nonhuman animals retain some form of cognitive map of events and objects, connect these objects and events to each other in some relational/

temporal fashion, and in some way reflect on the content of their experience. This larger matter of animal thought is of central concern to cognitive ethologists and is the issue to which we now turn.

Animal Thought

Except for hardcore behaviorists who doubt the existence of any form of subjective phenomena in either humans or nonhuman animals, most analysts acknowledge that some form of cognitive process goes on within animals.[60] Most basically, cognition entails acquiring information from the environment, relating pieces of information in new ways, and applying these relationships adaptively.[61] Cognition, therefore, requires that the being have some mode of mental representation in order to store information in memory. In turn, cognitive activities would necessitate consciousness, at least to the degree that the being is aware of its sensory experiences and purposefully involved in doing things. Acknowledging that nonhuman animals—principally vertebrates—are *conscious* is not conventionally presumed to be the same as conceding that animals *think*. Being rudimentarily conscious, displaying the ability to learn, and appearing to act in a purposive manner are not necessarily seen to be reliable indicators that animals actually think.

In contrast to this traditional skepticism about animal thought, cognitive ethologists use observations of animal behavior to advance the proposition that nonhuman animals possess *awareness* in the sense that they hold "interrelated mental images of the flow of events."[62] They act intentionally in the sense that they picture events in which they could be involved, choose event images from among the various alternatives, and act so as to make the chosen event happen. To the extent that intentional awareness directs future action, therefore, nonhuman animals can be defined as thinking—at least in some circumstances and within the constraints imposed by their inability to symbolize and consequently to think about the process of thinking.[63]

The ethologist Shirley Strum offers an interesting example of animal thinking drawn from her observations of baboon social activities. Peggy, a high status female in the troop with which Strum worked, wanted some of the Thompson's gazelle carcass in the possession of a male named Dr. Bob. Peggy cleverly acquired the meat by grooming Dr. Bob until he fell into a stupor and then stealing it from his lap. In a similar situation a few days later, Dr. Bob refused to fall for this ploy, accepting Peggy's grooming but keeping his hand on the carcass. Peggy then exploited the friendship structure of the troop in devising an effective strategy to achieve her goal:

> Peggy would get away with stealing once but no more. Thwarted but not defeated, she looked around until she found Dr. Bob's closest female friend: Peggy herself was a friend but not as high on Dr. Bob's list as this female. Deserting Dr. Bob, Peggy rushed to the female and in a very un-Peggy-like manner attacked her without provocation. Dr. Bob was in a quandary. He should go to support his friend, at least to reassure her after such an attack, but it was too far to drag the carcass. He looked back and forth between the female and the meat, obviously trying to make up his mind. Finally, deserting the meat, he started toward his friend—passing Peggy, going in the other direction on her way to the carcass![64]

Based on rich examples such as this, ethologist and others who regularly observe and intimately interact with animals propose that animals think and purposively construct goal-directed action. The issue, once again, hinges on *degree* rather than qualitative difference. Humans are not unique in possessing consciousness and having the ability to construct and carry out coherent plans of action—that is, to think. This is not to deny that humans are unique—with the possible exception of the language trained primates discussed below—in their ability to use socially constructed symbols to separate intention from action and reflect on the process of consciousness. But acknowledging the general inability of nonhuman animals to do this is not the same as saying that they are unconscious, unaware, or unthinking. Not thinking *like* humans is *not* not thinking.[65]

Granting that nonhuman animals engage in the modes of thinking briefly described above—that they can imagine possible events in the context of the present situation and devise and execute certain plans of action so as to achieve anticipated ends—continues to leave a considerable gap between animal and human thought. One of the factors traditionally presented as characterizing this presumed gap is that nonhuman animals are incapable of forming concepts, that is, they do not divide experienced reality into discernable categories and employ those categories as elements of thought.[66] In fact, considerable evidence exists indicating that nonhuman animals are capable of classifi-catory thinking and use conceptual categories as frames of reference.

Researchers working with a variety of animals have, for example, ef-fectively taught their "subjects" the basic concept of *difference*. Irene Pepperberg[67] has taught an African grey parrot named Alex to "use the sounds of English speech," as she cautiously puts it, to categorize ob-jects and respond to questions regarding the concepts of "same" and "different." Alex can use words to request objects he desires and of-fers a loud "NO!" when he is given something different from what he requested. When shown pairs of both familiar and unfamiliar objects, Alex is able to differentiate between those that are similar or different relative to the attributes of color, shape, and form. He makes the correct determination in over 80 percent of trials.

Karen Pryor,[68] a dolphin researcher, trained a captive rough-toothed dolphin named Hou to perform complicated action sequences to ob-tain food. Later, Pryor withheld rewards until Hou performed a trick that was *different from* any previously displayed. Though he initially ap-peared rather confused, within a few weeks the dolphin had success-fully grasped the concept of novelty and was inventing new maneu-vers.[69] (We will return to these issues of conceptualization later in this chapter when the matter of the animal's ability to differentiate between self and other is discussed and when the primate language research is presented in more detail.)

Being able to *pretend* is another form of thought activity convention-ally viewed as a capability unique to humans. However, primates raised in close association with people do seem able to behave in this sophis-ticated "as-if" manner. For example, having received a plastic tea set as a present, Koko presented Patterson with the empty tea pot and, employing a signing style she had devised when she wanted people to pretend, asked the trainer if she wanted a "sip" of imaginary tea.[70]

An even more striking example of this form of complex thinking is seen in the classic case of the imaginary pull-toy invented by the home-raised chimp Viki Hayes. Viki's "mother," Cathy Hayes,[71] describes the young chimpanzee playing in the bathroom and trailing one arm behind her as if pulling a toy. One day the imaginary string on the toy became entangled on the bathroom plumbing and Viki spent some time pantomiming the process of trying to untangle it. One day when Cathy was in the bathroom with Viki, the toy became "stuck"—the chimp sat with her arms extended as if pulling a rope—and Viki plaintively called for assistance. After Hayes made the motions of dislodging the toy, Viki ran off, once again pulling her imaginary plaything.[72]

In the specific realm of peoples' relationships with dogs, owners, trainers, and veterinarians rarely express doubt about whether the canines with whom they routinely interact have (wordless) concepts, think situations through, solve problems, or, in other ways, possess and demonstrate minded behavior.[73] Rhoda Lerman offers a revealing example of her Newfoundland Toby's thought process and problem-solving behavior:

> We halfheartedly train the dogs to sit on the floor in a long stay while we eat our meal. I think sharing food is very important; so do they. It becomes, how-ever, too disturbing, and we've limited them to table food at the end of the meal. But Toby has problems with waiting when there's butter on the table. Toby lies down, hops up, drops his head on the table, positions it next to the butter—it is always the butter—sighs over the butter. . . . He must think we are awfully stupid not to understand what he wants. . . . Once, though, the temptation being overwhelming, Toby thought through the problem of how to get the bread and butter. He did not lie down on command but left the room. We hear him rummaging around in the house, up and down the stairs, until he finally appeared with a treasure: a roasted pig ear. . . . Toby is allowed to take one out of the box each day. He had obviously hidden this one. He laid it at my feet. Naturally Toby received a piece of bread with slabs of but-ter. Toby reasoned and came up with the idea of trade.[74]

Animal Communication

"Dumb" animals are not stupid; they are without language.[75] Despite this inability, which many writers see as the most significant factor separating humans from nonhuman animals, all animals actively communicate. The most basic definition of communication—and one that avoids confronting the issue of animal consciousness—presents it as a causal process in which the emitter and the receiver are linked and their subsequent behaviors are predictable.[76] Animal communication is a major issue upon which ethologists focus.[77] For cognitive ethologists, animal communication is of special interest since it is an activity that provides, in Donald Griffin's apt phrase, a "window on animal minds."[78]

Analysts, especially those with a social scientific orientation, present animal communication as simply the emission of signs—as behavior that is the involuntary byproduct of internal (though unnamed) experience. As George Herbert Mead put it:

> It is quite impossible to assume that animals do undertake to express their emotions. They certainly do not undertake to express them for the benefit of other animals. The most that can be said is that the "expressions" did set free a certain emotion in the individual, an escape valve, so to speak, an emotional attitude which the animal needed in some sense, to get rid of.[79]

This anthropocentric perspective is not supported by numerous ethological studies. The evidence drawn from research with social animals demonstrates that communicative acts *are* directed at others, signals are constructed and emitted relative to particular referents,[80] vocalizations are produced and altered in light of the social and physical situation,[81] and the communication precipitates predictable responses by the recipients.[82]

Central to this issue of animal communication is the conventional distinction between symbol and sign. The philosopher Susanne Langer[83] stresses that symbols refer to ideas whereas signs compel action. A related distinction emphasizes that signs refer only to elements in the immediate situation in which they are emitted. Symbols, on the other hand, are socially constructed and shared and are, therefore, abstractions free from the constraints imposed by the here-and-now.[84] In drawing the distinction between signs and symbols Mead emphasized that the latter "tend" to elicit in the mind of the actor the same response as is generated in the recipient/other.[85] In this light, the communicative behavior of nonhuman animals represents "mere" signaling while human beings engage in the complex social activity of symbol use.

This conventional position is premised on an overly restrictive definition of language—that it is a mode of expression exclusively used by humans.[86] The view that humans are unique in possessing the genetic propensity for language is called into serious question by the primate language research conducted now for more than half a century. These studies are of particular importance since primates are "border animals" and the evidence of their linguistic potential seriously threatens the presumed qualitative sociobiological distinction between humans and nonhuman animals.[87]

Building on the initial efforts of Winthrop Kellogg[88] in the 1920s, the Hayeses[89] attempted to raise a chimpanzee named Viki in their home. While Viki displayed remarkable abilities, she was unable to speak more than a handful of words such as "Mama," "Papa," and "cup." Assuming that nonhuman primates do not possess the vocal apparatus necessary for speech, subsequent researchers taught various gorillas, chimpanzees, and orangutans other means of manipulating symbols. Some primates were taught to arrange lexigrams manually—for example, by placing variously shaped magnetized tiles on a metal board[90] or by pressing keys on a computerized keyboard.[91] An alternative approach involved teaching primates the gestural symbol system of American Sign Language.[92]

Though they have been the focus of considerable controversy, language trained primates have demonstrated remarkable abilities. Washoe, the ASL-trained chimpanzee who first worked with the Gardners and then with their colleague Roger Fouts,[93] acquired a vocabulary of 140 sign gestures and was observed to use close to 300 two-sign combinations. By age seven Koko, the gorilla taught by Penny Patterson,[94] had used 645 different signs and had a working vocabulary of about 375 signs. Kanzi, a pygmy chimpanzee who was taught to manipulate arbitrary symbols on the computer console at the Yerkes Primate Research Center in Georgia, had a working vocabulary of 90 lexigrams and understood 200 spoken words.[95]

In addition to acquiring useable vocabularies, the language trained primates displayed the ability to innovate and to arrange symbols syntactically. For example, Lucy, another chimpanzee working with Roger Fouts, knew the difference between "me tickle you" and "you tickle me." Fouts observes, "She does seem to follow rules. She uses the word 'you' before verbs or the pronoun 'me' in a way which at least looks like syntax."[96] David Premack is somewhat less cautious in describing the abilities of his lexigram trained chimp Sarah to use syntax. Sarah could manage plurals and respond to the interrogative, and she appeared to understand "if . . . then" constructions.[97]

One of the major ways in which language trained apes display innovation is by spontaneously combining symbols in order to describe objects for which they have no pre-existing label. Fouts's chimpanzee Lucy, for example, creatively dubbed radishes "cry hurt fruit" and referred to watermelons as "drink fruit."[98] Similarly, Patterson's Koko referred to a mask as an "eye hat" and called a Pinocchio doll an "elephant baby."[99] Koko also devised insults. She constructed epithets such as "dirty toilet" and used the signs for "nut" and "bird" in insulting ways.[100]

These innovations and other evidence from the activities of language trained primates indicate that they are able to engage effectively in the rather complex activities of joking and lying. Here, for example, is an exchange recorded between Koko and one of Patterson's assistants:

> The dispute began when Koko was shown a poster of herself that had been used during a fund-raising benefit. Manipulating hands and fingers, Cathy had asked Koko, "What's this?"
>
> "Gorilla," signed Koko.
>
> "Who gorilla?" asked Cathy.
>
> "Bird," responded a bratty Koko, and things went downhill from there.
>
> "You bird?" asked Cathy.
>
> "You," countered Koko.
>
> "Not me, you are bird," rejoined Cathy, mindful that "bird" can be an insult in Koko's lexicon.
>
> "Me gorilla," asserted Koko.
>
> "Who bird?" asked Cathy.
>
> "You nut," replied Koko, resorting to another of her insults. (For Koko, "bird" and "nut" switch from descriptive to pejorative terms by changing the position in which the sign is made.)
>
> "Why me nut?" asked Cathy.
>
> "Nut, nut," signed Koko.
>
> "You nut, not me," Cathy replied.

Finally Koko gave up. Plaintively she signed, "Damn me good," and walked away signing, "Bad."[101]

Patterson sees humorous exchanges such as this as being of particular importance since they require that the primate have sufficient knowledge of the rules to purposefully violate them. "It presumes an understanding of certain norms, which are then distorted in recognizable but preposterous ways."[102]

Rule violation is also seen in those situations in which ASL-trained primates lie. Fouts, Patterson, Rumbaugh, and other researchers have reported incidents of purposive deception on the part of the animals with whom they worked.[103] For example, when Koko was reprimanded after she broke a kitchen sink while jumping on it, she blamed one of Patterson's assistants, pointing to her and signing, "Kate there bad."[104]

An actor's ability to deal with abstract concepts is of special significance. Temporal displacement—the ability to dislodge one's self from the confines of the here-and-now—has routinely been seen as requiring symbolic abilities[105] and, therefore, to be a uniquely human attribute.[106] Language trained apes display clear understandings of past and future: they retain memories of past events; correctly employ time-words such as "now," "then," and "later"; and understand temporal sequencing as encoded in the words "before" and "after."[107]

The primates also use their acquired symbol systems to converse with each other. The Rumbaughs' keyboard-trained chimps would punch out messages to each other requesting that food be passed through an opening.[108] Following the introduction of a young male gorilla named Michael, Koko took it upon herself to coach him in signing. Understandably, she first taught him the most important words—her own name and the sign for "tickle." Patterson describes another interesting exchange between the two companions:

Early this year Mike was fumbling for the right sign to convince Ann to let him in to play with Koko. After Mike signed, "Out," Koko, waiting in her own room, began to get impatient. She signed to Mike through the wire mesh, "Do visit Mike hurry, Mike think hurry," imploring him to come up with the right sign. Then she said, "Koko good hug," and it finally dawned on Mike to say, "Koko." A relieved Koko signed, "Good know Mike," and then, "In Mike."[109]

Similarly, Fouts reports that Washoe taught a variety of signs to her adopted son Loulis and other chimpanzees in the colony in which she was eventually placed.[110]

Even more important are observations of language trained primates using signs to talk to themselves when they are alone. Washoe, for example, was observed signing "quiet" to herself as she went into an area she had been forbidden to enter.[111] Patterson once saw Koko sitting by herself and looking at a magazine. She touched a picture and signed "There flower."[112] This form of solitary self-talk was commonly seen with the language trained apes[113] and demonstrates that these primates possessed some degree of self-awareness. In a remarkable display of this key ability to conceptualize a self, Koko was once asked by a reporter if she was "an animal or a person." Koko quickly replied, "Fine animal gorilla."[114] (We will return to this issue of animal self-definition in a later section of this chapter.)

Critics attempt to discredit the ape language studies by characterizing them as elaborate examples of the "Clever Hans Effect."[115] The term refers to a famous German horse in the early 1900s who was apparently able to solve mathematical problems, stamping out the correct answers with his hoof. Skeptical critics eventually discovered that Hans could not work the problems when his owner, retired schoolteacher Wilhelm Von Osten, was not present. The horse read what were to human observers imperceptible cues (such as involuntary tensing of muscles and tiny head movements) given off by Von Osten.[116]

While some of the work with primates who are raised in close proximity to humans may be somewhat affected by the intense desires of some researchers to clearly demonstrate the humanlike propensities of their nonhuman colleagues, most researchers are trained in experimental techniques and take great pains to avoid bias effects. Certainly the computer communication studies and the more carefully controlled ASL research are least subject to criticism based on the effects of cuing. Hidden observations and videotapes of solitary animals conversing with themselves or primate companions provide data that is difficult to tar with the brush of "Clever Hansing."[117] Even if many of the apparently thoughtful and symbolically mediated activities of these primates *were* in response to the animals reading subtle cues from their human co-actors, why should this be seen as discrediting? The close attention and response to interactional cues such as tone of voice, physical movement, posture, and direction of gaze are key features of human communication. If the nonhuman animals involved in these studies are "only" responding to the subtle cues of humans, this would mean that they must be exceptionally aware, carefully calculating, and, in all, wonderfully skilled observers.[118]

Even when one moves away from our primate relatives to examine the communicative talents of other animals, the evidence that animals possess considerable expressive skill continues to be quite persuasive. For example, Alex, the African grey parrot trained by Irene Pepperberg, acquired a vocabulary of more than one hundred words referring to objects in his environment. Alex even learned to make verbal requests for things he desired ("I want banana") or certain types of assistance or interaction he wanted ("Wanna go gym," "You tickle me"). When his human associates offered something he did not want, he would loudly say, "NO" and repeat his request.[119] In one instance Alex demonstrated an especially poignant example of his communicative ability. When Pepperberg was leaving him at a veterinary clinic in which he was scheduled to undergo surgery, Alex cried, "Come here. I love you. I'm sorry, I want go back."[120]

Although they lack the physical abilities to produce human language, dogs are skilled intentional communicators. They employ a variety of vocal signals (growls, barks, howls, sighs, and so forth) to express their experiences, desires, or emotions. In addition, dogs are adept users of body language, effectively communicating what Erving Goffman calls "embodied messages"[121] through body postures, and movement of their eyes, ears, tails, and mouths.[122] Further, the dog's ability to comprehend and respond to human vocal signals is quite good. The psychologist Stanley Coren lists more than sixty words that his dogs understand and cites researchers who estimate that dogs have the ability to discriminate among over a hundred words.[123]

Animal Constructions of Meaning and Plans of Action

As we have seen, the sociological emphasis on language as the basis for conscious thought, self construction, and role-taking effectively excludes nonhuman animals (with the occasional exception of language trained primates) from serious consideration as parties in authentic social interaction with humans. The counter perspective to this conventional view is presented by Griffin:

> The most essential aspect of consciousness . . . is the ability to think about objects and events, whether or not they are part of the immediate situation. It seems likely that animals understand, at least to a limited degree under some circumstances, how their mental experiences relate to objects and events in the world around them. The animal's understanding may be accurate or misleading, and the relationships may be simple or complex. The content of conscious thinking may consist of immediate sensations, events remembered from the past, or anticipations of the future. . . . Complex animals obtain most of [their] information through their sense organs, including those that signal conditions within their bodies, but some important information may be based on past sensory input, and some may arise through recombination into new patterns of information already present in the central nervous system. . . . Animal thoughts and subjective feelings are almost certainly simpler than ours, and the content must be relevant to the animal's own situation rather than to human concerns.[124]

Not only does the single-minded sociological focus on symbolization discount the considerable abilities of nonhuman animals as conscious, intentional actors, it also leads to a misrepresentation of much human behavior. Accounts of artists and others engaged in creative activities bear witness to how the complex process of creativity does not always proceed through conscious, self-conversing.[125] Further, a considerable amount of everyday, practical human activity is not the consequence of the carrying out of rationally constructed plans of action. If possession of a socially shared conventional symbol system were the necessary antecedent to memory and other complex mental activities, human infants would be unable to learn language.[126]

Based on extensive observation of his dog's behavior and on examination of their human-animal interactions, the psychologist Kenneth Shapiro[127] offers propositions about the means through which his canine companion draws meaning from his world and constructs his everyday activity. Shapiro proposes that dogs—and, in all likelihood, other complex nonhuman animals—premise their construction of the world on information drawn from bodily experience. This experience is implicitly meaningful and acts as the basis for what Shapiro refers to as "endomesothought"—a mode of thought that does not consist of mentally constructing fact-objects but, instead, bases understanding on immediate practical concerns and physically acquired impressions. The "thought-world" of the dog, therefore, is oriented toward *place* rather than reproducing the temporal orientation of humans. The dog's knowledge is focused on "knowing how" rather than "knowing about":

> I would speculate that spatiality may ground the being of Sabaka [Shapiro's dog] in the way that it is often claimed that temporality grounds human beings. . . . This is not to say that there are not temporal structures operative in his experience, but I would suggest that place primarily grounds being for him. He belongs in the place and relates to others from and through that place. . . . His is a spacial identity. In contrast to a reflective self that is constituted and developed as a unity through and over time, his is a self constituted through association with a space. Sabaka's habitat is his self. The space he has and holds is his appropriated self.[128]

Based on observations of her own dogs, Rhoda Lerman came to see her Newfoundlands as orienting their present behavior through using mental maps constructed from prior experience. Significant incidents in the past were remembered and thus shaped their activities during walks:

> Since we take the same trail a few times a week, the dogs know it intimately and are aware of any change. The smallest limb fallen on the path is a momentous event and requires circling, sniffing, investigating in the extreme. For months I walked behind them, watching them explore, sniff the same place each time, examine the same log, the same bush for last spring's strawberries, the burrow hole from which a chipmunk had dashed four months before, the rock where Toby and Pippa discovered a box turtle. I realized that they make maps in their heads—scent maps, event maps, thing maps, texture maps, sequential maps—that much of their activity on the trails is mapmaking and map following.[129]

Clearly, dogs' heads are not empty. They understand place and situations, recall past events, and use these mental representations to make decisions about how to act in the present. These constructions of meaning and the plans of action based on these constructions are practical and highly situated. Though focused primarily on the local and immediate circumstance (as is typical of much human behavior), dogs and other social nonhuman animals may reasonably be seen as being aware that acts are linked together—that practically devised intentions

The "perfect" stick selected as a play object.
Photographer: Clinton Sanders

can be realized through the playing out of certain constructed actions.[130] Animals unable to engage in this linking together of acts would not survive very long.

The evidence is also persuasive that social animals share situated meanings and thoughtfully coordinate their plans of action.[131] Basic problems of survival make it essential that animals "in the wild" be able to share meaning effectively with others of their kind and thereby engage in coordinated behavior. Shapiro's observations of Sabaka and the numerous examples offered in this book provide persuasive evidence that dogs and other companion animals construct and share definitions of situations and objects.[132]

Because of human devotion to language, people typically use words to communicate their own understandings and expectations to their animal companions. As seen earlier in this chapter, dogs are quite adept at recognizing and responding appropriately to these verbalizations. In turn, dog owners routinely use their knowledge of their animals to ascertain their perceptions and intentions. Animals and humans ground and coordinate their interactions on these shared understandings. While it is typically simple, immediate, and practically oriented, the collective action mutually constructed by dogs and their human associates is not appreciably different from that which flows from human to human in their social exchanges.

Animal Definitions of Self and Other

From the symbolic interactionist sociological perspective, founded in large part on the ideas of George Herbert Mead, the "self" is the focal point of social exchanges and the essential element of consciousness. Since it is an object constructed in the course of interaction, having a self requires that one be able to "take the role of the other" and from that imaginative perspective look back upon one's self. As conventionally conceived, this process of self-construction requires that the social actor possess some degree of facility with a shared symbol system since this is the vehicle that makes role-taking possible.[133] From this perspective it is, therefore, impossible for nonhuman animals (with the possible exception of language trained apes) to have a social self.[134]

Ethological studies indicate that nonhuman animals in natural settings do demonstrate some degree of self-recognition. The most obvious indication is seen when animals hide from predators. This behavior shows an awareness that the "embodied self" is in danger and that concealment is in order. Ethologists who have studied grizzly bears, for example, describe incidents of bears hiding from humans in order to observe them.[135] Bears have also been reported to purposefully avoid leaving tracks in order to elude hunters.[136]

Hiding is one indication that an animal is aware of itself as an object in the world separate from the physical environment and from others.[137] Be it linguistically mediated—as with humans—or not—as with nonhuman animals, this separate self is integrally related to social experience. Recognition of self is intimately tied to the recognition of others and the related understanding that one is in turn recognized by others:

> To have such a concept [of self] one must recognize other beings in the
> world, distinguish what is self and what is not-self, and lay claim to pasts and

futures of the single being one is. To have a concept of the self is, in part at least, to do these things: to show awareness of the world as being more than one's immediate perception of it, to recognize other beings as being the same as some past acquaintances, to admit responsibility for past action and to intend some future.[138]

Systematic observations in natural settings persuasively indicate that nonhuman animals are recognized as individuals by their colleagues and are adept at identifying each other. One of the most common indications of other- and self-recognition is seen in dominance relationships within animal social groups. An individual's status in the social organization of the pack or tribe commonly is based on his or her relationships. Especially in primate groups, one's social position depends on who one's parents are and with whom one had built friendship bonds.[139] In short, nonhuman animals—like the human beings in which sociologists have traditionally been interested—situate themselves in networks of relationships.

In the relationships between people and companion animals, recognition of self and other and mutual adjustment of goals and behavior are of central importance. The literature on dog training, for example, consistently presents the process as involving teaching the canine other to *mind* or to knowingly exercise *self*-control. Professional trainers routinely couch the training process in moral terms. Training involves a "moral" transformation in that "good" canine companions respect the human other and value the relationship.[140] Violations of these expectations, in turn, often precipitate the submissive and avoiding behavior well-known by most dog owners who have returned home to find that their dogs have destroyed the carpet or "had an accident" on the living room floor. The dog's apparent display of shame may reasonably be interpreted as demonstrating a recognition of imposed rules and that violations reflect on the violator's self.[141] As seen in earlier chapters, dog owners and trainers interpret these displays of guilt as arising from the animal's "conscience."

Those who live and work with canine companions regard them as individuals who display the unique habits, traits, and perspectives that compose personality.[142] They define and interact with them as individuals who recognize themselves in relationship to others and to the expectations that others impose upon them. The relationship between dogs and their people, then, is optimally one of mutual orientation, or, as D. Lawrence Wieder[143] puts it, "being for one another." Like effective and mutually satisfying relationships between people, interactions between dogs and their human associates are conceived—certainly by the human party and, I submit, by the nonhuman co-actor as well—as existing between selves and others. Owner-animal interactions are mutually oriented and collectively defined.

The charge that the work of cognitive ethologists and primate language researchers, and others with extensive first-hand familiarity with animal behavior, is "simply" an example of the use of science to legitimate anthropomorphic ideology is consistently offered in an attempt to discredit the investigations briefly described above. But numerous sociological studies have demonstrated the essential importance of drawing information from ongoing, intimate, and disciplined interactions with others. As seen in this and earlier chapters, the most knowledgeable human analysts—ethologists, animal trainers, veterinarians, and others routinely involved with nonhuman animals in everyday settings—consistently see animals as conscious of themselves and their situations and "intelligent manipulators of their social world."[144] Fear of anthropomorphism is, as Pierre van den Berghe points out, an unnecessary limitation. As he succinctly puts it, "If the fear of anthropomorphism were to stifle any attempt at cross-specific comparisons of behavior, then the fear of ethnocentrism should have killed off anthropology long ago."[145] Observations of animals in laboratories, in the wild, and in our own homes acting "as if" they were thoughtful, aware, actively involved in weighing ends and means, responding to memories of past events, behaving innovatively, deceiving and otherwise manipulating co-interactants, and displaying other manifestations of consciousness (to say nothing of effectively employing learned complex symbol systems) are compelling. It would seem most sensible to interpret these activities in the same way we interpret them during our interactions with fellow humans. This approach to understanding—and appreciating—animals does not necessarily mean that they should be seen as "people in disguise."[146] It seems reasonable and functional for analysts intent upon understanding the activities of nonhuman animals—

and their social interactions with people—to adopt the stance Gordon Burghart[147] calls "critical anthropomorphism." By interpreting carefully collected observations with the aid of sympathetic insights and thoughtful intuitions shaped by information drawn from previous studies, we can begin the process of constructing a sociological understanding of interactions between people and animals. In the remainder of this chapter, I will focus primarily on human exchanges with dogs in an attempt to take a few steps further along this path.

Social Interaction between People and Companion Animals

At its most elemental, social interaction involves conscious beings who are co-present. For successful interaction to take place, these actors must possess certain basic abilities and share fundamental understandings. The foundation for this exchange is the mutual definition of the immediate situation in which the interaction is taking place. Central to this situational definition is a mutual understanding of who the actors are in the specific context and the purpose of the exchange—each actor is aware of his or her definition of the situation and goals and, in turn, estimates the understandings and goals of the other. Of key importance then is the ability of each actor to take the role of the other, to imaginatively see things from the other's point of view.

Some mode of communication is necessary to establish and sustain interaction. Most immediately, co-actors interpret each other's "bodily movements"[148] in order to ascertain goals, understandings, feelings, and intentions. Some of these bodily expressions are, as Erving Goffman[149] emphasized, consciously constructed and "given" while other elements of bodily expression are "given off" without the actor's overtly conscious intent.

Speech is the central communicative vehicle in human-to-human interaction. The ability to use and understand language allows human actors to more or less efficiently share information about their situational definitions, goals, emotions, and intentions. Since language, as well as physical gestures, allows the communication of both truths and lies, and human interactants are, at least at some level, aware that others are rarely entirely honest in their situated presentations of their selves and motivations, social interaction always has a rather tentative character. Nonetheless, the intersubjectivity of social exchanges is based on the practical working assumption that one can ascertain, or at least estimate with some degree of certainty, the feelings, thoughts, and intentions of the other. Each actor presumes that the internal representations of the other have some general similarity to his or her own feelings, goals, and so forth.

This intersubjective dance of social interaction, in short, involves each actor interpreting the situation, developing plans of action, and constructing behavior intended to achieve defined goals while, at the same time, attempting to gain an understanding of the plans, goals, and definitions of the other. On this intersubjective foundation co-actors construct what they determine to be reasonable and situationally appropriate courses of action. Interaction is a thoughtful, emotionally laden and communicative collective endeavor.

As I have stressed throughout this book, the conventional sociological focus on language as the communicative vehicle by which the essential meanings at the heart of interaction are shared has virtually excluded the social exchanges that take place between people and nonhuman, nonlinguistic animals from serious consideration and analysis. This conventional exclusion from serious consideration persists despite the fact that the majority of people share their homes with animals, feel intensely positive emotions for them, and routinely express their most intimate thoughts and feelings to them. As definedly wordless, thoughtless, emotionless, selfless, and planless *organisms*, dogs and other companion animals are discounted as viable members of society and authentic interactants. However, as amply demonstrated in this book, those who regularly interact with companion canines typically assume a practical "as if" stance with regard to the thoughts, feelings, and interactional abilities of their nonhuman intimates. Further, as seen in the preceding sections of this chapter, there is considerable empirical ground upon which to base a persuasive argument that, despite conventional sociological skepticism, dogs and other nonhuman animals do, in

fact, possess the faculties and abilities deemed necessary for viable social interaction and the construction of authentic and rewarding intimate relationships.

Like other primary relationships, those between people and their
animal intimates are laden with shared emotion and experienced by the
parties involved—certainly from the human's perspective and, it is reasonable to assume, on the part of the animal companion as well—as
having intrinsic value. The animal-human bond is founded on effective intersubjectivity. Rather than this connectedness being based on
verbal exchanges, it is an attachment in which "actions speak louder
than words." [150]

In his discussion of his relationship with his dog Sabaka, Ken Shapiro
stresses the kinesthetic basis of the mutual empathetic exchanges between people and their dogs. As he describes it:

> Sabaka will seek affection or solicit care as a complex function of a number of
> conditions, such as the amount of time we have been apart or . . . his sense of
> my feelings toward him. . . . When I have reprimanded Sabaka, or I am upset,
> or when the rest of the family is away, Sabaka is clearly riveted on me. I di-
> rectly sense his searching for my bodily attitude to him. He is, as it were,
> studying my kinesthetics—my posture, bearing, incipient movements, and
> the like. . . . Sabaka does not predicate or register or refer or depict or repre-
> sent. He is, rather, always concernfully absorbed. The question that we are
> raising here is whether that concernful absorption can contain a sense of a
> relationship. My empathetic sense of Sabaka suggests that it might—that Sa-
> baka carries with him a sense of how it is between us and that this is an im-
> portant feature of his world. [151]

Within animal-human interactions typifications are based on the
experience of each with the other. As Shapiro emphasizes, these exchanges are founded on shared physical grammars through which interactants communicate their intentions and thereby "reciprocally
motivate" [152] one another. The potential for this effective mode of communication is enhanced by the fact that mammals share a general tendency to employ similar physical gestures to express their subjective
experience. Like humans and other primates, for example, dogs hunch
their bodies, smile, wrinkle their foreheads, scowl, and use other physical modes of expression. In turn, they read information from the similar
bodily attitudes of their human associates: [153]

Paying close attention to the owner's facial expression.
Photographer: Caroline Abst

The dog's emotional expressions of anxiety, happiness, peace of mind, anger, affection, jealousy, embarrassment, and hostility are not too different from our own ways of communicating our feelings by face and body. The ability of the dog to read our feelings seems like mental telepathy until we observe what we are saying with body and face.[154]

As in human-with-human interactions,[155] gaze is a key element in the situated exchanges between people and their nonhuman co-interactants. Like human infants,[156] dogs and the other animals with whom people routinely interact display considerable interest in human facial expression and direct their own gaze in the directions indicated by human attention. Mutual directing of gaze is a display of mutual attentiveness as well as a means by which dogs and other companion animals indicate their understanding of relative status.[157] Looking where the other looks shows recognition of what the other is attending to and experiencing.[158]

Where dogs look and how they attend to where we are looking provide evidence that dogs have the intersubjective abilities that lie at the core of social interaction. Early in my systematic observations of my dogs I noticed the central importance of their gaze:

When Emma and Isis look at me they usually pay attention to my eyes. I have noticed on walks how important looking is to them. A common way that one will communicate to the other that she wants to play is by staring. During play they have a variety of ways of signaling "time out." In addition to stopping and avidly sniffing someplace, a player can effectively suspend the game by staring fixedly off into the middle distance. The other dog typically responds to this move by looking to see if there is actually anything important to look at. They do the same with me. If on the walk I stop and look in a particular direction, they will stop, glance at me, and gaze off in the direction I am looking. This seems a fairly clear indication of their elemental ability to put themselves into my perspective. In a literal sense they attempt to assume my "point of view." If I look at something they conclude that it is probably something important.[159]

Play is another form of interaction that has central social significance. It requires that the players engage in the most elemental form of intersubjectivity—taking the role of the other.[160] In order for mutual play to take place, the players must be aware of each other's definition of the situation—that the interaction is play, that there are certain constraining rules, that there is a specific goal, and so forth—and construct their

"Defining the situation" with a typical play bow.
Photographer: Marc Bekoff

behaviors so as to sustain the collective action of the game. In her observational study of play between boys and girls, Barrie Thorne discusses a feature of play that is of relevance to our interest in human interactions with companion animals. She maintains that play is a form of "border work." On the one hand, play invokes and highlights the differences between classes of players. At the same time, play demonstrates that certain forms of difference are irrelevant within the limits of the playing situation.[161] As a form of border work, people's play with dogs and other companion animals highlights the differences between the players and necessitates that players adjust their behaviors so as to limit the differences and maintain the playful exchange.

Typically, play—both animal with human and animal with animal—is initiated when one of the interactants solicits the other through the use of signaling moves—making "play" faces, assuming certain postures, presenting certain objects, or offering special verbal cues.[162] These initiatory sounds or gestures communicate to the other potential player that what will follow is not serious and that the interaction will be bounded by certain rules.[163]

Playful exchanges are central to the interactions of people and dogs. Both the human and the canine co-actors orient their play behaviors to the other. This is necessary since both have certain advantages over the other—the person is more devious and the dog is more agile, for example. Overuse of advantage is mutually agreed to be "against the rules" since the basic purpose of the "game" is to keep playing.[164]

Dog-human play typically entails some measure of pretense—each player presents a simple false "reality" to the other as part of the game. The person motions as if to throw an object and then hides it, for example. Or the animal player "fakes" a movement in one direction and then takes another course.[165] Play is, therefore, a mutual project in which both the companion animal and person hold compatible definitions of the situation and engage in tactical maneuvers that necessitate recognizing the intentions of the other and purposefully manipulating the expectations and subsequent actions of the other. Central to this exchange are mutual presentations of situational definitions and the players' abilities to take the role of the other.[166] As stated by Kenneth Shapiro following his description of playing with his dog Sabaka:

> At first glance, this activity hardly seems worth mentioning—a simple game of keep-away and chase. However, on reflection, the invitation ritual, the play itself, the implicit rules and regulations governing the legitimate play area, permitted and prohibited moves, and the object of the game, as well as the conditions ending it, were all quite intricate and yet easily maintained by both players. Even more subtle were the postures, feints, and deceits, the half-executed moves during what might look, to the uninitiated, like time-outs from the game.[167]

In a recent paper, Robert Mitchell and Elizabeth Edmunson examined the verbal elements of play interactions between people and their dogs. The human player's verbalizations typically involved his or her getting the dog's attention, asking for information, praising the dog, and describing what was happening or about to happen. They conclude that during play interactions owners talk to their dogs because they want to shape their behavior and because they see the exchange as demonstrating a communicative connection with their animals.[168]

Play behavior and mutual gaze provide persuasive evidence that dogs have the ability to take the role of the (human) other and share in authentic social interactions. As eminently social beings and the animals with whom people have the closest and most emotionally involving relationships, dogs consistently, and effectively, employ their intersubjective skills as they share in our everyday lives. It is reasonable to conclude that, like us, they know that putting one's self into the perspective of the other is essential if one is to act socially. Assuming the viewpoint of others is essential if actors—be they canine or human—are to anticipate behavior and manipulate it to their own ends. In turn, by imaginatively putting ourselves into the perspectives of the dogs with whom we have relationships we shape our encounters with them and, if we remain open to the practical evidence afforded by our experience, can reasonably come to see dogs as intelligent and full-fledged partners in social interaction.[169]

The dog owners, trainers, and veterinarians presented in this book are practical actors and consistently remain open to the evidence. Their daily experiences with dogs persuade them that it is reasonable to see their canine companions, trainees, and patients as emotional, thoughtful, and perceptive associates. The evidence is as persuasive as that one commonly employs to attribute thinking, planning, and feeling to fellow humans. Stanley Coren makes just this point after describing seeing his dog Wiz go into the bathroom, return with a towel, arrange it in a spot of sunlight, and contentedly lay down on it:

> If my young child had done this, I would have said that he felt the warmth of the sun and thought that it would be nice to take a nap in it. Then, remembering the towel in the bathroom, he went and retrieved it so that he could sunbathe more comfortably. All this requires consciousness, intelligence, and planning. Does my dog Wiz have it? It is easier for me simply to recognize that my dog's behaviors in this situation were similar to behaviors that are accompanied by consciousness in a human faced with the same situation. In the absence of any evidence to the contrary, I will presume that I am dealing with consciousness and intelligent behavior in my dog as well.[170]

Conclusion

What distinguishes men from animals is born of our relationship with them.
John Berger, About Looking

The skeptical reader may well dismiss the discussion above and the views of those presented in this book as mere anthropomorphic delusions. Our emotional attachment to dogs and other companion animals does make it tempting to see them as "cleverer than they really are,"[171] and some of the more extremely anthropomorphic portrayals of dogs do tend to present them as essentially small people with fur.[172] On the other hand, fear of having one's analysis labeled as anthropomorphic should not stifle the analyst's search for an understanding of animal mental capabilities or the intricacies of their interactions with humans.[173] Adhering to the rigid canons of scientific skepticism—seeking what is narrowly regarded as scientific "proof"—may blind us to the ways in which the real world actually operates. Bluntly put, it is stupid to assume that a perspective is false simply because we are not entirely sure that it is true.[174] Grounding inferences about animal mentality and behavior on our routine and intimate experiences with them—using what John Andrew Fisher[175] calls "interpretive anthropomorphism"—leads, in the end, to supportable and practical conclusions.

The dog owners, trainers, veterinarians, and others presented in this book are, in essence, "folk ethologists." They allow their canine companions to be subjects rather than objects; they listen as their dogs speak to them through their behavior[176] and draw reasonable conclusions from the "data" offered by their intimate familiarity with their animal companions.[177] Those of us devoted to describing and understanding the shared social world of people and animals must use the same evidence and be led to similar conclusions. Intimate familiarity with others—be they human or nonhuman—offers the richest of information. This information, I submit, is persuasive in demonstrating that our animal companions are thoughtful, emotional, intentional, and empathetic partners with us in our social world. However, our recognition of the consciousness and purposefulness of dogs and other companion animals—of their ability to be full-fledged social interactants with us in our daily lives—must be tempered with a recognition and appreciation of their difference. This appreciative understanding of the other-in-interaction is the most essential goal of social science. Our relationships with animals can only speak to us if we are open to listening.

Notes

Preface

1. While I recognize that "canid" is the proper designation for members of the dog-family, I have chosen to employ "canine" since it is the commonplace usage.

2. Academic examinations of human interactions with companion animals are based on a wide variety of types of data. Harriet Ritvo's (1987) work on petkeeping in Victorian England, James Serpell's (1986) overview of human-animal relationships, and Kathleen Kete's (1994) study of pets in nineteenth-century Paris exemplify this historical focus. "Serious" discussions of human-animal interactions done by social and behavioral scientists have tended to be based on data derived through the use of conventional methods such as survey research; for example, Jeffrey Rasmussen, D. W. Rajecki, and H. D. Craft (1993) and Nienke Endenburg (1991). The use of interpretive, phenomenologically sensitive approaches that tap more directly into the experience of people as they interact with their animal companions—the kind I have chosen to use—also have their advocates. Anthropologist Tom Ingold (1988a), cognitive ethologist Donald Griffin (1976:87–90), and psychologists Harold Herzog and Gordon Burghart (1988) have championed the use of qualitative approaches. Arnold Arluke and I (1996) have recently offered an extended testimony to the virtues of using ethnographic research as a means of exploring human relationships with animals.

3. As described by one of its contemporary advocates (Denzin 1989:34), auto-ethnography is

> An ethnographic statement which writes the ethnographer into the text in an autobiographical manner. . . . This is an important variant in the traditional ethnographic account which positions the writer as an objective outsider in the texts that are written about the culture, group, or person in question. . . . Such an auto-ethnography would be descriptive and interpretive.

While auto-ethnography has become something of a fad in postmodernist ethnographic circles, the basic approach is hardly new. The term was coined by David Hayano (1979), and the Chicago School sociologist Charles Horton Cooley (1964:

149

6–7) advocated a similar approach that he called "sympathetic introspection" almost a century ago (see also Ellis 1992).

4. This unusual denial of access involved a situation in which the client was a Ph.D. psychotherapist who was under considerable stress because his dog was experiencing severe seizures.

5. For an eloquent statement of the view that human relationships with animals are parallel to those between slaves and masters, see Spiegel 1988.

6. See Budiansky 1992.

7. In speaking of pets as members of the family, I am using a fairly broad definition of this sort of social arrangement. As Gubrium and Holstein (1990:139) state, "Family provides a reference point that is commonly shared and tacitly agreed upon, against which other relationships and behaviors are interpreted."

8. A sizeable body of research is currently drawing the connection between abuse of animals and other forms of violence in the family. For an overview see Akrow (1997).

9. This methodological stance is based on my distaste for conventional prescriptions about "scientific" detachment. I am committed to an understanding based on direct involvement with the actors and phenomena of interest. Positivistic approaches that stress the collection of data "at a distance" merely cast those the researcher is trying to understand as *objects* and, in so doing, obstructs the process of acquiring knowledge. See Costall 1998:24–25, Bekoff 1998, Jamieson and Bekoff 1993:117–118.

Chapter 1: Introduction: The Relationship between People and Pets

1. Rowan 1990:142.

2. Montgomery 1991:xvii–xviii.

3. While the "approved" generic term for dogs who assist those with visual impairments is "dog guides" (Putnam 1979:ix), "guide dog" is most commonly used and understood by the general public. Since guide dog is also the designation most often used by the owners and trainers with whom I worked, I will employ it in this book.

4. For general overviews of pet keeping see Council for Science and Society 1988:8–10; Fogle 1985; Serpell 1986, 1988; Fisher 1983; Tuan 1984; Manning and Serpell 1994. For an interesting historical and cross-cultural discussion that highlights the ambivalent ways in which dogs have been and are socially defined, see Menache 1998.

5. See Tuan 1984:110, Serpell 1986:38–47, ten Bensel 1984, Bustad and Hines 1984, Ritvo 1988.

6. Ritvo 1988:27–28; see also Spiegel 1988.

7. In his observational study of the social contacts dog owners had when walking their dogs, Peter Messent (1983:46) found that "pedigree dogs were more likely to elicit interest and contact from others than nonpedigree dogs."

8. Harry Truman is reputed to have observed, "If you want a friend in politics, get a dog" (quoted in Klein 1995:21).

9. Fogle 1985:50, 84–86.

10. Cited in Serpell 1986:28–29.

11. Serpell 1981, Hart and Hart 1984. It seems that dogs are more highly regarded by the general public than are cats. One study (Selby and Rhoades 1981) found that only 4 percent of those questioned expressed dislike for dogs while 28 percent disliked cats. Consequently, it would be reasonable to conclude that dog owners enjoy a higher degree of positive social regard than do cat owners.

12. Lockwood 1983.

13. As discussed in Chapter 2, in certain situations companion animals can *degrade* the owner's social identity. When the animal acts aggressively toward others, destroys property, is problematically noisy, or presents some other form of social nuisance, its owner commonly is defined as being overly permissive, uncaring, or otherwise lacking in appropriate control (see Borchelt et al. 1983; Beck 1983). The personal and interpersonal difficulties associated with pet possession lead to considerable ambivalence on the part of owners. One consequence of this ambivalence is that nearly one third of the dogs owned by Americans end their lives in animal shelters (Serpell 1986:15).

14. Covert et al. 1985.

15. Mary B. Harris 1983.

16. Salmon and Salmon 1983. One large-scale survey commissioned by the Pet Food Institute (Wilber 1983) grouped dog owners on the basis of their dominant attitudes toward their pets. Nineteen percent of those questioned were defined as "Valued Object Owners" characterized by their lack of emotional connection to the dog or their view of it as a functional provider of security. These kinds of owners regarded the dog as "an object that should be given the same quality care that their owner gives to other persons and possessions in the home."

17. Adell-Bath et al. 1979.

18. Cain 1983.

19. Messent 1983, 1984.

20. Goffman 1963:131–139; cf. Sanders 1989:57–61.

21. Cooley 1964.

22. Serpell 1981.

23. Cited in Cusack 1988:18.

24. While this research did not connect the development of a positive self definition specifically to increased affirmative encounters derived from association with companion animals, it is likely that this is an important aspect of the process by which these influential respondents constructed and maintained a positive definition of self (see Feldmann 1983:134). Another way in which companion animals affect social encounters is by providing the caretaker with information useful in defining other people with whom he or she has contact. Dog owners commonly pay attention to and interpret the meaning of the ways their dogs respond to those they encounter, since the "special" abilities of dogs to judge the character and intentions of people is a popular piece of folk knowledge shared by "dog lovers." Friendly displays signal the acceptability of the other person, while aggressive or fearful responses from the dog are commonly interpreted as grounds for suspicion and exercising caution (see Gillespie, Leffler, and Lerner 1996; Hearne 1987:77–116).

25. Gans 1974.

26. See Gillespie, Leffler, and Lerner 1996; Veevers 1985:15–19.

27. The social definition of the dog as a *companion* has class-based and historical roots. When dog ownership was predominantly an upper-class phenomenon, the animal was typically defined as a possession symbolizing the owner's social rank. Late in the seventeenth century dogs increasingly came to be incorporated into middle-class households. Within this social context they came to be regarded as companions and members of the family rather than as prized property symbolizing social position (Tuan 1984:111–114).

28. Katcher, Friedmann, et al. 1983.

29. Cain 1985.

30. Beck and Katcher (1983:44) found that 80 percent of the veterinary clients they studied talked to their pets "in the same way they talked to people."

31. Cain 1985:7, Macdonald cited in Beck and Katcher 1983:44.

32. See Veevers 1985:19–26, Beck and Katcher 1983:39–58.

33. Brickel 1985:45.

34. See also Cusack 1988:39–45.

35. Beck and Katcher 1983:59, Voith 1983.

36. Nieburg and Fischer 1982, Bryant 1982.

37. Serpell 1986:114. Garber (1996:73) puts it nicely when she writes that "the dog has become the repository of those model human properties which we have cynically ceased to find among human beings."

38. Wilber (1983), for example, found "Companionship Owners"—those who emphasized the friendship and affection afforded by their pet—to make up the largest "attitudinal segment" of dog owners (27 percent of those studied). Similarly, of the pet owners questioned by Bulcroft and his associates (1986), 94 percent agreed that "pets are an importance source of affection," 85 percent agreed that "my pet accepts me no matter what I do," and 83 percent agreed with the statement, "my pet makes me feel loved" (see also Fogle 1987:18–21, 41–62; Serpell 1983b; Sinrod 1993:91; Okoniewski 1984). At the most extreme, 3 percent of the pet owners surveyed by Sinrod (1993:88) said that they loved their pets more than any other member of their families.

39. Brickel 1985:44, 45.

40. Beck and Katcher 1983:202–204. See also Fogle 1987:114–126; Mechling 1989; Mitchell and Thompson 1986, 1990, 1991.

41. Smith 1983, Beck and Katcher 1983:112–119. A growing number of studies indicate that physical contacts between humans and companion animals have mutually beneficial physiological consequences as well as positive socioemotional rewards. See Katcher, Segal, and Beck 1984; Katcher and Beck 1988; Friedmann and Thomas 1985; Serpell 1986:87–99.

42. Smith 1983:35. Of course, not all of the discussions of pet-keeping and human-animal interaction present such a rosy picture. Tuan (1984), for example, emphasizes the rewards of dominance and power that human beings draw from their encounters with animals (see also Verney 1979). A number of writers focus on the presumed disadvantages of and social problems generated by pet ownership (see Simon 1984; Voith 1983; Beck and Katcher 1983:220–255; Serpell 1988:12–

13, 19–33). It is clear from the massive rate at which pets are discarded and destroyed that, like all relationships in which humans are involved, animal-human interactions lead to negative consequences as well as positive ones (see Akrow and Dow 1984).

43. See Budiansky 1992; Clutton-Brock 1995; Ginsburg and Hiestand 1992; Serpell 1986, 1988; Tuan 1984; Ritvo 1988.

44. Fogle 1987:50; see also Hearne 1987:192–223.

45. See Warnath and Seyfarth 1982, Gibbs 1982, Curtis 1981, Cusack 1988: 201–207. Since the pioneering work of Boris Levinson (1969) almost three decades ago, the functional use of animals in therapeutic situations has been a major focus of interest among those working in the area of animal-human relationships. Interactions with companion animals—even as simple an activity as observing fish in an aquarium (Riddick 1985; Katcher, Segal, and Beck 1984)—have been shown to have beneficial physical and psychological effects on people suffering from stress, depression, hypertension, withdrawal associated with advanced age, and a variety of other social, physical, and emotional dysfunctions (see Friedmann et al. 1984; Brickel 1984; Baun et al. 1984; Tolliver 1984; Olsen, Mandel, and Bender 1984; Hendy 1984; Cusack 1988; Rochberg-Halton 1985; Friedmann and Thomas 1985).

46. Serpell 1983a:7, emphasis added. Investigators of the psychotherapeutic benefits of animals stress a similar, though not as obvious, point. They argue that depressed, withdrawn, mentally disordered individuals largely suffer from feeling rejected and alienated. Interaction with the accepting, genuine, loving companion animal counteracts, to some degree, the negative self definition that is an important element of the person's feelings of "dis-ease." It is here in the area of pet-facilitated therapy that we can see one of the most dramatic ways in which companion animals extend and bolster the socially constituted human self. See Cusack 1988.

47. See Stewart 1983, Belk 1988:142–144.

48. In her comparison of human-to-human and animal-to-human relationships, Lisa Okoniewski (1984) observes that, because of these factors, her respondents found communication with animals to be "easier" and "less threatening" than communication with other people.

49. Scheff 1966.

50. See Cooley 1964 [1902]:89.

51. Beck and Katcher 1983:44.

Chapter 2: The Everyday Dog Owner: Knowing and Living with Dogs

1. "Pampering your Pets," *The Hartford Courant*, February 10, 1998, p. D1.

2. *Anthrozoös* 8(1), 1995, pp. 55–56.

3. See Arluke and Sanders 1996:61–81.

4. Terrace 1987.

5. See the discussion of "self-handicapping" as an element of canid social play in Allen and Bekoff 1997:108.

6. Some of the best work on play interactions between people and their dogs

has been done by Robert Mitchell and Nicholas Thompson (1986, 1990, 1991). See also Mechling 1989. For related discussions of dog-with-dog play see Allen and Bekoff 1997:87–113 and Bekoff 1995.

7. In the course of the fieldwork in the veterinary hospital, I was interested to hear the veterinarians regularly describe animals as "depressed." I asked a number of them what they meant when they employed the term—whether it referred to a physical or psychological state. The vets agreed it was a label that indicated *both* emotional and physiological characteristics:

> Depression refers to both (mental and physical attributes). It refers to the animals' attitude. [I responded, "That sounds pretty psychological."] I guess. If an animal is behaviorally depressed it usually means that it is psychologically depressed as well. When you see a dog that is usually active, who wags his tail when you come in, and he just lies there, that's one I would call depressed. Have you seen the abbreviation B.A.R.? It means "bright, active, and responsive." It's the opposite of depressed.

8. See Becker 1974.

9. For sociological discussions of these matters see Ostrow 1990:35–45 and Schutz 1970. For a specific description of the importance of the dog's body movements as the basis for intimate communication see Ken Shapiro's (1990) discussion of "kinesthetic empathy." Myers (1996) offers an interesting ethnographic study of nonverbal interactions between children and animals.

10. Related to the issue of communication of emotion through the use of proto-speech acts is Susan Langer's (1951:86–88) discussion of "non-discursive symbols" (cf. George 1985).

11. Seventy-eight percent of the owners surveyed by Sinrod (1995:37) said that their dogs talked to them.

12. Ongoing systems of intimate relationships are eminently political. In the interactions of people with their canine companions, the former is—at least ideally—involved in teaching the latter the basic rules to which the animal is expected to adhere. In essence, *training* is a power relationship between people and dogs. Desired behavior is rewarded while proscribed behavior is punished (e.g., Koehler 1962 and most informational literature on dog training). This basic characterization does not differentiate significantly between human-to-human and dog-to-human interactions. The structuring and maintenance of human relationships centrally involves interactants providing positive or negative feedback, expressing interest in the other, providing support or criticism, and through a variety of similar exchanges shaping the ongoing behavior of the other (see Goffman 1959).

13. See Goffman 1959.

14. For interesting discussions of deception as a central element in the play of dogs and people, see the work of Mitchell and Thompson (1990, 1991).

15. See Spiegel 1988.

16. For example, Goffman 1961, Vail 1966, Bogdan et al. 1974.

17. Bogdan and Taylor 1989.

18. Seventy-two percent of the owners interviewed by Cain (1985) said that their dog usually or always had "people status" (see also Veevers 1985).

19. Eight-year-old John Morrison described the intrinsic value of this relationship most simply when he wrote:

> My dog means somebody nice and quiet to be with. He does not say "Do" like my mother, or "Don't" like my father, or "Stop" like my brother. My dog, Spot, and I sit together quietly and I like him and he likes me. The end. (Quoted in Fogle 1985:76)

20. For example, one malamute breeder described the dog she brought to the veterinary clinic as being an atypical representative of the breed:

> She wanted to be Shirley Temple, but was born a dog instead. . . . Malamutes are peculiar dogs. Some people just don't know how to deal with them. They expect them to be like a golden or something—"Go over there and sit in the corner!"—and they just do it. You have to be strong with a Malamute. They aren't that domesticated. They are raised to pull sleds and you want them to be able to decide things like if the ice is too thin—to think for themselves. If you aren't strong with them then they think they are the boss and you are going to have real trouble. She's not like that. She's just the sweetest. She is like that in the show ring. She makes eyes at the judges and charms them. She's sweet with most people. There are some people though that she just doesn't like. Dogs have a sense of people like that. When she doesn't like someone it usually turns out that they weren't very likeable or worth knowing. It's interesting how dogs know things like that.

21. One of my interviewees responded to the question of whether she saw her dogs as "persons" by saying:

> They are. They have feelings. There is a mutual caring for one another and although they may hurt one another it is done in a playful manner. Yeah, they are people, but I hesitate to say that to too many individuals because they would think I am nuts. Because I don't think many people think of animals as being people. The majority of people think of animals as pets and they are to be kept at a distance. It is very important to me to have these "kids" portrayed as part of my family. Because they are part of my family. I do treat them as people. I care about them and I would never deliberately hurt them. It is very important for me to convey to them that I do care very much for them. I'm sure they understand that.

22. For example, Collins 1975:364–380 and Durkheim 1964.

23. Fifty-eight percent of the owners surveyed by Sinrod (1993) celebrated their dogs' birthdays (p. 35), 74 percent give their dogs birthday or Christmas gifts (p. 24), and 39 percent give birthday cards or presents to others in their dogs' names (p. 67).

24. The following letter "written" by a dog to one of the veterinarians at the clinic and "signed" with a paw-print, provides a vivid illustration of the defined personhood of the companion animal and its incorporation into the intimate network of the family:

Dear Dr. XXXXXX,
Christmas was a real drag for me this year, but thanks to you my future is looking bright. I was pretty darn scared when that big truck hit me. Mom completely lost it and was ready to call Life Star. Good thing Dad kept her together and we made it to the hospital. Just wanted to let you know that we are all very grateful for all you did and to also thank all those cute nurses for being so nice to me. I told all my buddies about you and they plan to give you a call if ever they feel a bit under the weather. I'll see you in 6 months when I come in for my shots.
Thanks again, Doc . . .
Your Pal Gretta

25. Glazer and Strauss 1972.
26. For discussions of dogs as the focus of public interaction see Robbins, Sanders, and Cahill 1991; Gillespie, Leffler, and Lerner 1996; Bekoff and Meany 1997, West 1997.
27. Goffman 1971:19.
28. Goffman 1971:65.
29. Goffman 1971:188–237.
30. See Hickrod and Schmitt 1982:64–66. The ultimate example of animals and humans collectively acting as a "with" is seen in the cooperative activity of a guide dog and his or her visually impaired owner in public settings. This special situation is discussed in the following chapter.
31. Goffman 1971:121.
32. When the animal acts aggressively toward others, destroys property, is problematically noisy, or presents some other form of social nuisance, its owner commonly is defined as being overly permissive, uncaring, or otherwise lacking in appropriate control (see Borchelt et al. 1983; Beck 1983). The personal and interpersonal difficulties associated with pet possession often lead owners to experience considerable ambivalence. One consequence of this ambivalence is seen in the millions of pets that are destroyed in the United States each year. In 1996 some 2.4 million abandoned dogs were euthanized (Derr 1997:42). Serpell (1986:15) estimates that nearly one-third of the dogs owned by Americans eventually end their lives in animal shelters.
33. See Goffman 1982.
34. Goffman (1971:95–187) refers to these kinds of interactional repair as "remedial interchanges." Alternatively, Stokes and Hewitt (1976) discuss "aligning actions" used by interactants to reestablish identities and relationships disrupted by problematic events. Discussions of "disclaimers" (prospective justifications presented to explain potential problems) (Hewitt and Stokes 1975), "accounts" (retrospective explanations) (Scott and Lyman 1968), "neutralization techniques" (ex-

planations presented to self and others in order to ease feelings and ascription of guilt) (Sykes and Matza 1957), and other "aligning actions" are oriented around the symbolic interactionist perspective on motives. Rather than being seen as initiatory "motors" of human action, motives, from this standpoint, are regarded as *verbal* presentations offered to the self and others that are intended to situate the behavior in question in an *understandable* context (see Mills 1940, Blum and McHugh 1971, Perinbanayagam 1977).

35. This discussion of excusing tactics is an extension of the general literature on aligning actions and vocabularies of motive in two significant regards. Prior discussions have focused on the process of offering motive statements to restore identities and realign interaction as, in essence, an individual activity (see Cahill 1987 for an exception). This presentation focuses on tactics employed by one (or more) members of a publicly identifiable group in response to disruption caused by another—and, in some regards, less culpable—member of the acting unit. In addition, this is, to the best of my knowledge, the first sociological discussion linking motive ascription and interactional realignment to the general topic of animal-human relationships.

36. For related psychological discussions of excuses, see Weiner, Figueroa-Munoz, and Kakihara 1991 and Snyder and Higgins 1988.

37. Hewitt and Hall 1973:367–368.

38. See Arkow and Dow 1984, Voith 1983, Borchelt 1983, Houpt 1983.

39. See, for example, Cahill 1987, Dixon 1978, Denzin 1977:64–75.

40. Cahill 1987:313, emphasis added.

41. Cahill 1987:315.

42. Dixon 1978:131–134.

43. Cahill 1987:315.

Chapter 3: The Guide Dog Owner: Dependence and Love

1. See Belk 1988.

2. See Chevigny 1946, Zee 1983.

3. Scott 1989.

4. See Deshen and Deshen 1989. Three of the interviewees volunteered that they initially had reservations about acquiring a dog because they felt that the service animal would be even more stigmatizing than a cane while, at the same time, requiring considerably more care and attention.

5. In speaking about the increased mobility afforded by working with an assistance dog (especially in contrast to using a cane), one interviewee admiringly spoke of the guide dog as "a blind man's Cadillac."

6. Kuusisto (1998:170) poetically captures the change in one's experience and self-definition precipitated by working with a guide dog:

The next morning in White Plains, Corky pulls me back from a Jeep that is cutting the curb.
She moves straight back. With strength.

Two pedestrians applaud. One says she'd like to get a guide dog too. I
laugh. But I can taste my lungs, as if I've been running at Pamplona.

For the first time I feel the sunken lanes under my feet.

The street is more my own. I belong here.

I'm walking without the fight-or-flee gunslinger crouch that has been the
lifelong measure of blindness.

I'm not frightened by the general onslaught of sensation.

The harness is a transmitter, the dog is confident.

At every curb we come to a reliable and firm stop. I cannot fall.

7. This distinction between "hard" and "soft" dogs is discussed in more detail
in Chapter 5.

8. It is reasonable to assume that the guide dog has a basic awareness of his or
her role, especially in making the distinction between "working" and "not working." I noticed this early in my observations of trainers in the field:

> The change in the dogs' demeanor is obvious when they are put into their
> harnesses. Without the harness they cavort, sniff, lick, and engage in typical
> doggy behavior. As soon as they are in the harness they change. Their ears go
> up, they stare straight ahead, and they assume a look of serious and focused
> attention. It is time to work.

9. Kuusisto (1998:179–180) makes a similar point in his description of accom-
panying his guide dog Corky in public.

10. Goffman 1963:126. See also Gardner 1993, Cahill and Eggleston 1995.

11. Cahill and Eggleston 1994, 1995.

12. Cahill and Eggleston 1995:685–686.

13. Cahill and Eggleston 1994:307–308, 1995:686–695.

14. Hochschild 1979.

15. Cahill and Eggleston 1994:309.

16. An article from the *Tallahassee Democrat* sent to Ann Landers (*The Hartford
Courant*, October 7, 1995, p. E6) provides an extreme example of the ignorance and
thoughtlessness of some members of the public when encountering a guide dog
user and his assistance animal:

> A minister and his wife sued a guide-dog school for $160,000 after a blind
> man learning to use a seeing-eye dog trod on the woman's toes in a shopping
> mall. . . . The $160,000 lawsuit was brought by Carolyn Christian of Ellenton
> and her husband, the Rev. William Christian. Each sought $80,000. The
> couple filed suit 13 months after Carolyn Christian's toe was stepped on and
> reportedly broken by a blind man who was learning to use his new guide dog,
> Freddy, under the supervision of an instructor. They were practicing at a Bra-
> denton shopping mall. According to witnesses, Carolyn Christian made no ef-
> fort to get out of the blind man's way because she wanted "to see if the dog
> would walk around me."

17. Of the seven guide dog users interviewed, three were currently living with
their first dog while four had owned two or more. Interviewees had lived and
worked with a total of thirteen guide dogs.

Chapter 4: The Veterinarian: Caring for Canine Patients

1. Mennerick 1974.
2. Davis 1959.
3. Cassell 1991.
4. Lazare et al. 1987.
5. Shurtleff 1983.
6. Stanford Gregory and Stephen Keto (1991) provide an insightful discussion of the significant differences between interactions in human medical settings and those that take place in veterinary settings. They emphasize the lack of ritual and mystery, open emotionality, use of "plain language," overt discussion of death, and negotiability of diagnosis and treatment that differentiate veterinary exchanges from those between a physician and human patient.
7. Strauss et al. 1985.
8. Dooley 1979.
9. See Owens 1986. The survey of pet owners conducted by Sinrod (1993) reveals that pet owners are relatively faithful in exposing themselves and their animals to the "art of veterinary practice." Forty percent of the dog owners questioned went to a veterinarian once a year and 25 percent went twice a year (p. 61). Sixty-seven percent of pet owners said that they would take care of their animal companion first if both they and their pet "needed non-emergency treatment" (p. 60).
10. Herzog, Vore, and New 1989; cf. Dingwall and Murray 1983; Becker et al. 1961:329–330.
11. See Danziger 1981, Friedson 1987.
12. In questioning pet owners about their animals' responses to veterinarians, Sinrod (1993:61) found that 45 percent of cats regularly hissed and 34 percent of dogs growled.
13. See Becker and Geer 1957.
14. Most of the veterinarians mentioned cat scratches as a common occupational hazard. Large animal practices, especially equine specialties, were generally regarded as the most dangerous.

> Yeah, equine practice can be dangerous. One time I was in a stall helping with breeding and the horse started rearing up and there just wasn't any place I could go. I really got scared. There's this fairly young guy, Dr. B_____, out in S_____ who has an equine practice. His wife would help out sometimes. One time she got kicked in the head and eventually died. It does happen. When you look at the obits in the journals and you see notices on fairly young people, you will see that they usually did equine work.

15. See Hart et al. 1983, Houpt 1983, Landsberg 1991.
16. Sometimes the tranquilizers routinely used to control aggression in patients could have unexpected consequences, as in the following (rather extreme) account from my field notes:

> I used to use Promazine but sometimes it has just the opposite effect on these [pit bulls]. I actually had one get aggressive on me so I switched to In-

novar. I shot one up and he jumped off the table and went for me. He came at me and I kicked him so that he hit the wall over there under the fire extinguisher. He just jumped up and came at me again and I kicked him again. The third time he arched up and hit the wall and then ran into X-ray. I got him with a capture loop. By that time my adrenaline was so up that I just went BAM! onto the table. Later we took him back to the client and I said, "You better watch this dog. He's getting kind of aggressive." It was her son's dog and she was scared shitless of him.

17. Bryant and Snizek 1976.

18. As members in a general practice, the veterinarians in the clinic I studied engaged in work with both "small" (companion) animals and "large" animals (principally cows and horses). When I told them about Bryant and Snizek's explanation for vets' presumed preference for office work as opposed to farm work, they tended to respond with some amusement. While agreeing that clients in the clinic tended to treat them with somewhat more respect than did dairy farmers or "horse people" encountered on the farms, they were quick to point out the routine dirty work involved in dealing with companion animals. For the most part, they tended to describe their large animal work with considerable pleasure since they enjoyed interactions with the dairy farmers ("horse people" were not so highly regarded) and "being on farm" freed them from the physical confines and routines of the clinic.

19. Hughes 1971:343–345.

20. The veterinary technicians who were given the most unsavory of the routine janitorial tasks in the clinic and were responsible for the macabre job of filling and emptying the cremation furnace also found the dirty work features of their job to be trying. I quote from field notes:

As I come in the back door through the garage, I am greeted by Bonnie who is in the room with the freezer along with Jennie. They are taking what remains in the crematorium, processing it in the blender and putting the resulting powder into the blue cardboard boxes in which they give the ashes to the owners. For the first time I see the end product of cremation—actually sizeable chunks of bone from 4 inches long to powder. Initially the leavings are put into a plastic trash can and pounded with a length of 2x4 to break up the largest chunks. The techs are careful to make sure that the name of the owner is always attached to the ashes—they know where the body was because they have labeled the various trays that go into the furnace. All in all it is a pretty grizzly business. I mention this to Bonnie who says, "When I first got here 20 years ago I lost 9 pounds in a couple of weeks. My husband told me not to come back here anymore but I told him I would get used to it." [I asked, "What was it that affected you like that?"] "It was mostly the smell— the medicinal smell. The only thing that really gets to me now is when I come in in the morning and reach into a cat cage and stick my hand into warm cat poop. That makes me gag. It is kind of disgusting here [in the cremation area] when the animal doesn't burn all the way and you have to deal with partially burned entrails."

Because they were primarily responsible for routine microscopic analyses of stool samples brought in by clients, the techs also jokingly commented on the pungent aspects of this task.

21. This particular incident and the admission of a dog infected with Canine Parvovirus—a highly communicable viral disease—made me realize that this project held an unanticipated danger that was novel to my research experience. Not only could I be exposed to disease, but I could potentially expose my own dogs. When I mentioned this concern to one of the techs she assured me that they were all quite careful when animals with communicable diseases were in the hospital and that I would be informed if there was some potential for exposure.

22. In a study of canine behavior problem cases referred to three practices, Landsberg (1991) found that 59 percent of the referrals were precipitated by problematically aggressive behavior.

23. Sudnow 1967, Coombs and Powers 1977, Zussman 1992.

24. Benrubi 1992.

25. See Bernards 1989, Angell 1988, Cassel and Meier 1990, Singer and Siegler 1990.

26. See Kahler 1992, Cantanzaro 1992, Duvin 1992, Stone, 1992.

27. For discussions of this general issue see Tuan 1984, Serpell 1986, Phillips 1993, Noske 1989, Rollin 1990.

28. See Shapiro 1990, Bekoff and Gruen 1993, Linden 1993.

29. For discussions of owners' emotional responses to the death of their pets see Gerwolls and Labott 1994, Gosse and Barnes 1994.

30. Medical sociologist John Moneymaker (1988:45) focuses on the dichotomous social definition of animals and its moral implications in relationship to euthanasia decisions when he observes:

> If an animal is not conscious of self and its future appears miserably wretched, then the only humane, compassionate course is to alleviate the creature's suffering by euthanasia. The issue is not one of diminishing happiness, but of eradicating further suffering through death. Even when consciousness of self is present, the animal is not capable of understanding its future prospects or of choosing whether to live or die; it should be deemed morally right and necessary for others to make this choice for the animal. This choice, however, is justifiable only if it is truly made out of compassionate interest for the being who is absolutely incapable of making the choice for itself. Whatever we choose, we are responsible for the foreseeable consequences that result, just as we are equally responsible for the fate of an animal we allow to continue to exist in a miserable state.

See also Stewart 1983.

31. American Veterinary Medical Association 1988, Fogle 1981, McCulloch and Bustad 1983, Harris, 1983.

32. A national survey commissioned by the American Veterinary Medical Association (1988) revealed that there were close to 35 million American households containing dogs and almost 28 million with cats. In 1987, 77.6 percent of dog-

owning households sought veterinary care an average of 2.37 times per household while 59.5 percent of cat owning households sought veterinary care an average of 1.62 times per household. This translates into some 26.75 million cat visits and 64 million dog visits per year and means that during the approximately 90.75 million combined veterinary encounters, between 1.8 million (at the 2 percent level) and 3.6 million (at the 4 percent level) dogs and cats were euthanized in veterinary practices during 1987. This is to say nothing of the somewhere between 2 and 25 million unwanted dogs and cats estimated to be euthanized each year in some 3,600 animal "shelters" in the United States (see Akrow 1993; Cantanzaro 1992; Kahler 1992; Patronek, Glickman, and Moyer 1995).

33. Sudnow 1967:43, Fogle and Abrahamson 1990:147.

34. My field notes record 37 euthanasia incidents that I observed as a researcher or, as I became more involved in the clinic as a direct participant, in which I assisted. According to my sampling of the clinic's computer records, during the time I was involved in the research an average of 4.6 euthanasias were performed each working day. This translates to each doctor in the clinic performing slightly over 11 euthanasias a month. A study of California veterinarians conducted by Hart, Hart, and Mader (1990) found that the doctors surveyed conducted an average of 8 euthanasias a month with a range of 3 to 20 per month.

35. One study of the reasons offered by veterinary clients in support of the euthanasia decision (McCulloch and Bustad 1983) found that 76 percent were performed for clinical reasons, 9 percent for economic reasons, 8 percent for reasons of "convenience" (such as the client's living quarters being too small or the client simply not wanting the animal any longer), and 4 percent because of the animal's behavioral problems.

36. Studies indicate that the vast majority of euthanasia decisions—from 70 to 80 percent—are precipitated by the animal's age and infirmity (Lago and Kotch-Jantzer 1988, McCulloch and Bustad 1983).

37. See Antelyes 1990, Landsberg 1991, Mugford 1981. Though McCulloch and Bustad (1983) found that only 4 percent of veterinary euthanasias were precipitated by behavioral problems (cf. Council for Science and Society 1988:41), a study of the reasons people delivered unwanted animals to humane societies (Akrow and Dow 1984) found that almost half of the mature animals were given up for this reason. Americans sustain more than four million dog bites a year, twelve of which result in the victim's death and close to three-quarters of a million of which require medical attention (Derr 1997:42). The Centers for Disease Control attributes the 37 percent increase in dog bites that occurred between 1986 and 1994 to the increased ownership of more ferocious dogs for protection (*The Hartford Courant,* May 29, 1997, p. A2).

38. Cantanzaro 1992:8.

39. It appears that there are significant cultural factors shaping veterinarians' agreement to euthanize healthy animals when requested to do so by owners. One study of British veterinarians found almost three-quarters willing to put down a healthy pet (Fogle and Abrahamson 1990), while another study of Japanese vets found only 44 percent willing to do so (Kogure and Yamazaki 1990).

40. Antelyes 1990; Hart, Hart, and Mader 1990; Soares 1990, 1991.
41. Harris 1984:272, Fogle 1981.
42. Shelp 1989.
43. Harris 1983:375.
44. I found the terms veterinarians used to refer to euthanasia to be of interest. When talking among themselves or making notations on records, the vets and their support staff employed the term "euth" as both a noun ("I have a euth in room 4") and as a verb ("I had to euth three dogs today"). However, when discussing the procedure with clients the doctors typically used the less harsh euphemistic terms "put down" or "put to sleep." When I asked one vet how she referred to euthanasia when talking with clients, she replied:

> I use "put to sleep." I don't think I ever use "euthanasia" with a client. If we are just doing it in the back we call it "euth," but with a client euthanasia just sounds too clinical, like you are hiding behind a white coat.

There was, however, some ambivalence among the doctors and staff around referring to being killed as being "put to sleep" since they recognized that the reference could be misunderstood by children and even some adult clients:

> I think it is a bad thing for young kids to see things like that. [The staff member with whom I was talking had been caring for a child while the family dog was euthanized.] When we came back [to the examination room] the first thing he said was, "Where's Salty?" I just told him that Salty had "gone away." I try not to use the term "put to sleep." I only use it out of habit. If you use it with little kids they wonder when the animal is going to wake up. If they get a sense of it they never will want to get back in their crib again.

See Fudin and Cohen 1988.
45. See Garcia 1991:126, DeGroot 1984:284–285.
46. Shelp 1989:192.
47. At the hospital in which I did fieldwork, there were three dispositional alternatives available to clients. Owners could choose to take their animal's lifeless body with them to be buried at their home or, more rarely, interred in a pet cemetery. (Forty-eight percent of dog owners surveyed by Sinrod [1993:52] said they gave their dogs funerals when they died, and 23 percent placed headstones over the graves.) Alternatively, the client could leave the animal's body at the clinic where it would be cremated and the ashes picked up and disposed of by a mysterious person routinely referred to as "Dead Dog Dave." These latter ex-patients were listed in the cremation records (the "burn book") as "ATWs" ("all the way"). More commonly, owners would have the body cremated and later pick up the ashes, contained in either a cardboard box or in a handmade pottery urn. Animals to be dealt with in this way were listed in the burn book as "saves."
48. See Coombs and Powers 1977:60, Sudnow 1967:36.
49. I encountered another (somewhat macabre) example of euthanasia humor posted one day on the staff bulletin board. Illustrated with crude drawings, the

single sheet offered instructions for the use of a "small rodent euthanasia device." This "device" consisted of two wooden blocks and the directions were:

1) Light joint; inhale once; exhale into bag.

2) Place rodent into bag for 30 seconds.

3) Play enclosed cassette tape.

4) Place subdued rodent on block A; as shown in figure A.

5) Tape rodent to block A; as shown in figure B.

6) Hold block B only as shown in figure C.

WARNING: DO NOT HOLD WITH FINGERS IN THE WAY OR SEVERE DAMAGE MAY RESULT!

7) Raise block B above block A; smash block B into block A.

WARNING: PROTECTIVE EYEWEAR MUST BE WORN FOR STEP 7

8) If euthanasia has not been achieved, repeat step 7.

WARNING: WE DO NOT RECOMMEND USE OF THIS DEVICE FOR WITNESS EUTHANASIA

50. It appears that, like the owners, other companion animals in the home grieve the passing of the nonhuman member of the household. A survey of 165 pet owners conducted by the American Society for the Prevention of Cruelty to Animals revealed that 46 percent of cats and 36 percent of dogs ate less than usual and over half were noticeably more affectionate to owners after the death of a same-species pet (*U.S. News and World Report*, May 13, 1996, p. 17).

51. Arluke 1991, Rollin 1988.

52. Hochschild 1979; see also Tolich 1993.

53. See Obenski 1988; Herzog, Vore, and New 1989; Fogle and Abrahamson 1990.

54. Eddy, Gallup, and Povenelli 1993; Rasmussen, Rajecki, and Craft 1993.

55. Cigman 1980:60, Frey 1980.

56. Shapiro (1989:187) captures this perspective in writing about his relationship with his dog Sabaka:

History informs the experience of a particular animal whether or not it can tell that history. Events in the life of an animal shape and even constitute him or her. . . . [Shared] events inform Sabaka's behavior, his personality, and partly constitute his individuality. Sabaka is an individual in that he is not constituted through and I do not live toward him as a species-specific behavioral repertoire or developmental sequence. More positively, he is an individual in that he is both subject to and subject of "true historical particulars." . . . I can not replace him, nor, ethically, can I "sacrifice" him for he is a unique individual being.

Chapter 5: The Guide Dog Trainer: Understanding and Teaching Dogs

1. A directory prepared by Rosemary Mathias (1997) of the University of South Florida for Project Action lists fourteen guide dog training programs.

Christy Hill's assistance dog directory (http://homepage.midusa.net/~kshaw/dogs/dirs.html#service) lists nineteen such programs in the United States.

2. See Hill and Jacobson 1985:61, Deshen and Deshen 1989:95–97. Given the popular image of the guide dog as *the* answer to a blind person's problems with mobility and the general increase of interest in the use of service dogs (in no small measure due to the efforts of the Delta Society of Renton, Washington), it is likely that the prevalence of guide dog use has increased somewhat during the 1990s. Despite the continued rarity of guide dog use, there is a significant body of general interest literature on the phenomenon (e.g., Emert 1985, Ireson 1991, Putnam 1979, Tucker 1984) and some "serious" discussions largely directed toward members of the helping professions (e.g., Lambert 1990; Orcutt 1980; Robson 1985; Valentine, Kiddoo, and LaFleur 1993; Warnath and Seyfarth 1982). Deshen and Deshen's (1989) discussion of the use of guide dogs in Israel is, to my knowledge, the only other ostensibly sociological discussion of this issue (but see Hart, Hart, and Bergin 1987; Eddy, Hart, and Boltz 1988).

3. For descriptions of this approach see Gibbs 1982, Kuusisto 1998:159–174, and Tucker 1984.

4. See Kuusisto 1998:167.

5. Wieder 1980.

6. For an overtly sociological discussion of training as social interaction see Crist and Lynch 1990.

7. This distinction is a common one in dog training circles. See Lenehan 1986, Hearne 1987:64.

8. All the trainers were aware of the significant stress the training process and the responsibilities of working as a guide generated for the dog. One way to think of this stress is to see many of the stresses of daily life experienced by the visually disabled as being placed on the shoulders of their assistance dog. One owner is very clear about this when he writes:

> One of the big things that assistance animals do for people with disabilities is that they take away some of the stress of daily living. . . . When you spend a lot of time trying to figure out how to get from point A to point B . . . you never have time to understand who you are and where you're going. . . . So, these animals serve many, many functions and allow . . . us to get in touch with who we really are. (Moran 1992:9)

9. See, for example, Lenehan 1986:93.

10. Goffman 1959.

11. Phillips 1994.

12. Arluke 1988.

13. See Lenehan 1986.

14. Arluke 1990.

15. See Thompson 1983, Lesy 1989:71–87.

16. See Arluke 1991, 1994.

17. See Broom 1989.

18. See Sykes and Matza 1957. In their recent study of the experience of veterinary students involved in "dog lab," Arluke and Hafferty (1996) discuss how the

students go beyond neutralization techniques (which largely center around one's acknowledgment of violations while presenting a reasonable justification for them) to "absolution." They not only find effective means of "rationalizing" their actions, but also find ways of defining these actions as nonviolative or, ideally, noble.

19. See Merton 1976:3–89 and Weigert 1991 for sociological discussions of ambivalence and its relationship to occupational experience.

Chapter 6: Animal Abilities and Human-Animal Interaction

1. See Hills' (1989) study of the person-thing distinction in people's orientation toward animals.

2. See Francione 1995 and Animal Welfare Institute 1990 for extended discussions of these matters. In a recent Florida divorce case in which the parties were contesting custody of their pet rottweiler, the judge awarded the dog to the husband and ruled that because the animal was legally an item of personal property, the wife was not allowed the visitation rights she requested (*The Hartford Courant*, January 26, 1995, p. A2). However, in another recent case a New York judge ruled that the plaintiff's dog was "somewhere between a person and personal property" and that he was eligible to receive more than the "fair market value" from the owners of the veterinary clinic in which the dog had died as the result of surgery (*Erwin v. The Animal Medical Center, New York Law Journal*, 8-29-96).

3. Tuan 1984.

4. See Barbara Noske's (1997) discussion of the ambivalence hunters feel about killing animals and the ritual practices employed to deal with this ambivalence.

5. See also Kete 1994 and Perin 1981 for similar explanations. Burt (1988) gives a psychoanalytic spin to the issue. She maintains (after Carl Jung) that our ambivalence toward animals derives from our unconscious fear of our own animal natures.

6. Williams 1997:60.

7. Descartes 1976:61–62.

8. For a general discussion of the Cartesian position see Walker 1985:1–38.

9. Quoted in Walker 1985:4.

10. In turn, Descartes was hardly charitable in pursuing the argument about the nature of animal thought and ability. In *Discourse on Method* he observed:

> Next to the error of those who deny God . . . there is none which is more effectual in leading feeble spirits from the straight path of virtue, than to imagine that the soul of the brute is of the same nature as our own, and that in consequence, after this life we have nothing to fear or to hope for, any more than the flies and ants. (Quoted in Regan and Singer 1976:62–63)

11. Darwin 1981 [1871], 1965 [1872].

12. See Allen and Bekoff 1997:25–26.

13. M. N. Branch quoted in Griffin 1984:22.

14. Hearne 1987.

15. Rollin (1990:106) emphasizes the narrowness of the behaviorist perspective and criticizes it for ignoring questions of morality that should be inherent in the exploration of animal abilities and actions.

16. Wieder 1980.

17. Wieder (1980) is rather charitable in his description of behavioristic operationalism and presents it as a kind of scientific agnosticism premised on a desire to achieve methodological rigor. The descriptions generated reflect a "neutrality toward subjectivity" that turns away from an analytic description which distinguishes between an automaton and an active subject (p. 100).

18. See Allen and Bekoff's (1997:25–29, 55–69) recent critique of behaviorist approaches to ethology.

19. Strum 1987:153–156.

20. Krebs 1978:23.

21. Wieder 1980:77.

22. Clark 1984:14.

23. Griffin 1984:18–24, 42.

24. See Bunge 1980. The label "purposive behaviorism" was coined by psychologist Edward C. Tolman. His advocacy of attending to subjective experience led ethologist Otto Koehler to refer to him derogatorily as a "cryptophenomenologist" (Griffin 1984:19, 42).

25. Present-day "neobehaviorists" adhere to behaviorist theory and method, but are willing to speculate about unobservable internal processes as "intervening variables" (Allen and Bekoff 1997:28).

26. See, for example, Mead 1964.

27. See Mead 1907.

28. Mead 1964:128, 154–155. See also Cook 1993:60–61, 81–82.

29. The early sociologist Charles Horton Cooley did present the possibility of rudimentary mind in the absence of speech. In typically elegant prose he observed:

> A word is a vehicle, a boat floating down from the past, laden with the thought of men we never saw. . . . [Words] are powerful makers of what they stand for. A mind without words would make only such feeble and uncertain progress as a traveller set down in the midst of a wilderness where there were no paths or conveyances and without even a compass. (Cooley 1962:69)

Mead, in contrast, did not acknowledge "wordless thought" (Terrace 1987):

> The animal does not think. . . . In order that thought may exist there must be symbols, vocal gestures generally, which arouse in the individual himself the response which he is calling out in the other, and such that from the point of view of that response he is able to direct his later conduct. (Mead 1962:73)

30. Miller 1973:31.

31. Mead 1964:158–159.

32. Mead 1964:180–181.

33. For related discussions of these issues, see Meddin 1979:104–105, Langer 1964, Becker 1981:94, Kaye 1982:127–138, Clark 1984:44–53.

34. Mead 1964:168; cf. Ingold 1988b:94–97.

35. Mead 1962:182–183. See Cook 1993:168. Alger and Alger (1997) offer an excellent critique of the Meadian perspective in their discussion of interactions between house cats and their owners.

36. Cathcart and Gumpert 1986, Turkle 1984. See also Wolfe 1993:55–81.

37. Cohen 1989. For a discussion of animals as consumer products, see Sanders and Hirschman 1996.

38. Noske 1989:82–83.

39. Writers interested in exploring the relationships between people and non-human animals increasingly are expressing concern over the ethical implications of this commonsensical scientific discounting of animal experience. Animals are excluded from the legal standing upon which individual rights are premised. Lacking a self to which to refer, they are unable to refer to their grievances (e.g., Shapiro 1989). This discounting of rights and experience due to the animal's presumed lack of a self and inability to speak is most poignantly encountered in scientistic notions of animal pain (or the absence thereof). A veterinarian recalls:

> I was taught by scientist mentors that nonhuman animal pain was an oxymoron, because pain is a subjective response which requires words to communicate its existence from the sufferer to the observer. I was taught, in other words, that only humans can be properly said truly to experience pain, because only humans have the capacity to translate the feeling into words such as "that hurts;" *ergo* as nonhuman animals can't speak, what they experience can't be called pain. (Feldmann 1990:133)

See also Rollin 1990:107–205.

40. Tinbergen 1972.

41. Lorenz 1971.

42. See Rollin 1990:209–221 and Allen and Bekoff 1997:29–31 for overviews.

43. To his credit, Lorenz was somewhat ambivalent in dismissing the view of animals as engaged in subjectively meaningful, purposive activities. One of his most insightful and accessible works—*Man Meets Dog* (1988)—was largely based on his experiences with his own companion animals. In this popular work he presents dogs and cats as lying, understanding, being faithful, displaying evidence of possessing a conscience, and otherwise behaving as intentional, individual, and insightful social actors. The difficulty of maintaining a skeptical behaviorist stance in the face of regular and intimate interactions with animals is a common theme in ethological writings (e.g., Strum 1987, Cheney and Seyfarth 1990).

44. Griffin 1984, 1985, 1991, 1992.

45. See Dawkins 1993, Ristau 1991.

46. Griffin 1984:37, emphasis in original.

47. Griffin 1991:5–6. Griffin's pioneering work has generated considerable criticism both from positivists who reject or are skeptical about the mental abilities of animals and those analysts who are generally sympathetic to a cognitive ethological perspective (see Allen and Bekoff 1997:32–37, 49–62). Those sympathetic to Griffin are concerned primarily with his failure to provide a rigorous theory that

connects animal consciousness to behavior and his reliance on a relatively unsystematic collection of "examples of clever behavior by animals" (Allen and Bekoff 1997:144; see also Jamieson and Bekoff 1993).

48. In his discussion of the subjective life of human infants, the psychologist Kenneth Kaye (1982) presents three different ways in which one may conceive of the relationship between physical expression and emotion. The facial gesture or other manifestation may be an "accurate index" of what the actor is feeling. Conversely, the behavior might be *assumed* by the observer to be an expression of the inner state of the other—an "interpreted index." Finally, the physical actions might be an expression of what the actor *wants* the observing other to believe that he/she/it is feeling.

49. See Allen and Bekoff 1997:115–123, Cheney and Seyfarth 1990:139–203.

50. For example, see Dunayer 1990 and many of the selections in Rockwell 1988 for tales of animal altruism.

51. To provide yet another example, one of the owners I interviewed spoke of her dog's ability to read and respond to both her and her husband's emotions:

> Ricki was always attuned to our feelings. He would try to get between us and get involved when we were affectionate, and he was always upset when we would fight. When we would start arguing he would whimper and crawl under the bed. It got so that we would have to go out for a walk if we wanted to have an argument. He was a good indicator of feelings. You couldn't deny using "that tone" because you could always tell by looking at the way he was acting.

52. Patterson 1978, Patterson and Linden 1981.

53. Goodall 1986:118.

54. See Clark 1990, Allen and Bekoff 1997:63–85.

55. Searle 1983:5.

56. Sinrod 1993:91.

57. Rasmussen and Rajecki 1995. See also Eddy, Gallup, and Povenelli 1993.

58. Whitney 1971.

59. See Clark 1987, Milani 1986, Caras 1992. For extended discussions of the emotional lives of nonhuman animals generally and dogs in particular see Masson and McCarthy 1995 and Masson 1997. An interesting example of the emotional expression of companion canines is the dog's "smile." Michael Fox (1987:138) observes that it is likely that this facial expression is an authentic demonstration of the dog's pleasure and that it most likely has been learned by canines in the course of interacting with humans.

60. See Walker 1985; Griffin 1984, 1992; Ristau 1991; Jamieson and Bekoff 1993; Bekoff 1995.

61. Cheney and Seyfarth 1990:9. Those interested in getting a taste of the lively philosophical debate regarding animal mind should see Dawkins 1993, Dupre 1990, Midgley 1983, Stebbins 1993, Sorabji 1993 and any issue of the journal *Between the Species*. Stephen Walker's *Animal Thought* (1989) provides an excellent overview of these matters from a psychological perspective.

62. Griffin 1976:9.

63. Ingold (1988b) observes that Griffin's proposition of thought preceding action presents a criterion for the conscious awareness of animals that is not required when considering human consciousness. Many human actions are not premised on "prior intent" (Searle 1984:65) but are spontaneous. Further, one of the key goals of human learning is to be able to engage in certain actions without thinking.

64. Strum 1987:133.

65. See Midgley 1988, Maggitti 1990, Walker 1983:386–388, Noske 1989: 128–132.

66. Lindesmith, Strauss, and Denzin 1977:94–99; Becker 1981.

67. Pepperberg 1991a, 1991b.

68. Pryor 1975.

69. See also Bateson 1974.

70. Patterson 1978:446–447.

71. Hayes 1951.

72. See Cheney and Seyfarth 1990:243–244 for a discussion of pretend play by primates.

73. For recent survey evidence of dog owners' perceptions of canine mental abilities see Fidler, Light, and Costall 1996.

74. Lerman 1996:112–113.

75. Lewis Henry Morgan (1868), a major figure in late nineteenth century anthropology, studied the interactions and engineering activities of beavers. Having developed considerable respect for beavers, he preferred to refer to them as "mute."

76. Clark 1984:14.

77. See Bright 1984, Evans 1987:31–47 for overviews.

78. Griffin 1984:154–164. For a critical evaluation of Griffin's claim see Allen and Hauser 1993.

79. Mead 1964:130–131; see also Langer 1951:95–96. Griffin (1985:615) refers to this view that verbal signals are reflexive expressions of animal arousal which are not socially directed as the "groans of pain" (GOP) concept of animal communication.

80. Cheney and Seyfarth 1990:98–174; Marler, Karakashian, and Guger 1991.

81. Strum 1987:262–274.

82. Griffin 1984:162–164.

83. Langer 1951:61–63; see also Kaye 1982:131–139.

84. Langer 1951:37.

85. Mead 1962:71–75. See also Lindesmith, Strauss, and Denzin 1977:117–121; Schutz 1967:118–126; Cohen 1989:201–210; Becker 1981.

86. Chomsky 1980; cf. Hummer 1985, Noske 1989:129–150.

87. See Haraway 1986.

88. Kellogg 1969.

89. Hayes 1951, Hayes and Hayes 1951.

90. Premack 1976.

91. Savage-Rumbaugh, Rumbaugh, and Boysen 1978.

92. For discussions of the primate language studies see Meddin 1979, Walker

1985:254–381, Griffin 1984:196–202, Evans 1987:202–208, Linden 1986, Gardner and Gardner 1969, Terrace 1979, Patterson 1978, Patterson and Linden 1981. For critiques of this work see Sebeok and Umiker-Sebeok 1980, Aitchison 1983: 32–58, Wallman 1992, Zuckerman 1991.

93. Fouts 1974.

94. Patterson 1978.

95. Golden 1991.

96. Jenkins 1976:90.

97. Premack and Premack 1972; see also Golden 1991, Patterson and Linden 1981:111–118.

98. Fouts 1974:479.

99. Patterson 1978:462.

100. Patterson 1978:456, Patterson and Linden 1981:146–151. Kanzi, the chimpanzee working with Sue Savage-Rumbaugh at the Yerkes Center, produced 2,805 multi-word sequences in the course of seventeen months. Only 10 percent of these lexigrams were initiated by his human co-interactants; the rest were innovative constructions (Evans 1987:206).

101. Patterson 1978:438–440; see also Patterson and Linden 1981:71–82.

102. Patterson and Linden 1981:81.

103. See Miles 1986.

104. Patterson 1978:459–462.

105. Cassirer 1944:53–55.

106. Mead 1964:180–182; Miller 1973:128–132; Lindesmith, Strauss, and Denzin 1977:67.

107. Patterson and Linden 1981:196–202, Meddin 1979:102–103, Aitchison 1983:46–52, Noske 1989:133–135.

108. Walker 1985:364–370. Menzel's research with chimpanzees who were not language trained is also relevant. He would release one of a group of chimps into an enclosure and show him or her a toy, some food, or a dangerous object. When returned to the company of the others, the "leader" chimp was able to communicate information about the relative location of the object and whether it should be sought or avoided (Menzel 1978).

109. Patterson 1978:465.

110. Fouts, Fouts, and Van Cantfort 1989.

111. Desmond 1979:30–31.

112. Patterson 1978:453, Patterson and Linden 1981:137–138.

113. Jolly 1991:237; cf. Lindesmith, Strauss, and Denzin 1977:146–154.

114. Patterson 1978:465. In perhaps what is the ultimate observation of solitary, self-directed behavior by a language-trained primate, the home-raised chimpanzee Lucy was seen masturbating with the aid of a vacuum cleaner hose while leafing through a copy of *National Geographic* (Temerlin 1975:105–108).

115. See Sebeok and Umiker-Sebeok 1980, Sebeok 1981:109–265.

116. Pfungst 1965 [1911].

117. See Griffin 1984:198–202, Meddin 1979, Walker 1983:372–381, Wilder 1990. See Stebbins 1990 for a critique of the "Clever Hans" perspective.

118. Crist and Lynch 1990, Shapiro 1990:187, Rollin 1990:147.

119. Barber 1993:4–8; Pepperberg 1991a, 1991b.
120. Masson and McCarthy 1995:229.
121. Goffman 1963:14.
122. See Coren 1994:91–115.
123. Coren 1994:93–98.
124. Griffin 1984:8–9.
125. See Dewey 1958:43–46, Hatterer 1965.
126. Rollin 1990:142.
127. Shapiro 1990.
128. Shapiro 1990:189.
129. Lehrman 1996:107.
130. See Cheney and Seyfarth 1990:15–18.
131. See Cheney and Seyfarth 1990, Strum 1987, Fossey 1983, Jolly 1991, Smith 1991.
132. My own observations provide a telling illustration of the dog's situated ability to discriminate among objects and select those that have preferred characteristics:

> Shadow demonstrates a compulsive attachment to sticks and has a clear preference for those with specific features. I have noticed that there is a difference between the "trail" sticks she prefers to chase and carry on a walk and the "water" sticks she likes to swim after. The best trail sticks are large and slightly rotted. She loves to carry these off into the woods, lie down, and with clear relish tear them to pieces. Good water sticks, on the other hand, are around two feet long, smaller in diameter, and solid. An incident on the walk today made her preferences clear. On the way to the reservoir I could only find a large rotted stick. I threw this into the water and she swam after it. While she was occupied I searched around and found another, more suitable, piece of pine branch. After she retrieved the "bad" stick I threw both out into the water curious about how she would respond. She swam first to the original rotted stick, grabbed hold of it, and then, seeing the "good" stick a few feet away, spit out the rotted one and brought back the other. I saw this as a pretty clear indication that she has certain preferences, makes discriminations among objects (good versus bad), and that her preferences vary with the situation. Not a bad display of mindedness.

133. Mead 1962:144–152, 200–209; Blumer 1966:80–82; Hewitt 1976:50–56; Cooley 1962:8–12; Humphrey 1986.
134. The work with primates taught to use sign language and other modes of symbolization is least controversial from the standpoint of conventional sociology (see Meddin 1979). While these studies call into question the presumed qualitative barrier between animals and humans, they do not threaten the sociological emphasis upon symbolization as the foundation of the self concept. The language-trained apes consistently refer to themselves and express some recognition of and ability to name their internal states; recall Koko's proud self-reference "Fine animal gorilla." When asked to sort a group of photos into those which showed animals and

those that showed people, Viki Hayes, the home-raised chimpanzee, placed a picture of the family dog in the animal pile but put her own photograph on the human pile (Rowan 1988:5).

Gordon Gallup's research relates directly to the issue of primate self-recognition. He presented mirrors to captive apes and determined that chimpanzees and orangutans (though, interestingly, not gorillas or monkeys) recognized their own reflections. When initially shown the mirror the chimps responded to the image with threatening gestures and other social behaviors indicating that they thought the image was another chimp. Eventually, however, they began to respond to the reflection as representations of themselves, using the image to look inside their mouths, as a grooming aid, and to try out various postures. Gallup later anesthetized some chimps and daubed their faces with paint. When awakened the animals used their mirror images to help clean off the spots (Gallup 1982). For a discussion of the relevance of primate recognition of mirrored images to self-recognition see Cheney and Seyfarth 1990:242–243.

135. Haynes and Haynes 1966. In her typically direct manner, Vickie Hearne acidly observes that university students are routinely cautioned by zoology professors and other academics not to draw the logical conclusions from examples of animal self-concealment:

> Students had . . . to be cured of . . . the habit of supposing that one animal might hide from another animal. (I have never known a hunter to be successfully cured of this habit of mind.) I was deeply intrigued by this, for what in the world was the puppy doing under the bed when you returned home to find an unwelcome monument on the broadloom, if not hiding? But it was sternly pointed out to me what a great and anthropomorphic mistake it was to say or think this. In order to be hiding, whether from predators or from the vexed owner of the carpet, a creature would have to have certain logical concepts that animals simply couldn't have. . . . In order to hide . . . one had to have a concept of self. Not only that, one had to have the concept of self given by the ability to speak academic language, or at least a standard human language—a concept of self that depends on the ability to think. (Hearne 1987:7)

136. Griffin 1984:72.

137. See Allen and Bekoff 1997:156–158.

138. Clark 1984:47.

139. See Cheney and Seyfarth 1990:58–97, Strum 1987, Tanner 1981:83–107.

140. Crist and Lynch 1990; see Koehler 1962, Hearne 1983:24–32.

141. See Masson and McCarthy 1995:190–191.

142. See Kando 1977:220–231. See Coren 1994:189–207 for a specific discussion of personality differences among dogs and Barber 1993:93–97 for a discussion of the personalities of individual birds.

143. Wieder 1980:96–97.

144. Strum 1987:156.

145. van den Berghe 1974:781.

146. Clark 1984:24. See also Barbara Noske's (1997) discussion of these matters within an anthropological framework.

147. Burghart 1991.

148. Schutz 1967:100.

149. Goffman 1959.

150. Dawkins 1987.

151. Shapiro 1990:189–190; see also Wieder 1980:96–97.

152. Schutz 1962:315.

153. See Dunbar 1979:61–96, Morris 1986.

154. George 1985:69; cf. McTear 1985:5–6, 61; Griffin 1984:176–185.

155. Duncan and Fisk 1977:80–88, Kendon 1977:13–51.

156. McTear 1985:60, Brazelton 1984:25–26, Kaye 1982:147.

157. Serpell 1983b:62.

158. Walker 1985:370–371. Nonhuman primates are especially adept at reading gaze, at seeing what the other sees. When Menzel (1978) showed a single chimpanzee where food items were hidden, the knowledgeable chimp was adept at using direction of gaze to communicate to others where the caches could be located.

159. Also from my field notes on the topic of gaze is this excerpt:

> I have noticed that the dogs use where they look to inform me about their desires and what they expect of me. For example, they have learned that soon after I use the blow drier I will be leaving the house. Just before leaving I give them each a handful of popcorn, a favorite treat that I take from a jar on the kitchen counter. When they hear the hair drier they position themselves near the counter, eyes wide and ears up with happy expectation. As I come out of the bedroom they gaze longingly at the popcorn container and then glance at me. They continue this until they receive their treats. The communicative meaning of these actions is quite clear. The dogs know the location of what they want, they expect that I can and will provide them with what they want, and they attempt to affect my behavior through their own actions. In this and many similar ways they demonstrate their ability to involve themselves in mutually meaningful social exchanges.

For a general discussion of gaze as an element of social interaction see Kendon 1990:51–89. In a recent study Deborah Goodwin and John Bradshaw (1997) observed gaze in human-cat interactions. They emphasize the significance of people's staring as affecting cat behavior. Cats apparently interpret being stared at as threatening and tend to respond by avoiding the looker. When people looked at cats and then looked away, on the other hand, the cats typically returned the looks and approached the people who had glanced at them.

160. Denzin 1977:143, Musolf 1996:306–308. For a general discussion of the significance of play in human interactions see Millar 1969.

161. Thorne 1993:64–88.

162. Simonds 1974:198–200; Strum 1987:46–47, 272–274; Lorenz 1988:154–160; Cheney and Seyfarth 1990:244.

163. Bekoff 1993:28–30, Clark 1984:30–31, Allen and Bekoff 1997:98–112.

164. Smith 1983:31–33.

165. See Mitchell and Thompson 1986, 1990; Allen and Bekoff 1997:107.

166. Allen and Bekoff 1997:109.

167. Shapiro 1990:186. Mead (1962:48–51) would, of course, disagree with Shapiro's analysis of this exchange since, from his perspective, the dog is "mindless" and is therefore incapable of imagining actions in such a way that he can call up in his own mind the anticipations of the other player which are at the heart of the playful interaction.

168. Mitchell and Edmunson 1997.

169. For discussions of the central importance of empathy as an approach to understanding the mental experience of animals, see Jamieson and Bekoff 1993: 114 and Bekoff 1998. Armstrong (1997) offers an interesting description of empathy as a source for James Audubon's presentations of bird behavior.

170. Coren 1994:75.

171. Dawkins 1993:178.

172. Thomas (1993) is a notable example of this offense.

173. See Meijsing 1997 and Bekoff's (1998:12–13) discussion of the heuristic utility of anthropomorphism.

174. Clarke 1990, Vorstenbosch 1997.

175. Fisher 1991:60.

176. See Wemelsfelder 1997.

177. Allen and Bekoff (1997:53), in making this basic point, advocate an understanding of animal mental abilities based on "inference to the best explanation," that is, "the selection of the most plausible hypothesis among competing alternatives for the explanation of observable phenomena." See also Costall's (1998) related discussion of Lloyd Morgan and his celebrated "canon."

References

Adell-Bath, M., A. Krook, G. Sanqvist, and K. Skantze. 1979. *Do We Need Dogs? A Study of Dogs' Social Significance to Man*. Gothenburg: University of Gothenburg Press.

Aitchison, Jean. 1983. *The Articulate Mammal: An Introduction to Psycholinguistics* (2nd ed.). New York: Universe.

Akrow, Phillip. 1993. "New Statistics Challenge Previously Held Beliefs about Euthanasia." *The Latham Letter* 14(2): 1, 10–11.

Akrow, Phillip. 1997. "The Relationship between Animal Abuse and Other Forms of Family Violence." *The Latham Letter* 18(1): 1, 6–11, 14.

Akrow, Phillip, and Shelby Dow. 1984. "The Ties That Do Not Bind: A Study of the Human-Animal Bonds That Fail," pp. 348–354 in Anderson, Hart, and Hart (eds.), *The Pet Connection*.

Alger, Janet, and Steven Alger. 1997. "Beyond Mead: Symbolic Interaction between Humans and Felines." *Society and Animals* 5 (1): 65–81.

Allen, Colin, and Marc Bekoff. 1997. *Species of Mind*. Cambridge: MIT Press.

Allen, Colin, and M. Hauser. 1993. "Communication and Cognition: Is Information the Connection?" *Philosophy of Science* 1992: 81–91.

American Veterinary Medical Association. 1988. *The Veterinary Services Market for Companion Animals*. Prepared by Charles, Charles Research Group, Overland Park, Kansas.

Anderson, Robert, Benjamin Hart, and Lynette Hart (eds.). 1984. *The Pet Connection*. Minneapolis: University of Minnesota Center to Study Human-Animal Relationships and Environments.

Angell, M. 1988. "Euthanasia." *New England Journal of Medicine* 319: 1348–1350.

Animal Welfare Institute. 1990. *Animals and Their Legal Rights*. Washington, D.C.

Antelyes, Jacob. 1990. "Client Relations when the Animal Dominates." *Journal of the American Veterinary Medical Association* 196(4): 578–580.

Arluke, Arnold. 1988. "Sacrificial Symbolism in Animal Experimentation: Object or Pet?" *Anthrozoös* 2(2): 98–117.

Arluke, Arnold. 1990. "Uneasiness Among Laboratory Technicians." *Lab Animal* 19(4): 20–39.

Arluke, Arnold. 1991. "Coping with Euthanasia: A Case Study of Shelter Culture." *Journal of the American Veterinary Medical Association* 198(7): 1176–1180.

Arluke, Arnold. 1994. "Managing Emotions in an Animal Shelter," pp. 145–165 in A. Manning and J. Serpell (eds.), *Animals and Human Society.*

Arluke, Arnold, and Frederic Hafferty. 1996. "From Apprehension to Fascination with 'Dog Lab': The Use of Absolutions by Medical Students." *Journal of Contemporary Ethnography* 25(2): 201–225.

Arluke, Arnold, and Clinton Sanders. 1996. *Regarding Animals.* Philadelphia: Temple University Press.

Armstrong, James. 1997. "Audubon's Ornithological Biography and the Question of 'Other Minds,'" pp. 103–126 in Jennifer Hamm and Matthew Senior (eds.), *Animal Acts.* New York: Routledge.

Barber, Theodore. 1993. *The Human Nature of Birds.* New York: Penguin.

Bateson, Gregory. 1974. "Observations of a Cetacean Community," pp. 146–168 in Joan McIntyre (ed.), *Mind in the Waters.* New York: Scribner's Sons.

Bateson, P. P. G., and Peter Klopfer (eds.), *Perspectives in Ethology (Vol. 9): Human Understanding and Animal Awareness.* New York: Plenum.

Baun, Mara, Nancy Bergstrom, Nancy Langston, and Linda Thoma. 1984. "Physiological Effects of Petting Dogs: Influences of Attachment," pp. 162–170 in Anderson, Hart, and Hart (eds.), *The Pet Connection.*

Beck, Alan. 1983. "Animals in the City, pp. 237–243 in Katcher and Beck (eds.), *New Perspectives on Our Lives with Companion Animals.* Philadelphia: University of Pennsylvania Press.

Beck, Alan, and Aaron Katcher. 1983. *Between Pets and People.* New York: Putnam's.

Becker, Ernest. 1981. "From Animal to Human Reactivity," pp. 91–95 in Gregory Stone and Harvey Farberman (eds.), *Social Psychology Through Symbolic Interaction* (2nd ed.). New York: Wiley.

Becker, Howard. 1974. "Art as Collective Action." *American Sociological Review* 39(6): 767–776.

Becker, Howard, and Blanche Geer. 1957. "Participant Observation and Interviewing: A Comparison." *Human Organization* 16(3): 28–32.

Becker, Howard, Blanch Geer, Everett Hughes, and Anselm Strauss. 1961. *Boys in White: Student Culture in Medical School.* Chicago: University of Chicago Press.

Bekoff, Marc. 1993. "Cognitive Ethology and the Empirical Analysis of Nonhuman Social Behavior." *Etologica* 3:23–39.

Bekoff, Marc. 1995. "Play Signals as Punctuation: The Structure of Social Play in Canids." *Behavior* 132:419–429.

Bekoff, Marc. 1998. "Deep Ecology." *The AV Magazine* (Winter), pp. 10–19.

Bekoff, Marc, and Lori Gruen. 1993. "Animal Welfare and Individual Characteristics: A Conversation Against Speciesism." *Ethics and Behavior* 3(2): 163–180.

Bekoff, Marc, and Dale Jamieson (eds.). 1990. *Interpretation and Explanation in the Study of Animal Behavior* (Vol. 1). Boulder: Westview.

Bekoff, Marc, and Carron Meaney. 1997. "Interactions Among Dogs, People, and the Environment in Boulder, Colorado: A Case History." *Anthrozoös* 10(1): 23–31.

Belk, Russell. 1988. "Possessions and the Extended Self." *Journal of Consumer Research* 15:139–168.

Benrubi, Guy. 1992. "Euthanasia—The Need for Procedural Safeguards." *New England Journal of Medicine* 326(3): 197–198.

Berger, John. 1980. *About Looking.* New York: Pantheon.

Bernards, Neal (ed.). 1989. *Euthanasia: Opposing Viewpoints.* San Diego: Greenhaven.

Blakemore, Colin, and Susan Greenfield (eds.). 1987. *Mindwaves: Thoughts on Intelligence, Identity, and Consciousness.* New York: Basil Blackwell.

Blum, Alan, and Peter McHugh. 1971. "The Social Ascription of Motives." *American Sociological Review* 36:98–109.

Blumer, Herbert. 1969. *Symbolic Interactionism.* Englewood Cliffs, N.J.: Prentice-Hall.

Bogdan, Robert, and Steven Taylor. 1989. "Relationships with Severely Disabled People: The Social Construction of Humanness." *Social Problems* 36(2): 135–148.

Bogdan, Robert, Steven Taylor, Bernard deGrandpre, and Sandra Haynes. 1974. "Let Them Eat Programs: Attendants' Perspectives and Programming on Wards in State Schools." *Journal of Health and Social Behavior* 15:142–151.

Borchelt, Peter. 1983. "Separation-Elicited Behavior Problems in Dogs," pp. 187–196 in Katcher and Beck (eds.), *New Perspectives on Our Lives with Companion Animals.*

Borchelt, Peter, Randall Lockwood, Alan Beck, and Victoria Voith. 1983. "Dog Attack Involving Predation on Humans," pp. 219–234 in Katcher and Beck (eds.), *New Perspectives on Our Lives with Companion Animals.*

Brazelton, T. Berry. 1984. "Four Stages in the Development of Mother-Infant Interaction," pp. 19–34 in Noboru Kobayashi and T. B. Brazelton (eds.), *The Growing Child in Family and Society.* Tokyo: University of Tokyo Press.

Brickel, Clark. 1985. "Initiation and Maintenance of the Human-Animal Bond: Familial Roles from a Learning Perspective," pp. 31–48 in Sussman (ed.), *Pets and the Family.*

Bright, Michael. 1983. *Animal Language.* London: British Broadcasting Corporation.

Broom, Donald. 1989. "Ethical Dilemmas in Animal Usage," pp. 80–86 in David Paterson and Mary Palmer (eds.), *The Status of Animals.* Oxon, U.K.: CAB International.

Bryant, B. K. 1982. "Sibling Relationships in Middle Childhood," pp. 87–122 in M. E. Lamb and B. Sutton-Smith (eds.), *Sibling Relationships: Their Nature and Significance Across the Lifespan.* Hillsdale, N.J.: Lawrence Erlbaum.

Bryant, Clifton, and William Snizek. 1976. "Practice Modes and Professional Role Playing Among Large and Small Animal Veterinarians." *Rural Sociology* 41(2): 179–193.

Budiansky, Stephen. 1992. *The Covenant of the Wild.* New York: William Morrow.

Bulcroft, Kris, George Helling, and Alexa Albert. 1986. "Pets as Intimate Others." Paper presented at the meetings of the Midwest Sociological Society, Des Moines, Iowa, March 28.

Bunge, M. 1980. *The Mind-Body Problem: A Psychological Approach*. New York: Pergamon.

Burghart, Gordon. 1991. "Cognitive Ethology and Critical Anthropomorphism: A Snake with Two Heads and Hog-Nosed Snakes that Play Dead," pp. 53–90 in Ristau (ed.), *Cognitive Ethology*.

Burt, Marianna. 1988. "The Animal as Alter Ego: Cruelty, Altruism and the Work of Art," pp. 117–136 in Rowan (ed.), *Animals and People Sharing the World*.

Bustad, Leo, and Linda Hines. 1984. "Historical Perspectives of the Human-Animal Bond," pp. 15–29 in Anderson, Hart, and Hart (eds.), *The Pet Connection*.

Cahill, Spencer. 1987. "Children and Civility: Ceremonial Deviance and the Acquisition of Ritual Competence." *Social Psychology Quarterly* 50(4): 312–321.

Cahill, Spencer, and Robin Eggleston. 1994. "Managing Emotions in Public: The Case of Wheelchair Users." *Social Psychology Quarterly* 57(4): 300–312.

Cahill, Spencer, and Robin Eggleston. 1995. "Reconsidering the Stigma of Physical Disability: Wheelchair Users and Public Kindness." *The Sociological Quarterly* 36(4): 681–698.

Cain, Ann. 1983. "A Study of Pets in the Family System," pp. 71–81 in Katcher and Beck (eds.), *New Perspectives on Our Lives with Companion Animals*.

Cain, Ann. 1985. "Pets as Family Members, pp. 5–10 in Sussman (ed.), *Pets and the Family*.

Cantanzaro, Thomas. 1992. "Why Are There Too Many Euthanasias?" *The Latham Letter* 13(4): 1ff.

Caras, Roger. 1992. *A Dog is Listening*. New York: Summit.

Cassel, C. K., and D. E. Meier. 1990. "Morals and Moralism in the Debate over Euthanasia and Assisted Suicide." *New England Journal of Medicine* 323:750–752.

Cassell, Joan. 1991. *Expected Miracles: Surgeons at Work*. Philadelphia: Temple University Press.

Cassirer, Ernst. 1944. *An Essay on Man*. New Haven: Yale University Press.

Cathcart, Robert, and Gary Gumpert. 1986. "The Person-Computer Interaction: A Unique Source," pp. 323–332 in G. Gumpert and R. Cathcart (eds.), *Inter/Media: Interpersonal Communications in a Media World*. New York: Oxford University Press.

Cheney, Dorothy, and Robert Seyfarth. 1990. *How Monkeys See the World*. Chicago: University of Chicago Press.

Chevigny, Hector. 1946. *My Eyes Have a Cold Nose*. New Haven: Yale University Press.

Chomsky, Noam. 1980. *Rules and Representations*. New York: Columbia University Press.

Cigman, Ruth. 1980. "Death, Misfortune, and Species Inequality." *Philosophy and Public Affairs* 10(1): 47–64.

Clark, Stephen. 1984. *The Nature of the Beast*. New York: Oxford.

Clark, Stephen. 1987. "The Description and Evaluation of Animal Emotion," pp. 139–149 in Blakemore and Greenfield (eds.), *Mindwaves*.

Clark, Stephen. 1990. "The Reality of Shared Emotions," pp. 449–472 in M. Bekoff and D. Jamieson (eds.), *Interpretation and Explanation in the Study of Animal Behavior* (Vol. 1).

Clutton-Brock, Juliet. 1995. "Origins of the Dog: Domestication and Early History," pp. 7–20 in James Serpell (ed.), *The Domestic Dog.*

Cohen, Joseph. 1989. "About Steaks Liking to be Eaten: The Conflicting Views of Symbolic Interactionists and Talcott Parsons Concerning the Nature of Relations between Persons and Non-Human Objects." *Symbolic Interaction* 12(2): 191–214.

Collins, Randall. 1975. *Conflict Sociology.* New York: Academic Press.

Comfort, David. 1994. *The First Pet History of the World.* New York: Simon and Schuster.

Conrad, Peter, and Rochelle Kern (eds.). 1981. *The Sociology of Health and Illness: Critical Perspectives.* New York: St. Martin's.

Cook, Gary. 1993. *George Herbert Mead: The Making of a Social Pragmatist.* Urbana: University of Illinois Press.

Cooke, David. 1988. "Animal Disposal: Fact and Fiction," pp. 224–234 in Kay et al. (eds.), *Euthanasia of the Companion Animal.*

Cooley, Charles Horton. 1962. *Social Organization.* New York: Schocken.

Cooley, Charles Horton. 1964. *Human Nature and the Social Order.* New York: Schocken.

Coombs, Robert, and Pauline Powers. 1977. "Socialization for Death: The Physician's Role," pp. 58–66 in H. Paul Chalfant, Ebans Curry, and C. Eddie Palmer (eds.), *Sociological Stuff,* Dubuque, Iowa: Kendall/Hunt.

Coren, Stanley. 1994. *The Intelligence of Dogs.* New York: The Free Press.

Costall, Alan. 1998. "Lloyd Morgan and the Rise and Fall of 'Animal Psychology.'" *Society and Animals* 6(1): 13–29.

Council for Science and Society. 1988. *Companion Animals in Society.* New York: Oxford University Press.

Covert, Anita, A. Whiren, J. Keith, and C. Nelson. 1985. "Pets, Early Adolescents, and the Family," pp. 95–108 in Sussman (ed.), *Pets and the Family.*

Crist, Eileen, and Michael Lynch. 1990. "The Analyzability of Human-Animal Interaction: The Case of Dog Training." Paper presented at the meetings of the International Sociological Association, Madrid, Spain.

Curtis, Patricia. 1981. *Cindy: A Hearing Ear Dog.* New York: Dutton.

Cusack, Odean. 1988. *Pets and Mental Health.* New York: Haworth.

Danziger, Sandra Klein. 1981. "The Uses of Expertise in Doctor-Patient Encounters During Pregnancy," pp. 359–376 in Peter Conrad and Rochelle Kern (eds.), *The Sociology of Health and Illness: Critical Perspectives.*

Darwin, Charles. 1965 [1872]. *The Expression of Emotions in Man and Animals.* Chicago: University of Chicago Press.

Darwin, Charles. 1981 [1871]. *The Descent of Man and Selection in Relation to Sex.* Princeton: Princeton University Press.

Davis, Fred. 1959. "The Cabdriver and His Fare: Facets of a Fleeting Relationship." *American Journal of Sociology* 65: 158–165.

Dawkins, Marian Stamp. 1987. "Minding and Mattering," pp. 151–160 in Blakemore and Greenfield (eds.), *Mindwaves.*

Dawkins, Marian Stamp. 1993. *Through Our Eyes Only?: The Search for Animal Consciousness.* New York: W. H. Freeman.

DeGroot, Alice. 1984. "Preparing the Veterinarian for Dealing with the Emotions of Pet Loss," pp. 283–291 in Anderson, Hart, and Hart (eds.), *The Pet Connection.*

Denzin, Norman. 1977. *Childhood Socialization.* San Francisco: Jossey-Bass.

Denzin, Norman. 1989. *Interpretive Biography.* Newbury Park, Calif.: Sage.

Derr, Mark. 1997. "Psychology: So Long to Bad Dogs." *The Atlantic Monthly* (May), pp. 41–46.

Descartes, Rene. 1976. "Animals are Machines," pp. 60–66 in Regan and Singer (eds.), *Animal Rights and Human Obligations.*

Deshen, Shlomo, and Hilda Deshen. 1989. "On Social Aspects of the Usage of Guide-Dogs and Long-Canes." *Sociological Review* 37(1): 89–103.

Desmond, Adrian. 1979. *The Ape's Reflection.* New York: Dial.

Dewey, John, 1958. *Art as Experience.* New York: Capricorn.

Dingwall, Robert, and T. Murray. 1983. "Categorization in Accident Departments." *Social Health and Illness* 5: 121–148.

Dixon, Carol. 1978. "Guided Options as a Pattern of Control in a Headstart Program," pp. 121–134 in John Lofland (ed.), *Interaction in Everyday Life.* Beverly Hills: Sage.

Dol, Marcel, Soemini Kasanmoentalib, Susanne Lijmbach, Esteban Rivas, and Ruud van den Boss (eds.). 1997. *Animal Consciousness and Animal Ethics.* Assen, The Netherlands: Van Gorcum.

Dooley, D. R. 1979. "Client Relations," pp. 121–134 in Paul Pratt (ed.), *Veterinary Practice Management.* Santa Barbara: American Veterinary Publications.

Dunayer, Joan. 1990. "The Nature of Altruism." *Animal Agenda* (April), pp. 27ff.

Dunbar, Ian. 1979. *Dog Behavior.* Neptune, N.J.: TFH Publications.

Duncan, Starkey, and Donald Fisk. 1977. *Face-to-Face Interaction.* Hillsdale, N.J.: Lawrence Erlbaum.

Dupre, John. 1990. "The Mental Lives of Nonhuman Animals," pp. 428–448 in M. Bekoff and D. Jamieson (eds.), *Interpretation and Explanation in the Study of Animal Behavior* (Vol. 1).

Durkheim, Emile. 1964. *Elementary Forms of Religious Life.* New York: Humanities Press.

Duvin, Edward. 1992. "Getting Out of the Killing Business." *The Animals' Voice Magazine* 5(3): 17–20.

Eddy, Jane, Lynette Hart, and Ronal Boltz. 1988. "The Effects of Service Dogs on Social Acknowledgements of People in Wheelchairs." *Journal of Psychology* 122(1): 39–45.

Eddy, Thomas, Gordon Gallup, and Daniel Povenelli. 1993. "Attributions of Cognitive States to Animals: Anthropomorphism in Comparative Perspective." *Journal of Social Issues* 49(1): 87–101.

Ellis, Carolyn. 1991. "Sociological Introspection and Emotional Experience." *Symbolic Interaction* 14(1): 23–50.

Emert, Phyllis. 1985. *Guide Dogs*. Mankato, Minn.: Crestwood House.

Endenburg, Nienke. 1991. *Animals as Companions*. Amsterdam: Thesis Publishers.

Evans, Peter. 1987. *Ourselves and Other Animals*. New York: Pantheon.

Feldmann, Bruce. 1983. "Why People Own Pets: Pet Owner Psychology and the Delinquent Owner," pp. 133–134 in Quigley (ed.), *Perspectives: Interrelationships of People and Animals in Society Today*.

Feldmann, Bruce. 1990. "Common Sense and Nonsense" (review of B. Rollin, *The Unheeded Cry*). *Between the Species* 6(3): 130–136.

Fidler, Margaret, Paul Light, and Alan Costall. 1996. "Describing Dog Behavior Psychologically: Pet Owners Versus Non-Owners." *Anthrozoös* 9(11): 196–200.

Fisher, John Andrew. 1991. "Disambiguating Anthropomorphism: An Interdisciplinary Review," pp. 49–85 in Bateson and Klopfer (eds.), *Perspectives in Ethology* (Vol. 9): *Human Understanding and Animal Awareness*.

Fisher, Maxine. 1983. "Of Pigs and Dogs: Pets as Produce in Three Societies," pp. 132–137 in Katcher and Beck (eds.), *New Perspectives on Our Lives with Companion Animals*.

Fogle, Bruce (ed.). 1981. *Interrelations between People and Pets*. Springfield, Ill.: Charles C. Thomas.

Fogle, Bruce. 1981. "Attachment—Euthanasia—Grieving," pp. 331–344 in Fogle (ed.), *Interrelations between People and Pets*.

Fogle, Bruce. 1985. *Pets and Their People*. New York: Pocket Books.

Fogle, Bruce. 1986. *Games Pets Play*. New York: Viking.

Fogle, Bruce, and David Abrahamson. 1990. "Pet Loss: A Survey of the Attitudes and Feelings of Practicing Veterinarians." *Anthrozoös* 3 (3): 143–150.

Fossey, Dian. 1983. *Gorillas in the Mist*. Boston: Houghton Mifflin.

Fouts, Roger. 1974. "Language: Origins, Definitions, and Chimpanzees." *Journal of Human Evolution* 3:475–482.

Fouts, Roger, D. H. Fouts, and T. E. Van Cantfort. 1989. "The Infant Loulis Learns Signs From Cross-Fostered Chimpanzees," pp. 280–292 in R. Gardner, B. Gardner, and T. Van Cantfort (eds.), *Teaching Sign Language to Chimpanzees*. Albany: State University of New York Press.

Fox, Michael. 1987. *The Dog: Its Domestication and Behavior*. Malabar, Fla.: Krieger.

Francione, Gary. 1995. *Animals, Property, and the Law*. Philadelphia: Temple University Press.

Frey, Raymond G. 1980. *Interests and Rights: The Case Against Animals*. Oxford: Clarendon Press.

Friedmann, Erika, Aaron Katcher, Muzza Eaton, and Bonnie Berger. 1984. "Pet Ownership and Psychological Status," pp. 300–308 in Anderson, Hart, and Hart (eds.), *The Pet Connection*.

Friedmann, Erika, and Sue Thomas. 1985. "Health Benefits of Pets for Families," pp. 191–204 in Sussman (ed.), *Pets and the Family*.

Friedson, Eliot. 1987. "Client Control and Medical Practice," pp. 179–191 in John Stoeckle (ed.), *Encounters between Patients and Doctors*.

Fudin, Carole, and Susan Cohen. 1988. "Helping Children and Adolescents Cope with the Euthanasia of a Pet," pp. 79–86 in Kay et al. (eds.), *Euthanasia of the Companion Animal.*

Gallup, George. 1982. "Self-Awareness and the Emergence of Mind in Primates." *American Journal of Primatology* 2:237–248.

Gans, Herbert. 1974. *Popular Culture and High Culture.* New York: Basic Books.

Garber, Marjorie. 1996. "Dog Days." *The New Yorker* (August 8), pp. 72–78.

Garcia, Eddie. 1991. "Pet Loss Considered from the Veterinary Perspective," pp. 119–132 in Latham Foundation (ed.), *Universal Kinship.*

Gardner, Carol Brooks. 1993. "Kinship Claims: Affiliation and the Disclosure of Stigma in Public Places," pp. 203–228 in James Holstein and Gale Miller (eds.), *Perspectives on Social Problems* (Vol. 4). Greenwich, Conn.: JAI Press.

Gardner, R. Allen, and Beatrice Gardner. 1969. "Teaching Sign Language to a Chimpanzee: A Standard System of Gestures Provides a Means of Two-Way Communication with a Chimpanzee." *Science* 165:664–672.

George, Jean. 1985. *How to Talk to Your Animals.* New York: Harcourt Brace Jovanovich.

Gerwolls, Marilyn, and Susan Labott. 1994. "Adjustment to the Death of a Companion Animal." *Anthrozoös* 7(3): 172–187.

Gibbs, Margaret. 1982. *Leader Dogs for the Blind.* Fairfax, Va.: Denlinger's.

Gillespie, Dair, Ann Leffler, and Elinor Lerner. 1996. "Safe in Unsafe Places: Leisure, Passionate Avocations, and the Problematizing of Everyday Public Life." *Society and Animals* 4(2): 169–188.

Ginsburg, Benson, and Laurie Hiestand. 1992. "Humanity's 'Best Friend': The Origins of Our Inevitable Bond with Dogs," pp. 93–108 in Hank Davis and Dianne Balfour (eds.), *The Inevitable Bond: Examining Scientist-Animal Interactions.* Cambridge: Cambridge University Press.

Glazer, Barney, and Anselm Strauss. 1972. "Awareness Contexts and Social Interaction," pp. 447–461 in J. Manis and B. Meltzer (eds.), *Symbolic Interaction* (2nd ed.). Boston: Allyn and Bacon.

Goffman, Erving. 1959. *The Presentation of Self in Everyday Life.* Garden City, N.Y.: Doubleday.

Goffman, Erving. 1961. *Asylums.* Garden City, New York: Doubleday.

Goffman, Erving. 1963. *Behavior in Public Places.* New York: Free Press.

Goffman, Erving. 1971. *Relations in Public.* New York: Basic Books.

Goffman, Erving. 1982. "Embarrassment and Social Organization," pp. 97–112 in E. Goffman, *Interaction Ritual.* New York: Pantheon.

Golden, Frederic. 1991. "Clever Kanzi." *Discover* (March), p. 20.

Goodall, Jane. 1986. *The Chimpanzees of Gombe.* Cambridge: Harvard University Press.

Goodwin, Deborah, and John Bradshaw. 1997. "Gaze and Mutual Gaze: It's Importance in Cat/Human and Cat/Cat Interaction." Paper presented at the meetings of the International Society for Anthrozoology, Boston, July 24–25.

Gosse, Gerald, and Michael Barnes. 1994. "Human Grief Resulting from the Death of a Pet." *Anthrozoös* 7(2): 103–112.

Gregory, Stanford, and Stephen Keto. 1991. "Creation of the 'Virtual Patient' in Medical Interaction: A Comparison of Doctor/Patient and Veterinarian/Client

Relationships." Paper presented at the meetings of the American Sociological Association, Cincinnati, August.

Griffin, Donald. 1976. *The Question of Animal Awareness*. New York: Rockefeller University Press.

Griffin, Donald. 1984. *Animal Thinking*. Cambridge: Harvard University Press.

Griffin, Donald. 1985. "Animal Consciousness." *Neuroscience and Behavioral Reviews* 9:615–622.

Griffin, Donald. 1991. "Progress Toward a Cognitive Ethology," pp. 3–18 in Ristau (ed.), *Cognitive Ethology*.

Griffin, Donald. 1992. *Animal Minds*. Chicago: University of Chicago Press.

Gubrium, Jaber, and James Holstein. 1990. *What is Family?* Mountain View, Calif.: Mayfield.

Haraway, Donna. 1986. "Primatology is Politics by Other Means," pp. 77–118 in Ruth Bleier (ed.), *Feminist Approaches to Science*. New York: Pergamon.

Harris, James. 1983. "A Study of Client Grief Responses to Death or Loss in a Companion Animal Veterinary Practice," pp. 370–376 in Katcher and Beck (eds.), *New Perspectives on Our Lives with Companion Animals*.

Harris, James. 1984. "Understanding Animal Death: Bereavement, Grief, and Euthanasia," pp. 261–275 in Anderson, Hart, and Hart (eds.), *The Pet Connection*.

Harris, Mary B. 1983. "Some Factors Influencing Selection and Naming of Pets." *Psychological Reports* 53:1163–1170.

Hart, Benjamin, and Lynette Hart. 1984. "Selecting the Best Companion Animal: Breed and Gender Specific Behavioral Profiles," pp. 180–193 in Anderson, Hart, and Hart (eds.), *The Pet Connection*.

Hart, Benjamin, Sybil Murray, Margaret Hahs, Bernadine Cruz, and Michael Miller. 1983. "Breed Specific Behavior Profiles of Dogs: Model for a Quantitative Analysis," pp. 47–56 in Katcher and Beck (eds.), *New Perspectives on Our Lives with Companion Animals*.

Hart, Lynette, Benjamin Hart, and Bonita Bergin. 1987. "Socializing Effects of Service Dogs for People with Disabilities." *Anthrozoös* 1(1): 41–44.

Hart, Lynette, Benjamin Hart, and Bonnie Mader. 1990. "Humane Euthanasia and Companion Animal Death: Caring for the Animal, the Client, and the Veterinarian." *Journal of the Veterinary Medical Association* 197(10): 1292–1299.

Hatterer, Lawrence. 1965. *The Artist in Society*. New York: Grove Press.

Hayano, David. 1979. "Auto-Ethnography: Paradigms, Problems, and Prospects." *Human Organization* 38(1): 99–104.

Hayes, Catherine H. 1951. *The Ape in Our House*. New York: Harper and Row.

Hayes, K. J., and C. Hayes. 1951. "The Intellectual Development of a Home Raised Chimpanzee." *Proceedings of the American Philosophical Society* 95:105–109.

Haynes, B. D., and E. Haynes (eds.). 1966. *The Grizzly Bear: Portraits from Life*. Norman, Okla.: University of Oklahoma Press.

Hearne, Vickie. 1987. *Adam's Task*. New York: Knopf.

Hendy, Helen. 1984. "Effects of Pets on the Sociability and Health Activities of Nursing Home Residents," pp. 430–437 in Anderson, Hart, and Hart (eds.), *The Pet Connection*.

Herzog, Harold, and Gordon Burghart. 1988. "Attitudes Toward Animals: Origins and Diversity," pp. 75–94 in Rowan (ed.), *Animals and People Sharing the World.* Hanover, N.H.: University Press of New England.

Herzog, Harold, Tamara Vore, and John New, Jr. 1989. "Conversations with Veterinary Students." *Anthrozoös* 2(3): 181–188.

Hewitt, John, 1976. *Self and Society.* Boston: Allyn Bacon.

Hewitt, John, and Peter Hall. 1973. "Social Problems, Problematic Situations, and Quasi-Theories." *American Sociological Review* 38(3): 367–374.

Hewitt, John, and Randall Stokes. 1975. "Disclaimers." *American Sociological Review* 40:1–11.

Hickrod, Lucy, and Raymond Schmitt. 1982. "A Naturalistic Study of Interaction and Frame: The Pet as 'Family Member.'" *Urban Life* 11(1): 55–77.

Hill, Everett, and William Jacobson. 1985. "Controversial Issues in Orientation and Mobility: Then and Now." *Education of the Visually Handicapped* 17(2): 59–70.

Hills, Adelma. 1989. "The Relationship between Thing-Person Orientation and the Perception of Animals." *Anthrozoös* 3(2): 100–110.

Hochschild, Arlie. 1979. "Emotion Work, Feeling Rules, and Social Structure." *American Journal of Sociology* 85:551–575.

Houpt, Katherine. 1983. "Disruption of the Human-Companion Animal Bond: Aggressive Behavior in Dogs," pp. 197–204 in Katcher and Beck (eds.), *New Perspectives on Our Lives with Companion Animals.*

Hughes, Everett C. 1971. *The Sociological Eye.* Chicago: Aldine.

Hummer, John. 1985. "Human and Animal Intelligence: A Question of Degree and Responsibility." *Between the Species* 1(2): 28–36.

Humphrey, N. K. 1986. *The Inner Eye.* London: Faber and Faber.

Ingold, Tom (ed.). 1988. *What Is An Animal?* London: Unwin Hyman.

Ingold, Tom. 1988a. "Introduction," pp. 1–16 in Ingold (ed.), *What Is An Animal?*

Ingold, Tom. 1988b. "The Animal in the Study of Humanity," pp. 84–99 in Ingold (ed.), *What Is An Animal?*

Ireson, Peter. 1991. *Another Pair of Eyes.* New York: Penguin.

Jamieson, Dale, and Marc Bekoff. 1993. "On the Aims and Methods of Cognitive Ethology." *Philosophy of Science Association* 2:110–124.

Jenkins, Peter. 1976. "Teaching Chimpanzees to Communicate," pp. 85–92 in Regan and Singer (eds.), *Animal Rights and Human Obligations.*

Jolly, Alison. 1991. "Conscious Chimpanzees? A Review of Recent Literature," pp. 231–252 in Ristau (ed.), *Cognitive Ethology.*

Kahler, Susan. 1992. "Stalking a Killer: The 'Disease' of Euthanasia." *Journal of the American Veterinary Association* 201(7): 973–975.

Kando, Thomas. 1977. *Social Interaction.* St. Louis: Mosby.

Katcher, Aaron, and Alan Beck (eds.). 1983. *New Perspectives on Our Lives with Companion Animals.* Philadelphia: University of Pennsylvania Press.

Katcher, Aaron, and Alan Beck. 1988. "Health and Caring for Living Things," pp. 53–74 in Rowan (ed.), *Animals and People Sharing the World.*

Katcher, Aaron, Erika Friedmann, Alan Beck, and James Lynch. 1983. "Looking, Talking, and Blood Pressure: The Physiological Consequences of Interaction with the Living Environment," pp. 351–362 in Katcher and Beck (eds.), *New Perspectives on Our Lives with Companion Animals.*

Katcher, Aaron, Herman Segal, and Alan Beck. 1984. "Contemplation of an Aquarium for the Reduction of Anxiety," pp. 171–178 in Anderson, Hart, and Hart (eds.), *The Pet Connection.*

Kay, William, Susan Cohen, Carole Fudin, Austin Kutscher, Herbert Nieburg, Ross Grey, and Mohamed Osman (eds.). 1988. *Euthanasia of the Companion Animal.* Philadelphia: Charles Press.

Kaye, Kenneth. 1982. *The Mental and Social Life of Babies.* Chicago: University of Chicago Press.

Kellogg, Winthrop. 1969. "Research on the Home Raised Chimpanzee." *The Chimpanzee* (Vol. 1), pp. 369–392. New York: Karger.

Kendon, Adam. 1977. *Studies in the Behavior of Social Interaction.* Bloomington: Indiana University Press.

Kendon, Adam. 1990. *Conducting Interaction.* Cambridge: Cambridge University Press.

Kete, Kathleen. 1993. *The Beast in the Boudoir: Petkeeping in Nineteenth-Century Paris.* Berkeley: University of California Press.

Klein, Richard. 1995. "The Power of Pets." *The New Republic* (July 10), pp. 18–23.

Koehler, William R. 1962. *The Koehler Method of Dog Training.* New York: Howell.

Kogure, Norio, and Keiko Yamazaki. 1990. "Attitudes to Animal Euthansia in Japan: A Brief Review of Cultural Influences." *Anthrozoös* 3(3): 151–154.

Krebs, J. R. 1978. "Optimal Foraging: Decision Rules for Predators," pp. 23–63 in J. R. Krebs and N. B. Davies (eds.), *Behavioral Ecology.* Oxford: Blackwell.

Kuusisto, Stephen. 1998. *Planet of the Blind: A Memoir.* New York: The Dial Press.

Lago, Dan, and Catherine Kotch-Jantzer. 1988. "Euthanasof of Pet Animals and the Death of Elderly Owners: Implications for Support of Community-Dwelling Elderly Pet Owners," pp. 148–156 in Kay et al. (eds.), *Euthanasia of the Companion Animal.*

Lambert, Robert. 1990. "Some Thoughts about Acquiring and Learning to Use a Dog Guide." *Re:view* 22(3): 151–158.

Landsberg, Gary. 1991. "The Distribution of Canine Behavior Cases in Three Behavior Referral Practices." *Veterinary Medicine* (October), pp. 1011–1018.

Langer, Susanne. 1951. *Philosophy in a New Key.* New York: New American Library.

Latham Foundation (ed.). 1991. *Universal Kinship: The Bond between All Living Things.* Saratoga, Calif.: R and E Publishers.

Lazare, Aaron, S. Eisenthal, Arthur Frank, and John Stoeckle. 1987. "Studies in a Negotiated Approach to Patienthood," pp. 413–432 in John Stoeckle (ed.), *Encounters between Patients and Doctors.*

Lenehan, Michael. 1986. "Four Ways to Walk a Dog." *The Atlantic Monthly* 257 (April), pp. 35–48, 89–99.

Lerman, Rhoda. 1996. *In the Company of Newfs.* New York: Henry Holt.

Lesy, Michael. 1989. *The Forbidden Zone.* New York: Anchor.

Levinson, Boris. 1969. *Pet-Oriented Child Psychotherapy.* Springfield, Ill.: Charles C. Thomas.

Linden, Eugene. 1986. *Silent Partners: The Legacy of the Ape Language Experiments.* New York: Random House.

Linden, Eugene. 1993. "Can Animals Think?" *Time Magazine* 22 (March), pp. 54–61.

Lindesmith, Alfred, Anselm Strauss, and Norman Denzin. 1977. *Social Psychology* (5th ed.). New York: Holt, Rinehart and Winston.

Lockwood, Randall. 1983. "The Influence of Animals on Social Perception," pp. 64–71 in Katcher and Beck (eds.), *New Perspectives on Our Lives with Companion Animals.*

Lorenz, Konrad. 1971. *Studies in Animal and Human Behavior.* Cambridge: Harvard University Press.

Lorenz, Konrad. 1988. *Man Meets Dog.* New York: Penguin.

Maggitti, Phil. 1990. "Animal Thinking." *The Animals' Agenda* (April), pp. 24ff.

Manning, Aubrey, and James Serpell (eds.). 1994. *Animals and Human Society.* New York: Routledge.

Marler, Peter, Stephen Karakashian, and Marcel Guger. 1991. "Do Animals Have the Option of Withholding Signals When Communication is Inappropriate? The Audience Effect," pp. 187–208 in Ristau (ed.), *Cognitive Ethology.*

Masson, Jeffrey. 1997. *Dogs Never Lie About Love.* New York: Crown.

Masson, Jeffrey, and Susan McCarthy. 1995. *When Elephants Weep: The Emotional Lives of Animals.* New York: Delacorte.

Mathias, Rosemary. 1997. *Assisting Passengers Traveling with Service Animals.* Washington, D.C.: Project Action.

McCulloch, Michael, and Leo Bustad. 1983. "Incidence of Euthanasia and Euthanasia Alternatives in Veterinary Practice," pp. 366–369 in Katcher and Beck (eds.), *New Perspectives on Our Lives with Companion Animals.*

McTear, Michael. 1985. *Children's Conversation.* New York: Basil Blackwell.

Mead, George Herbert. 1907. "Concerning Animal Perception." *Psychological Review* 14:383–390.

Mead, George Herbert. 1962. *Mind, Self, and Society.* Chicago: University of Chicago Press.

Mead, George Herbert. 1964. *George Herbert Mead on Social Psychology.* Edited by Anselm Strauss. Chicago: University of Chicago Press.

Mechling, Jay. 1989. "'Banana Cannon' and Other Folk Traditions between Human and Nonhuman Animals." *Western Folklore* 48:312–323.

Meddin, Jay. 1979. "Chimpanzees, Symbols, and the Reflective Self." *Social Psychology Quarterly* 42:99–109.

Meijsing, Monica. 1997. "Awareness, Self-Awareness and Perception: An Essay on Animal Consciousness," pp. 48–61 in Dol et al. (eds.). *Animal Consciousness and Animal Ethics.*

Menache, Sophia. 1998. "Dogs and Human Beings: A Study of Friendship." *Society and Animals* 6(1): 67–86.

Mennerick, Lewis. 1974. "Client Typologies: A Method for Coping with Conflict in the Service Worker-Client Relationship." *Sociology of Work and Occupations* 1: 396–418.

Menzel, E. W. 1978. "Cognitive Mapping in Chimpanzees," pp. 375–422 in S. H. Hulse, H. Fowler, and W. K. Honig (eds.), *Cognitive Processes in Animal Behavior.* Hillsdale, N.J.: Lawrence Erlbaum.

Merton, Robert. 1976. *Sociological Ambivalence and Other Essays.* New York: Free Press.

Messent, Peter. 1983. "Social Facilitation of Contact with Other People by Pet Dogs," pp. 37–46 in Katcher and Beck (eds.), *New Perspectives on Our Lives with Companion Animals.*

Messent, Peter. 1984. "Correlates and Effects of Pet Ownership," pp. 331–340 in Anderson, Hart, and Hart (eds.), *The Pet Connection.*

Midgley, Mary. 1983. *Animals and Why They Matter.* Athens: University of Georgia Press.

Midgley, Mary. 1988. "Beasts, Brutes and Monsters," pp. 35–46 in Ingold (ed.), *What Is An Animal?*

Milani, Myrna. 1986. *The Body Language and Emotion of Dogs.* New York: Morrow.

Miles, H. Lyn. 1986. "How Can I Tell a Lie? Apes, Language, and the Problem of Deception," pp. 245–266 in Mitchell and Thompson (eds.), *Deception: Perspectives on Human and Nonhuman Deceit.*

Millar, Susanna. 1969. *The Psychology of Play.* Baltimore: Penguin.

Miller, David. 1973. *George Herbert Mead: Self, Language, and the World.* Chicago: University of Chicago Press.

Mills, C. Wright. 1940. "Situated Actions and Vocabularies of Motive." *American Sociological Review* 5:904–913.

Mitchell, Robert, and Elizabeth Edmunson. 1997. "What People Say to Dogs When They are Playing with Them." Paper presented at the meetings of the International Society for Anthrozoology, Boston, July 24–25.

Mitchell, Robert, and Nicholas Thompson (eds.). 1986. *Deception: Perspective on Human and Nonhuman Deceit.* Albany: State University of New York Press.

Mitchell, Robert, and Nicholas Thompson. 1986. "Deception in Play between Dogs and People," pp. 193–204 in Mitchell and Thompson (eds.), *Deception: Perspective on Human and Nonhuman Deceit.*

Mitchell, Robert, and Nicholas Thompson. 1990. "The Effects of Familiarity on Dog-Human Play." *Anthrozoös* 4(1): 24–43.

Mitchell, Robert, and Nicholas Thompson. 1991. "Projects, Routines, and Enticements in Dog-Human Play," pp. 189–216 in Bateson and Klopfer (eds.), *Perspectives in Ethology: Human Understanding and Animal Awareness.* New York: Plenum.

Moneymaker, James. 1988. "Euthanasia and the Human/Animal Compassion Bond," pp. 42–46 in Kay et al. (eds.), *Euthanasia of the Companion Animal.*

Montgomery, Sy. 1991. *Walking with the Great Apes.* New York: Houghton Mifflin.

Moran, Michael. 1992. "The New Jersey Knight." *InterActions* 10(1): 8–9.

Morgan, Lloyd H. 1868. *The American Beaver and His Works.* Philadelphia: Lippincott.

Morris, Desmond. 1986. *Dog Watching.* New York: Crown.

Mugford, Roger. 1981. "Problem Dogs and Problem Owners: The Behavior Specialist as an Adjunct to Veterinary Practice," pp. 295–317 in Fogle (ed.), *Interrelations between People and Pets.*

Musolf, Gil. 1996. "Interactionism and the Child: Cahill, Corsaro, and Denzin on Childhood Socialization." *Symbolic Interaction* 19(4): 303–321.

Myers, Olin E., Jr. 1996. "Child-Animal Interaction: Nonverbal Dimensions." *Society and Animals* 4(1): 19–36.

Nieburg, H., and A. Fischer. 1982. *Pet Loss*. New York: Harper and Row.

Noske, Barbara. 1989. *Humans and Other Animals*. London: Pluto Press.

Noske, Barbara. 1997. "Speciesism, Anthropocentrism, and Non-Western Cultures." *Anthrozoös* 10(4): 183–190.

Obenski, Michael. 1988. *The Best of Mike Obenski, VMD*. Cleveland: Business Information Services.

Okoniewski, Lisa. 1984. "A Comparison of Human-Human and Human-Animal Relationships," pp. 251–260 in Anderson, Hart, and Hart (eds.), *The Pet Connection*.

Olsen, Geary, Jack Mandel, and Alan Bender. 1984. "Evaluating Pet Facilitated Therapy in Long Term Care Facilities," pp. 399–406 in Anderson, Hart, and Hart (eds.), *The Pet Connection*.

Orcutt, Stephen. 1980. "The Role of a Mobility Instructor in a Dog Guide School." *Visual Impairment and Blindness* 74(7): 266–268.

Ostrow, James. 1990. *Social Sensitivity*. Albany: State University of New York Press.

Owens, Jerry. 1986. "The Art of Practice." *Proceedings of the 53rd Annual Meeting of the American Animal Hospital Association*, New Orleans, pp. 585–593.

Patronek, Gary, Larry Glickman, and Michael Moyer. 1995. "Population Dynamics and the Risk of Euthanasia for Dogs in an Animal Shelter." *Anthrozoös* 8(1): 31–43.

Patterson, Francine. 1978. "Conversations with a Gorilla." *National Geographic* (October), pp. 438–465.

Patterson, Francine, and Eugene Linden. 1981. *The Education of Koko*. New York: Holt, Rinehart, and Winston.

Pepperberg, Irene. 1991a. "Learning to Communicate: The Effects of Social Interaction," pp. 119–164 in Bateson and Klopfer (eds.), *Perspectives in Ethology (Vol. 9): Human Understanding and Animal Awareness*.

Pepperberg, Irene. 1991b. "A Communicative Approach to Animal Cognition: A Study of Conceptual Abilities of an African Grey Parrot," pp. 153–186 in Ristau (ed.), *Cognitive Ethology*.

Perin, Constance. 1981. "Dogs as Symbols in Human Development," pp. 68–88 in Fogle (ed.), *Interrelations between People and Pets*.

Perinbanayagam, Robert. 1977. "The Structure of Motives." *Symbolic Interaction* 1: 104–120.

Pfungst, Otto. 1965 [1911]. *Clever Hans: The Horse of Mr. von Osten*. New York: Holt, Rinehart and Winston.

Phillips, Mary. 1993. "Savages, Drunks, and Lab Animals: The Researcher's Perception of Pain." *Society and Animals* 1(1): 61–82.

Phillips, Mary. 1994. "Proper Names and the Social Construction of Biography: The Negative Case of Laboratory Animals." *Qualitative Sociology* 17: 119–142.

Premack, Ann, and David Premack. 1972. "Teaching Language to an Ape." *Scientific American* 227: 92–99.

Premack, David. 1976. *Intelligence in Ape and Man*. Hillsdale, N.J.: Lawrence Erlbaum.

Pryor, Karen. 1975. *Lads Before the Wind*. New York: Harper and Row.

Putnam, Peter. 1979. *Love in the Lead*. New York: Dutton.

Quigley, Joseph (ed.). 1993. *Perspectives: Interrelationships of People and Animals in Society Today*. Center to Study Human/Animal Relationships and Environments, University of Minnesota.

Rasmussen, Jeffrey, and D. W. Rajecki. 1995. "Differences and Similarities in Humans' Perceptions of Thinking and Feeling of a Dog and Boy." *Society and Animals* 3(2): 117–137.

Rasmussen, Jeffrey, D. W. Rajecki, and H. D. Craft. 1993. "Human Perceptions of Animal Mentality: Ascriptions of Thinking." *Journal of Comparative Psychology* 107(2): 293–290.

Regan, Tom, and Peter Singer (eds.). 1976. *Animal Rights and Human Obligations*. Englewood Cliffs, N.J.: Prentice Hall.

Riddick, Carol. 1985. "Health, Aquariums, and the Non-Institutionalized Elderly," pp. 163–174 in Sussman (ed.), *Pets and the Family*.

Ristau, Carolyn (ed.), 1991. *Cognitive Ethology: The Minds of Other Animals*. Hillsdale, N.J.: Lawrence Erlbaum.

Ritvo, Harriet. 1987. *The Animal Estate*. Cambridge: Harvard University Press.

Ritvo, Harriet. 1988. "The Emergence of Modern Pet-Keeping," pp. 13–32 in Rowan (ed.), *Animals and People Sharing the World*.

Robbins, Douglas, Clinton Sanders, and Spencer Cahill. 1991. "Dogs and Their People: Pet-Facilitated Interaction in a Public Setting." *Journal of Contemporary Ethnography* 20(1): 3–25.

Robson, Howard. 1985. "Dog Guide and Blind Person: The Matching Process." *Journal of Visual Impairment and Blindness* 79(8): 356.

Rochberg-Halton, Eugene. 1985. "Life in the Treehouse: Pet Therapy as Family Metaphor and Self-Dialogue," pp. 175–190 in Sussman (ed.), *Pets and the Family*.

Rockwell, Jane (ed.). 1988. *Famous Authors Tell You About Their Beautiful, Loving, and Nutty Dogs*. New Canaan, Conn.: William Mulvey.

Rollin, Bernard. 1988. "Animal Euthanasia and Moral Stress," pp. 31–41 in Kay et al. (eds.), *Euthanasia of the Companion Animal*.

Rollin, Bernard. 1990. *The Unheeded Cry: Animal Consciousness, Animal Pain, and Science*. New York: Oxford University Press.

Rowan, Andrew (ed.). 1988. *Animals and People Sharing the World*. Hanover, N.H.: University Press of New England.

Rowan, Andrew. 1990. "Editorial: The Power of the Telling Anecdote." *Anthrozoös* 3(3): 141–142.

Salmon, Peter, and Ingrid Salmon. 1983. "Who Owns Who?: Psychological Research into the Human-Pet Bond in Australia," pp. 244–265 in Katcher and Beck (eds.), *New Perspectives on Our Lives with Companion Animals*.

Sanders, Clinton R. 1989. *Customizing the Body: The Art and Culture of Tattooing*. Philadelphia: Temple University Press.

Sanders, Clinton, and Elizabeth Hirschman. 1996. "Involvement with Animals as Consumer Experience." *Society and Animals* 4(2): 111–119.

Savage-Rumbaugh, E. Sue. 1986. *Ape Language: From Conditioned Response to Symbol*. New York: Columbia University Press.

Savage-Rumbaugh, E. Sue, Duane Rumbaugh, and Sally Boysen. 1978. "Linguistically Mediated Tool Use and Exchange by Chimpanzees (Pan troglodytes)." *The Behavioral and Brain Sciences* 4:539–554.

Scheff, Thomas. 1966. *Becoming Mentally Ill.* Chicago: Aldine.

Schutz, Alfred. 1962. *Collected Papers (Vol. 1): The Problem of Social Reality.* The Hague: Nijhoff.

Schutz, Alfred. 1967. *The Phenomenology of the Social World.* Evanston, Ill.: Northwestern University Press.

Schutz, Alfred. 1970. *On Phenomenology and Social Relations.* Chicago: University of Chicago Press.

Scott, Marvin, and Stanford Lyman. 1968. "Accounts." *American Sociological Review* 33:46–62.

Scott, Robert. 1989. *The Making of Blind Men.* New York: Russell Sage.

Searle, J. R. 1983. *Intentionality.* Cambridge: Cambridge University Press.

Searle, J. R. 1984. *Minds, Brains and Science.* London: BBC.

Sebeok, Thomas. 1981. *The Play of Musement.* Bloomington: Indiana University Press.

Sebeok, Thomas, and J. Umiker-Sebeok. 1980. *Speaking of Apes: A Critical Anthology of Two-Way Communication with Man.* New York: Plenum.

Selby, L. A., and J. Rhoades. 1981. "Attitudes of the Public Towards Dogs and Cats as Companion Animals." *Journal of Small Animal Practice* 22:129–137.

Serpell, James. 1981. "Childhood Pets and Their Influence on Adults' Attitudes." *Psychological Reports* 49:651–654.

Serpell, James. 1983a. "Pet Psychotherapy." *Pets-Animals-Environment* (Spring), pp. 7–8.

Serpell, James. 1983b. "The Personality of the Dog and Its Influence on the Pet-Owner Bond," pp. 57–63 in Katcher and Beck (eds.), *New Perspectives on Our Lives with Companion Animals.*

Serpell, James. 1986. *In the Company of Animals.* New York: Basil Blackwell.

Serpell, James. 1988. "Pet-Keeping in Non-Western Societies: Some Popular Misconceptions," pp. 33–52 in Rowan (ed.), *Animals and People Sharing the World.*

Serpell, James (ed.). 1995. *The Domestic Dog.* Cambridge: Cambridge University Press.

Shapiro, Kenneth. 1989. "The Death of the Animal: Ontological Vulnerability." *Between the Species* 5(4):183–193.

Shapiro, Kenneth. 1990. "Understanding Dogs through Kinesthetic Empathy, Social Construction, and History." *Anthrozoös* 3(3):184–195.

Shelp, Earl. 1989. "Active Infant Euthanasia is Acceptable," pp. 190–194 in Bernards (ed.), *Euthanasia: Opposing Viewpoints.*

Shurtleff, Robert. 1983. "In the Patient's Interest: Toward a New Veterinary Ethic," pp. 511–515 in Katcher and Beck (eds.), *New Perspectives on Our Lives with Companion Animals.*

Simon, Leonard. 1984. "The Pet Trap: Negative Effects of Pet Ownership on Families and Individuals," pp. 226–240 in Anderson, Hart, and Hart (eds.), *The Pet Connection.*

Simonds, Paul. 1974. *The Social Primates.* New York: Harper Row.

Singer, Peter, and M. Siegler. 1990. "Euthanasia: A Critique." *New England Journal of Medicine* 322:1881–1883.

Sinrod, Barry. 1993. *Do You Do It When Your Pet's In the Room?* New York: Fawcett Columbine.

Smith, Sharon. 1983. "Interactions between Pet Dog and Family Members: An Ethological Study," pp. 29–36 in Katcher and Beck (eds.), *New Perspectives on Our Lives with Companion Animals.*

Smith, W. John. 1991. "Animal Communication and the Study of Cognition," pp. 209–230 in Ristau (ed.), *Cognitive Ethology.*

Snyder, C. R., and Raymond Higgins. 1988. "Excuses: Their Effective Role in the Negotiation of Reality." *Psychological Bulletin* 104(1): 23–35.

Soares, Cecelia. 1990. "Supporting Clients at the Time of Euthanasia." *Scientific Proceedings, American Animal Hospital Association 57th Annual Meetings* (San Francisco, March 23–30), pp. 694–696.

Soares, Cecelia. 1991. "Grief Counseling for Euthanasia," pp. 133–142 in Latham Foundation (ed.), *Universal Kinship.*

Sorabji, Richard. 1993. *Animal Minds and Human Morals.* Ithaca: Cornell University Press.

Spiegel, Marjorie. 1988. *The Dreaded Comparison: Human and Animal Slavery.* Philadelphia: New Society Publishers.

Stebbins, Sarah. 1990. "Natural Acts: Doing What We do When We Talk," pp. 269–282 in M. Bekoff and D. Jamieson (eds.), *Interpretation and Explanation in the Study of Animal Behavior.*

Stebbins, Sarah. 1993. "Anthropomorphism." *Philosophical Studies* 69:113–122.

Stewart, Mary. 1983. "Loss of a Pet—Loss of a Person: A Comparative Study of Bereavement," pp. 390–406 in Katcher and Beck (eds.). *New Perspectives on Our Lives with Companion Animals.*

Stoeckle, John D. (ed.). 1987. *Encounters between Patients and Doctors.* Cambridge: MIT Press.

Stokes, Randall, and John Hewitt. 1976. "Aligning Actions." *American Sociological Review* 41:838–349.

Stone, Karen. 1992. "Begging the Question." *The Animals' Voice Magazine* 5(3): 21–23.

Strauss, Anselm, Shizuko Fagerhaugh, B. Seczek, and C. Weiner. 1985. *Social Organization of Medical Work.* Chicago: University of Chicago Press.

Strum, Shirley. 1987. *Almost Human.* London: Elm Tree.

Sudnow, David. 1967. *Passing On: The Social Organization of Dying.* Englewood Cliffs, N.J.: Prentice-Hall.

Sussman, Marvin (ed.). 1985. *Pets and the Family.* New York: Haworth.

Sykes, Gresham, and David Matza. 1957. "Techniques of Neutralization." *American Sociological Review* 22:667–669.

Tanner, Nancy, 1981. *On Becoming Human.* Cambridge: Cambridge University Press.

Temerlin, M. 1975. *Lucy: Growing Up Human.* Palo Alto, Calif.: Science and Behavior Books.

ten Bensel, Robert. 1984. "Historical Perspectives of Human Values for Animals and Vulnerable People," pp. 2–14 in Anderson, Hart, and Hart (eds.), *The Pet Connection*.

Terrace, Herbert. 1979. *NIM: A Chimpanzee Who Learned Sign Language*. London: Methuen.

Terrace, Herbert. 1987. "Thoughts Without Words," pp. 123–137 in Blakemore and Greenfield (eds.), *Mindwaves*.

Thomas, Elizabeth Marshall. 1993. *The Hidden Life of Dogs*. New York: Houghton Mifflin.

Thompson, William. 1983. "Hanging Tongues: A Sociological Encounter with the Assembly Line." *Qualitative Sociology* 6(3): 215–237.

Thorne, Barrie. 1993. *Gender Play*. New Brunswick, N.J.: Rutgers University Press.

Tinbergen, Niko. 1972. *The Animal in Its World*. Cambridge: Harvard University Press.

Tolich, Martin. 1993. "Alienating and Liberating Emotions at Work." *Journal of Contemporary Ethnography* 22(3): 361–381.

Tolliver, Lennie-Marie. 1984. "Perspectives of Aging and the Role of Companion Animals," pp. 366–371 in Anderson, Hart, and Hart (eds.), *The Pet Connection*.

Tuan, Yi-Fu. 1984. *Dominance and Affection*. New Haven: Yale University Press.

Tucker, Michael. 1984. *The Eyes that Lead*. New York: Howell.

Turkle, Sherry. 1984. *The Second Self*. New York: Simon and Schuster.

Vail, David. 1966. *Dehumanization and the Institutional Career*. Springfield, Ill.: Charles C. Thomas.

Valentine, Deborah, Mary Kiddoo, and Bruce LaFleur. 1993. "Psychosocial Implications of Service Dog Ownership for People Who Have Mobility or Hearing Impairments." *Social Work in Health Care* 19(1): 109–125.

van den Berghe, Pierre. 1974. "Bringing Beasts Back In: Toward a Biosocial Theory of Aggression." *American Sociological Review* 39: 777–788.

Veevers, Jean. 1985. "The Social Meaning of Pets: Alternative Roles for Companion Animals," pp. 11–30 in Sussman (ed.), *Pets and the Family*.

Voith, Victoria. 1983. "Animal Behavior Problems: An Overview," pp. 181–186 in Katcher and Beck (eds.), *New Perspectives on Our Lives with Companion Animals*.

Vorstenbosch, Jan. 1997. "Conscientiousness and Consciousness. How to Make Up our Minds About the Animal Mind?" pp. 32–47 in Dol et al. (eds.), *Animal Consciousness and Animal Ethics*.

Walker, Stephen. 1985. *Animal Thought*. London: Routledge and Kegan Paul.

Wallman, Joel. 1991. *Aping Language*. New York: Cambridge University Press.

Warnath, Charles, and Glenda Seyfarth. 1982. "Guide Dogs: Mobility Tool and Social Bridge to the Sighted World." *Journal of Rehabilitation* 48(2): 58–61.

Weigert, Andrew. 1991. *Mixed Emotions*. Albany: State University of New York Press.

Weiner, Bernard, Alice Figueroa-Munoz, and Craig Kakihara. 1991. "The Goals of Excuses and Communication Strategies Related to Causal Perceptions." *Personality and Social Psychology Bulletin* 17(1): 4–13.

Wemelsfelder, Francoise. 1997. "Investigating the Animal's Point of View. An Inquiry into a Subject-Based Method of Measurement in the Field of Animal Welfare," pp. 73–89 in Dol et al. (eds.), *Animal Consciousness and Animal Ethics*.

West, Candace. 1997. "Part 1: Public Spaces. Not Even a Day in the Life." *Qualitative Sociology* 20(4): 447–456.

Whitney, Leon. 1971. *Dog Psychology: The Basis of Dog Training.* New York: Howell.

Wieder, D. Lawrence. 1980. "Behavioristic Operationalism and the Life-World: Chimpanzees and Chimpanzee Researchers in Face-to-Face Interaction." *Sociological Inquiry* 50:75–103.

Wilber, Robert. 1983. "Pets, Pet Ownership, and Animal Control: Social and Psychological Attitudes, 1975," pp. 124–131 in Quigley (ed.), *Perspectives: Interrelationships of People and Animals in Society Today.*

Wilder, Hugh. 1990. "Interpretive Cognitive Ethology," pp. 344–368 in M. Bekoff and D. Jamieson (eds.), *Interpretation and Explanation in the Study of Animal Behavior* (Vol. 1).

Williams, Joy. 1997. "The Inhumanity of the Animal People." *Harper's* (August), pp. 60–67.

Wolfe, Alan. 1993. *The Human Difference: Animals, Computers, and the Necessity of Social Science.* Berkeley: University of California Press.

Zee, Alyse. 1983. "Guide Dogs and Their Owners: Assistance and Friendship," pp. 472–486 in Katcher and Beck (eds.), *New Perspectives on Our Lives with Companion Animals.*

Zuckerman, Lord. 1991. "Apes R Not Us." *New York Review of Books* May 30, pp. 43–49.

Zussman, Robert. 1992. *Intensive Care: Medical Ethics and the Medical Profession.* Chicago: University of Chicago Press.

Index

Abrahamson, David, 162 n
accounts, 156 n. *See also* aligning actions, disclaimers, excusing tactics, neutralization techniques, motives, remedial interchanges
Afghan, 6, 68
African grey parrot (Alex), 126, 133
Akrow, Phillip, 150 n, 162 n
Alger, Janet, 168 n
Alger, Steven, 168 n
aligning actions, 156–157 n. *See also* accounts, disclaimers, excusing tactics, neutralization techniques, motives, remedial interchanges
Allen, Colin, 153 n, 154 n
ambivalence: and disposition of pet animals, 151 n, 156 n; of hunters, 166 n; and social definitions of animals, 111–112; sociological discussions of, 166 n; and trainers' views of guide dogs, 108–110;
American Animal Hospital Association, 16
American Veterinary Medical Association, 16, 161–162 n
American Society for the Prevention of Cruelty to Animals (ASPCA), 164 n
American Sign Language (ASL), 122, 129–132
anal glands, 67
animal rights: view of guide dog use, 52; view of pet-keeping, xiv
Animal Welfare Institute, 166 n
animals: ability to fantasize, 126–127; altruism of, 169 n; conventional sociological view of, 117–119, 133–134, 141; emotions of, 121–124; as objects, 111–112, 114,

118–119, 166 n; pain of, 168 n; philosophical debates about, 169 n; self concept of, 132, 137–140, 173 n; as thinking, 119–121, 124–127, 133–137. *See also* cat, dogs, guide dogs, pets, primates
anthropomorphism, 139–140, 147–148; critical, 140; heuristic value of, 175 n; interpretive, 148
Anthrozoös, 1
Arluke, Arnold, 109, 149 n, 165 n
Armstrong, James, 175 n
Audubon, James, 175 n
auto-ethnography, xii, 149–150 n. *See also* research method

Barber, Theodore, 173 n
beagle, vii, 6
bears, 137
Beck, Alan, 15, 152 n
Bekoff, Marc, 150 n, 153 n, 154 n
behaviorism, 115–117; and "behavioristic operationalism," 115–116, 167 n; critiques of, 167 n, 168 n; as "mechanomorphic" perspective, 115; purposive versus inclusive, 116, 167 n. *See also* ethology, Wieder
Berger, John, 147
birds, personalities of, 173 n
Bogdan, Robert, 25–26, 30
Bradshaw, John, 174 n
Brickel, Clark, 10, 11
Bryant, Clifton, 67, 160 n
Budiansky, Stephen, 150 n
Bulcroft, Kris, 152 n
bull mastiff, vii–viii
Burghart, Gordon, 140, 149 n

197